AF654548

SUSTAINABLE LIVELIHOODS

About the Author

A. Vidya Sagar, is a Gold Medalist in Economics with M.A. and Ph.D. Degrees from Sri Venkateshwara University, Tirupati and Andhra University, Visakhapatnam.

Dr. Vidya Sagar, I.A.S., has worked in the Departments of Tribal Welfare Panchayati Raj and Rural Development and Social Welfare, Andhra Pradesh. He has also been Principal Secretary to the Government of Andhra Pradesh and has gained vast experience and expert knowledge in the Welfare and Development sectors.

During his academic career, he worked as a Lecturer in Development Economics, Sri Venkateshwara University and was the Resource Person in the National Seminar on People's Participation in Development Administration for Tribal Welfare, at the National Institute of Rural Development (NIRD), Hyderabad. Dr. Vidya Sagar, who hails from Prakasam district Andhra Pradesh has a deep concern for the marginalized sections of society and has always been sensitive about the lives of those hailing from rural, tribal, and backward areas.

His publications include a collection of short stories titled ***Bhachrachalam Mannem Kathalu*** (Vows of an underdeveloped area) translated and published in English by the National Book Trust and five collections of his poetry in Telugu, i.e., his mother tongue.

Sustainable Livelihoods

Collection and Marketing of NTFP by Scheduled Tribes with Special Reference to North Coastal Andhra Pradesh

A. Vidya Sagar, *IAS*

CONCEPT PUBLISHING COMPANY PVT. LTD.
NEW DELHI-110 059

© A. Vidya Sagar

All rights reserved. No part of this work may be reproduced, stored, adapted, or transmitted in any form or by any means, electronic, mechanical, photocopying, micro-filming recording or otherwise, or translated in any language, without the prior written permission of the copyright owner and the publisher. The book is sold subject to the condition that it shall not, by way of trade or otherwise, be lent, resold, hired out, or otherwise circulated without the prior publisher's written consent in any form of binding or cover other than that in which it is published.

The views and opinions expressed in this book are author(s) own and the facts reported by him/her have been verified to the extent possible, and the publishers are not in any way liable for the same.

ISBN-13 : 978-81-8069-864-4

First Published 2012

Published and Printed by

Concept
Since 1974

Concept Publishing Company Pvt. Ltd.
A/15-16, Commercial Block, Mohan Garden
New Delhi-110059 (India)
T: 25351460, 25351794, *F*: 091-11-25357109
E: publishing@conceptpub.com, W: www.conceptpub.com
Editorial Office: H-13, Bali Nagar, New Delhi-110 015, India.

Cataloging in Publication Data--*Courtesy:* D.K. Agencies (P) Ltd. <docinfo@dkagencies.com>

Vidyasagar, E., 1956-
Sustainable livelihoods : collection and marketing of NTFP by scheduled tribes with special reference to north coastal Andhra Pradesh / A. Vidya Sagar.
p. cm.
Includes bibliographical references (p.) and index.
ISBN 9788180698644

1. Non-timber forest products industry—Government policy—India—Andhra Pradesh. 2. Community forestry—India—Andhra Pradesh.3.Andhra Pradesh (India)—Scheduled tribes—Economic conditions. 4. Sustainable development—India—Andhra Pradesh. I. Title.

DDC 305.80095484 23

Acknowledgements

I take this opportunity to express my profound thankfulness and gratitude to my Research Director, Prof. C. Ratnam, Department of Economics and Honorary Director, Agro Economic Research Centre, Andhra University for his prudent and judicious guidance; for his encouragement and timely suggestions at different stages of my research work.

I express my gratitude and sincere thanks to the Government of Andhra Pradesh for permitting me to take up research work in Andhra University, Visakhapatnam.

I sincerely thank Prof. L. Venugopal Reddy, Vice Chancellor, Andhra University for permitting me to enroll as a Research Scholar (Part-time) in the Department of Economics and to avail the academic facilities of various Departments and Central Library.

I thank Prof. J.V. Prabhakar Rao, Principal, College of Arts & Commerce, Andhra University for extending cooperation in all the administrative procedures.

I thank the Doctoral Committee Members of Pre-Ph.D., Prof. K.C. Reddy and Dr. R. Sudarsana Rao.

My thanks are also due to Prof. G. Ramachandrudu, Head of the Department and all the faculty members of Department of Economics for their co-operation at various stages of my research work either directly or indirectly. I owe a lot to each one of them.

I thank Sri V. Krishna Rao, C.E.O., Kovel Foundation, Visakhapatnam, Andhra Pradesh for the timely support during my survey on NTFP based livelihoods of tribals in the North Coastal Andhra Pradesh.

I thank Sri Sanjay Patnaik and Sri Manoj Patnaik, RCDC, Bhubaneswar for their interactions on policy regulations on NTFP in the State of Orissa.

I would like to express sincere thanks to General Managers, Divisional Managers, and other staff of GCC for their support in providing me the data to carry out my research work.

I am very much obliged to Dr. S. Ashok Kumar, Divisional Manager, GCC, for his valuable contribution in the discussion on various issues relating to NTFP collection and marketing.

I am impressed by Mr. Gita Mohan, Research Scholar for providing me the benefit of his insights into the statistical techniques and I thank him for extending his services.

I thank Smt. B. Suneetha Raja Ratnam and Sri L.V.S. Ravi for computerizing the material and carrying out the work.

I thank Sri K. Sivaram and Mr. P. Devaraju for scheduling the time of my research work without affecting my regular work

I finally thank my wife, Smt. K. Ratna Prabha, IAS, Principal Secretary (IT), Government of Andhra Pradesh for her valuable contribution by sharing her ideas on my research work despite her hectic activities and busy schedules and allowing me to utilize my spare time for research work.

A. VIDYA SAGAR

Contents

List of Tables

List of Appendix Tables and Annexure

ANNEXURE

List of Abbreviations

AP	Andhra Pradesh
APCMS	Agricultural Primary Cooperative Marketing Society
APFDC	Andhra Pradesh Forest Development Corporation
APRLP	Andhra Pradesh Rural Livelihood Project
BCs	Backward Classes
CACP	Commission for Agricultural Cost and Prices
CBRTI	Central Bee Research and Training Institute
CCPA	Credit-cum-Purchase Assistant
CFM	Community Forest Management
CFTRI	Central Food Technological Research Institute
CMFPF	Chhattisgarh Minor Forest Produce (Trading & Development) Cooperative Federation
DFO	Divisional Forest Officer
DRDA	District Rural Development Agency
D.R.s	Domestic Requirements
D.R. Depot	Domestic Requirement Depot
EGS	Employment Guarantee Scheme
ECs	Essential Commodities
FD	Forest Department
FDC	Forest Development Corporation
GCC	Girijan Cooperative Corporation
GDP	Gross Domestic Product
GoI	Government of India
GPCMS	Girijan Primary Cooperative Marketing Society
GVVKS	Girijan Vidya Vikas Kendra School
IGP	Income Generation Programme
IIFM	Indian Institute of Forest Management
IKP	Indira Kranti Patham

ITDA	Integrated Tribal Development Agency
JFDC	Jharkhand Forest Development Corporation
JFM	Joint Forest Management
KL	Kendu Leaves
LPG	Liquefied Petroleum Gas
MADA	Modified Area Development Agency
MARKFED	Marketing (Cooperative) Federation
MCW	Measurer-cum-Watchman
MFP	Minor Forest Produce
MMUs	Mobile Medical Units
MoEF	Ministry of Environment and Forest
MoRD	Ministry of Rural Development
MoTA	Ministry of Tribal Affairs
MoU	Memorandum of Understanding
MPP	Minimum Purchase Price
MSP	Minimum Support Price
NABARD	National Agricultural Bank for Rural Development
NAFED	National Agricultural Cooperative Federation
NCA	North Coastal Andhra
NGO	Non-Governmental Organisation
NTFP	Non Timber Forest Produce
OCs	Other Castes
OFDC	Orissa Forest Development Corporation
ORMAS	Orissa Rural Marketing and Agricultural Society
PDS	Public Distribution System
PESA	Panchayat Extension to Scheduled Areas
PFPCS	Primary Forest Produce Cooperative Society
PSU	Public Sector Undertakings
QC	Quality Control
R & D	Research & Development
RMD	Retail Marketing Division
RR Labs	Regional Research Laboratories
SAP	Seasonal Agricultural Produce
SBU	Strategic Business Unit
SCs	Scheduled Castes
SERP	Society for Elimination of Rural Poverty

SGRY	Sampoorna Grameen Rozgar Yojana
SGSY	Swarnajayanti Gram Swarozgar Yojana
SHG	Self-Help Groups
STEP	Sustainable Tribal Empowerment Project
STs	Scheduled Tribes
TCDC	Tribal Cooperative Development Corporation
TDBs	Tribal Development Blocks
TDCCs	Tribal Development Cooperative Corporations
TFRI	Tropical Forest Research Institute
TP	Transit Pass
TRIFED	Tribal Cooperative Marketing Development Federation
TSP	Tribal Sub Plan
UNIFEM	United Nations Development Fund for Women
VC & MD	Vice Chairman & Managing Director
VSS	Vana Samrakshana Samithi
WTO	World Trade Organisation

List of Botanical Names/NTFP/ Medicinal Herbs/Agricultural Produce procured from Tribals by GCC

S.No.	Trade / Popular Name	Botanical Name
I. *Gums & Resins*		
1.	Gum Karaya	*Sterculia urens*
2.	Gum Kondagogu	*Cohlospermum religiasum*
3.	Gum Olibunam	*Boswellia serrata*
4.	Gum Dikamali	*Gardenia gummiferra*
5.	Gum Tiruman/ Gum Ghatti	*Anogessus latifolia*
II. *Food Items*		
6.	Honey/Honey wax	*Apis dorsata*
7.	Tamarind	*Tamarindus indica*
III. *Cosmetic Items*		
8.	Sheekakai	*Acacia concinna*
9.	Soapnuts	*Sapaindus emerginatus*
IV. *Tree Borne Oil Seeds*		
10.	Pungam seed	*Pungamia glabra*
11.	Mohua seed	*Maduca latifolia*
12.	Kusum seed	*Scheleichera oleosa*
13.	Neem seed	*Azadirachta indica*
V. *Nuts and Seeds*		
14.	Myrobalans	*Terminalia chebula*
15.	Marking nuts	*Semicarpus anacardium*
16.	Nux vomica	*Strychnus Nux vomica*

S.No.	Trade / Popular Name	Botanical Name
17.	Cleaning nuts	*Strychnus potatorum*
18.	Tamarind seed	*Tamarindus indica*
19.	Annato seed	*Bixa orellina*
VI. *Others*		
20.	Naramamidy	*Litsea glutinosa*
VII. *Medicinal Items*		
21.	Amla pulp	*Emblica officinalis*
22.	Thani	*Terminalia bellirica*
23.	Nannari/Maredu Geddalu	*Decalepis hamiltonii*
24.	Padapatri	*Gymnema sylvestre*
25.	R S Roots	*Rauwolfia serpentina*
26.	Palageddalu	*Holestema adakodien*
27.	Guruvinda seed	*Abrus precatorius*
28.	Tippa/Tippa Teega	*Tinospora cardifolia*
29.	Tantemu	*Casia tora*
VIII. *Agricultural Produce*		
30.	Rajmah/French beans	*Phaseolus vulgaris*
31.	Turmeric	*Curcuma longa*
32.	Cashew	*Anacardium occidentale*
33.	Chillies	*Capscium annum*
34.	Niger Seed	*Zingiber officianale*

1

Introduction

Role of Forests in the Economy

Forests contribute immensely to a country's economic development by providing valuable raw materials like: wood and non-timber forest produce (NTFP), protecting the environment through tree cover and water resources, and serve as a source of recreation. Wood consists of timber and firewood. Timber is the basic raw material for a number of cottage, small scale, and large scale industries in India, which generate considerable amount of income and employment. In India, firewood is a major source of energy for the households, especially in the rural areas. Forests also provide a large variety of NTFP, which have great economic value. Collection of the NTFP is the main economic activity of a large number of tribals and non-tribals living in the vicinity of forests. Certain types of NTFP constitute basic raw materials in a number of industries, which have great employment generating potential.

Therefore, forests are the main source of livelihood for a large number of people especially the poor, and a major source of raw materials for various economic activities undertaken by industrialists. Forest lands are also used for a number of developmental purposes like: crop cultivation, creation of infrastructure, construction of dams, building of townships, and rehabilitation of displaced persons. Forests also play a very important role in protecting the environment by controlling the green house effect, moderating climate, arresting the soil erosion, and regulating the water supplies. The importance of forests in environmental protection can be well appreciated from the estimates showing the environmental benefits of a medium sized tree of 50 tonnes during its 50-year life span.[1]

As per the 1997 statistics, India has a forest area of 76.5 million hectares, which accounts for 23 per cent of the geographical area. In the total forest area, 48 per cent area has a crown density of more than 40 per cent; 34 per cent between 10 and 40 per cent; and the rest 18 per cent has less than 10 per cent or no forest cover at all.[2] The overall productivity of forests is estimated to be 0.7 cum (cubic metres) of wood, which is much less than the potential of 2 cum.[3] The average annual production of wood from forests in India is 30 million cubic metres of which 12 million cubic metres is the timber and 18–19 million cubic metres is the fire wood. Timber is used as a raw material in a number of industries. The important timber-based industries in India are: pulp and paper, plywood and veneer, fibre board and particle board, match industry, railway sleepers and coaches, packaging, housing, agricultural implements and temporary construction, furniture and paneling, mining, wooden toys and sporting, and wood carving and engraving industry.

Until 1970, Indian foresters looked at forests as a source of revenue by maximizing timber output. It was only during the late seventies, that the Government of India realized that there was a tremendous increase in the revenues from NTFP which include: fire wood, fuel wood, bamboo, grasses, leaves, flowers, fruits, gums, seeds, roots, and barks, and other plant parts.

The contribution of forests to the GDP in India ranges from 1 per cent to 2 per cent. In 2000–01, income from forestry and logging at 1993–94 constant prices was Rs. 14,516 crore. The shares of timber, firewood, and minor forest products in it are 9.84 per cent, 79.65 per cent, and 10.49 per cent respectively. Thus 90 per cent of the income from forestry is contributed by NTFP. Forests in India are concentrated more in the economically poorer regions where agricultural productivity is low, and soil is generally poor. People live deep inside these forests and some even in remote interiors while some of them have been living traditionally and others were brought by the forest department in the colonial period and, were forced to settle there to ensure round the year availability of labour. Now more than 100 million forest dwellers in the country are living in and around forest lands, and another 275 million for whom forests have continued to be an important source of their livelihood and means of survival.[4] According to a study conducted by the World Resource Institute: in India, nearly 500 million people living in and around forests depend on NTFP as a critical component for their sustenance.[5] Firewood, a component of NTFP is used both by households and industries for hundreds of years until the advent of coal, oil, gas, electricity, etc. Wood constitutes man's chief source of fuel. Even today, more than half of the total world population uses wood for fuel, and it will continue to remain a major source of domestic fuel in India for many years to come.

Place and Role of Forests in Tribal Life—Dependence of Tribals on Forests

The tribal people recognized as Scheduled Tribes by the Constitution of India having abundant self-respect and are conscious to preserve their social and cultural identity. On account of various pressures exerted on them, they retreated into forests and hill tracts over the centuries. They are physically tough and adapted to the rugged terrain, which they inhabit. Their wants are primarily basic needs of life like food, shelter, and clothing. Forests are their cherished homes through generations; an abode of their mother-deity. The tribal communities could subsist for thousands of years with reasonable standards of health, mainly because forests provided them with food, water, shelter, clothing, medicines, and employment.

In times of distress like famine, forests are the last resort. Even in areas where forests do not exist, the tribals still visit the distant forests periodically and try to get their traditional requirements from there, however, insignificant they may appear to be. The Scheduled Tribes traditionally collect many items from the forests, which are necessary for their day-to-day existence. The young, old, and the women-folk gather food items from the forest. A survey done in the forest regions of

Gujarat revealed that nearly 22 to 27 per cent of the elderly persons and 70 to 72 per cent of the children go to forest for collection of tubers, leafy vegetables, bamboo shoots, and a host of other products.[6] Fuel wood in the context of tribal people is not merely used for cooking but also for generating heat and lighting: By and large, these people do not have any warm clothes to protect them from the harsh and cold winters and the only method by which they keep themselves warm is by lighting up bonfires. The fire also gives them light in the absence of any other means of lighting in the area. Fire also helps them in keeping the wild animals at bay. In fact, the material existence of these people depends on forest to such an extent that, this cannot be visualized in the absence of the forests.

Tribals and forests are ecologically and economically inseparable. They coexisted since times immemorial and will continue to coexist in a mutually reinforcing relationship. Tribals have always been sentimentally attached to the forests and considered them to be nature's gift. Their folklore is full of references to the forest. There are several rites and rituals, in which some forest produce is used one way or the other. Many of the leaves, climbers, etc., needed in magico- religious rites are procured from these forests. Few trees in the indigenous forests are considered to be the abode of deities and are worshipped as such.

Significance of NTFP in the Tribal Economy

The tribal economy being a subsistence economy, agriculture fails to provide full sustenance to the tribals. They depend upon the forest produce both for consumption and sale or market NTFP to augment their low incomes from agriculture. It is obtained through collection without causing much damage to the forest. Collection of forest produce also provides food security particularly during droughts or famines and generates more equitable distribution of forestry benefits within communities and families.[7] It also generates additional employment and income and offers opportunities for processing, enterprise, and contributes to foreign exchange earnings, and supports biodiversity conservation and other environmental objectives.[8] The forest products, tribals generally collect include: bamboo, grasses, leaves, flowers, fruits, gums, seeds, roots, barks, and other plant parts and fire wood which are termed as NTFP. The NTFP excluding firewood are called MFP.

The NTFP exhibit significant variation in their use. Some of them like fruits, fodder and wild roots, etc., are consumed immediately after the harvest. Products like edible nuts, bamboo, cane products, etc., are consumed after primary processing. On the other hand, many NTFP go through a series of downstream processing and in the process add value to the products. They are utilized at the subsistence and commercial levels. While wild seeds, nuts, roots, and tubers supply fats and carbohydrates, wild leaves and fruits contain many essential vitamins and mushrooms; gums, and saps provide protein as well as minerals. A large number of items of our regular use such as: medicines, perfumes, skin lotions, nail polish, mouth wash, hair conditioners, cheese, chewing gum, ice cream, edible nuts, breakfast cereals, soft drinks, fancy bags, etc., contain various proportions of NTFP. Besides, NTFP support, village-level artisanry and handicrafts activity and provide raw materials to support processing enterprises. The NTFP are also traded internationally.[9]

The contribution of NTFP to the tribal economy in terms of provision of food and nutrition security and generation of employment and income has been very well highlighted by a number of studies. In recent times, the most comprehensive treatment of these various aspects is proved in the studies of De Beer and McDermott,[10] Campbell,[11] and Malhotra *et al.*[12] A number of other studies also examined the contribution of NTFP to the local tribal economies, although not in a comprehensive manner. In order to highlight the contribution of NTFP for the sustenance of tribal livelihoods, an attempt has been made to present the results of some of these studies.

Mallik[13] in his work, "Sustainable Management of Non-Timber Forest Products in Orissa: Some issues and options," reviewed the research studies on contribution of NTFP to the tribal livelihoods, conducted in Orissa, Madhya Pradesh, Himachal Pradesh and Bihar. One of the observations he made in these studies is that, 80 per cent of the forest dwellers in these States depend exclusively on NTFP for their daily subsistence and livelihood. Gupta and Guleria[14] in their study "Non-Wood Forest Products in India" observed that, during drought and natural calamities; NTFP are a vital source of livelihood for the poor and underprivileged tribal people. About 60 per cent of the NTFP collection is consumed locally.

The NTFP is a good source of supplementing the incomes of the rural poor especially the tribals. About 35 per cent of the income of a tribal household in India comes from the collection of NTFP.[15] A study conducted in Orissa reveals that, income from the sale of NTFP to the total income of a household constitutes 38.8 per cent.[16] Another study on procurement and marketing of Kendu leaves in Orissa reveals that the income from sale of Kendu leaves alone constitutes 13.9 per cent of the total income of a tribal household.[17] There are also some studies,[18] which show that contribution of NTFP to the household income ranges from 10 per cent to 15 per cent. The differences in the estimates are mainly due to the regional variations in the availability of NTFP. Therefore, the results of aggregate studies on NTFP should be read with a caution, and more emphasis should be laid on it for the conduct of regional studies.

In addition to the income generating potential, NTFP provide great scope for employment generation also. Around three-fourths (57.6 per cent) of total mandays of employment to a forest dwelling household is available in the collection of NTFP in Orissa.[19] Some other studies[20] conducted in Orissa reveal that the percentage of employment available to a tribal household ranges from 23 per cent to 55 per cent. Apart from providing direct employment, NTFP also provide great scope for generation of indirect employment. For instance, forest based small scale enterprises, primarily based on NTFP, provide up tc 50 per cent of their income for 20 to 30 per cent of the rural labour forces in India.[21]

Although income and employment generating potential is very high, due to difficult terrains, weak marketing channels, and unremunerative prices offered to the products, the entire potential is not being exploited. A study[22] conducted in Orissa reveals that the primary gatherers collect only 27 to 34 per cent of the NTFP species. Some other studies[23] also got a similar result that only a fraction of harvestable NTFP is being collected. Apart from providing sustenance for many, management of forest resources for NTFP has great ecological significance. This is because many NTFP activities involve non-destructive harvesting of annual renewable plant parts in contrast with timber harvesting. Tribal communities have extracted NTFP for centuries without destroying the resource base. Also managing forests for NTFP implies greater biodiversity of both animal and plant species. Therefore, promoting sustainable production of NTFP assumes importance in the context of providing livelihood for the poor tribals and protecting the environment.

Scope of the Study

There has been an increasing recognition that NTFP play a crucial role in providing important community needs for improved rural livelihoods especially of the poor tribals. More specifically, as already mentioned, they contribute largely to household food security and nutrition, generate additional employment and income, offer opportunities for processing enterprises, contribute to foreign exchange earnings, and support biodiversity conservation and other environmental objectives. Therefore, for the sustenance of tribal livelihood, sustainable production of NTFP and its access to the tribals assume importance. This requires sustainable development of forests, improvement in silvicultural practices and promotion of scientific methods of collection. Tribals' access to NTFP to a large extent depends on the government policies relating to collection and marketing of NTFP.

Regarding the current state of forests in India, although different sources of data[24] present contradictory picture up to 1990, the contradiction has, however, disappeared in the nineties. Based on these different sources of data many studies reveal that area under the forests in India is more or less stable in the nineties. However, the compound growth rates during the period 1989–1993 show that the area under forest cover declined at the rate of 0.0459 per cent per year, while the area under open forests declined at the rate of 0.0936 per cent.[25] As the decline in different components of forest area is marginal, it can be said that forests in India were stable both in terms of quantity and quality during the nineties.

These positive trends in forest development might be the outcome of the changing forest policies. The forest policies that existed before 1970 focused on maximizing forest revenues through timber output and NTFP were not recognized as a source of income. With such an approach the Indian forests were exploited ruthlessly in both the pre- and post-independence eras. It was only in the 1970s that the Government of India realized that NTFP is also as important a source of revenue as timber. It was also then realized that about the tremendous importance of forests in maintaining ecological balance. Accordingly a change in the forest policy was brought about in 1988. The new policy clearly stated that forests of the country need to be looked upon as national assets; not only as sources of revenue but also for their ecological value. Under this policy the concepts and objectives of forest management have changed drastically during the last 10 to 20 years. Emphasis is now on the maximization of total benefits from forestry including timber, non-timber, and environmental benefits, rather than focusing only on timber. For achieving this goal an innovative programme known as Joint Forest Management Programme was introduced. This programme recognized the role of community participation in reviving India's degraded forests through aforestation. These policy changes have been yielding positive results.

On the silvicultural practices front, no significant change in favour of NTFP has occurred. Although the new forest policy of 1988, is more in favour of protection of the forests, the emphasis on increasing the production of NTFP through silvicultural practices did not find a significant place in it. In the Social Forestry Programme which is expected to promote the regeneration of NTFP, the staff who have ambitious targets to meet are not inclined to spend time on growing seedlings of NTFP species, as they require a relatively longer period at the seedling stage, compared with fast growing species such as

Eucalyptus, which can be planted only after a few months. This tendency of the staff can be clearly seen from the fact that in Orissa where the dependence of tribals on NTFP is high, only 4 per cent of the trees planted in 1986–87 are NTFP species.[26] Also in the new forest policy very little emphasis has been given for developing technology to promote the production of NTFP.

The collection of NTFP has been subjected to various regulations over the years. These regulations vary from State to State. For instance, the Bihar Forest Produce Act 1984 restricts the purchase or transport of specified forest products. Contrary to this, Jharkhand had created different kinds of rights for the tribals with regard to the collection of NTFP. In Andhra Pradesh there are many Acts and Rules that govern the management of NTFP.[27] Although these rules and regulations are framed for the noble cause of protecting the forests and making the production of NTFP sustainable, they are very often acting against the interests of the tribals. The complexity in understanding these rules and the way, in which they are being implemented, sometimes lead to corruption and harassment of NTFP gatherers.

The government had created rights for industrialists through long-term agreements for the supply of NTFP at a lower price. With the increase in profits, the forest based industries had an explosive growth and led to non-sustainable use of forest stocks. In order to maximize the collection of NTFP, the industries encouraged methods, which were destructive to the plants. Extraction of resin from pine tree is one such example. In *tendu* bush areas, all under-growth is slashed to promote better growth of *tendu* leaves. In this process many fruits, roots, and medicinal plants get destroyed. Thus the provision of NTFP to the industries at low prices is leading to destruction of the production cycle of NTFP.

Most of the NTFP are nationalized in the sense that they can be sold only to government agencies. For instance in Andhra Pradesh, the Andhra Pradesh Minor Forest Act 1971 and the Andhra Pradesh Scheduled Areas NTFP Act declare that, trade in NTFP is a State monopoly irrespective of ownership status of land where they occur. The tribals have no right to make any direct sale to outside party. Although the

State monopoly of the trade in NTFP was created in the interest of the tribals collecting NTFP, there are complaints against the functioning of these State organizations. The major complaint is that in some instances, the open market price is far greater than the price offered by government agencies.

All the aforementioned factors discussed here prompt us to believe that the tribals access to NTFP has been declining and posing a problem for their life sustenance. Therefore, there is a need for government intervention to reverse this trend and to improve the livelihood for NTFP gatherers. In this connection, a study examining in detail aspects such as: the status of the NTFP gatherers access to NTFP, whether it is declining or increasing as the time passes; factors responsible for such change, and suggestions on the ways and means of improving the livelihoods of NTFP gatherers, assumes much importance. As all these factors are region-specific, regional studies have assumed great significance. In Andhra Pradesh, the NCA region, which comprises the districts of Visakhapatnam, Vizianagaram, and Srikakulam, has a significant size of forest cover and the tribal population. A number of NTFP are produced in this region and they are the major sources of livelihood to a large percentage of tribals. The trade in NTFP in this region is done through a State controlled agency called the Girijan Cooperative Corporation (GCC). This study analyses the aforementioned aspects in the NCA region of Andhra Pradesh.

Objectives of the Study

The specific objectives of the study are :

(a) to examine the forest and NTFP policies and assess their impact on NTFP gatherers, i.e., tribals access to NTFP;
(b) to study the production related aspects of NTFP such as : the type of the tree, the conditions under which it grows, the months in which the product is available, method of extraction, and primary processing of the product;

(c) to examine the trends in growth, instability, and cyclical variations of the collection of NTFP;
(d) to assess whether the production/collection of NTFP is sustainable;
(e) to examine the marketing channels and price determination process of NTFP;
(f) to analyse the variations in the GCC's procurement and sale prices of NTFP;
(g) to document the origin, objectives, growth and various other activities undertaken by the GCC for the welfare of the tribals engaged in NTFP collection and identify the constraints, if any; and
(h) to suggest policy measures for the sustainable production/collection of NTFP and improve the economic condition of the NTFP gatherers.

Methodology

This study is exploratory in nature and is based on secondary as well as primary data. The data required for presenting the socio-economic profile of the study area are drawn from the population census and the reports of Mandal Statistics.[28] The information on types of NTFP available, total procurement of NTFP, their prices and value, market management, price fixation, value addition for NTFP, measures taken by the GCC for improving the welfare of the tribals, etc., are drawn from secondary sources. These data are obtained from the office of the Managing Director, GCC, Visakhapatnam. The information on NTFP policies is also drawn from secondary sources. The analysis of the production is related to aspects such as : methods of extraction of various types of NTFP, time spent on extraction, distance travelled for extraction, quantities extracted, problems involved in the sale, and extraction, prices received, number of days engaged in the collection, and incomes earned, is based on the primary data collected from a sample of households.

In this study, for selecting the sample households, a stratified random sampling design has been used, with each district in the region, viz., Visakhapatnam, Vizianagaram, and

Srikakulam, as a stratum. Again villages in each stratum, i.e., districts are classified into three strata, viz., villages in the interior forests, villages in the semi-interior forest area, and villages in the proximity of plains; and from each of these three strata, one village is selected at random. Altogether nine villages were selected and the data were obtained from all households in these villages by canvassing a pre-designed schedule during the months from August to September 2003. The villages selected for the study are: Nelapalem, Edulapalem, and Garikabanda in Visakhapatnam district; Katraguddi, Badnaikvalasa, and Madavalasa in Vizianagaram district; and Bennaduguda, Addakulaguda, and Gurunda in the Srikakulam district. The total number of households in the selected villages in Visakhapatnam, Vizianagaram, and Srikakulam are 91, 87, and 84 respectively.

As the conditions relating to the availability of NTFP collection, marketing, access to other sources of employment and income, life styles, etc., vary with the location of the village in the forest, analysis of the primary data is carried out separately for the households in the interior forest area, households in the semi-interior forest area, and households in the proximity of plain areas. The selected villages representing the interior forests are Nelapalem, Katraguddi and Bennaduguda and the number of households in these three villages is 62. The selected villages representing the semi-interior forest area are : Edulapalem, Badnaikvalasa, and Addakulaguda, and the total number of household in these villages is 103. The villages representing the area nearer to the plains are : Garikabanda, Madavalasa and Gurunda, and the number of households in these villages is 86. The statistical data are summarized in terms of percentages and averages, and the analysis is carried out in terms of these parameters.

The trends in the growth of procurement of the various NTFP are analysed in terms of trend growth rates. The instability in growth is analysed in terms of instability index. Cyclical variations are analysed using cyclical components estimated by both additive and multiplicative models. Using the same techniques, both procurement and sale prices of NTFP are also analysed. The time series analysis of trends in growth and fluctuations, cover the period from 1990–91 to 2002–03.

Chapterisation

The study is presented in eight chapters. Chapter 1 is the introduction which provides the background for the study, statement of the research problem, and objectives, and describes the methodology and chapter scheme. The socio-economic profile of the study area is presented in chapter 2. Chapter 3 documents the various forest policies and NTFP policies of the State and examines the impact of these policies on the access of the tribals to NTFP in the State. The analysis of the production related issues such as : the types of NTFP available in the region, the conditions under which they grow, the method of extraction of the products, the quantities extracted, their primary processing, time taken for the collection, distance travelled for collection, etc., trends in the growth and unstability and cyclical variations, etc., form the content of Chapter 4. Chapter 5 discusses the aspects relating to marketing of NTFP, price fixation, price spread, fluctuations in prices over time. Analysis of the origin, functions, administrative set-up and the activities taken up by the GCC for improving the welfare of the tribals is presented in Chapter 6. The policy options for achieving sustainable production of NTFP and improving the living conditions of NTFP gatherers, are discussed in Chapter 7. Chapter 8 provides a brief summary and conclusions.

NOTES

1. T.M. Das (1980) : The Value of a Tree. Proceedings of the Indian Science Congress.
2. Forest Survey of India (FSI) 1998, State of India's Forests 1997, Dehradun, India.
3. *Ibid.*
4. Lynch Owen J. (1992) , "Securing Community-based Tenurial Rights in the Tropical Forests of Asia" , *Issues in Development,* November, World Resource Institute, Washington.

5. World Resource Institute (1990), *World Bank in the Forest Sector : A Global Policy Paper*, World Resource Institute, Washington.
6. "Tribal Life in India" – In *Tribal Life and Forests* by Devendra Thakur and D.N. Thakur.
7. Food and Agricultural Organization (FAO) (1989), *Household Food Security and Forestry : An Analysis of Socio-Economic Issues*, F.A.O., Rome.
8. F.A.O. (1995) : *Report of the International Expert Consultation on Non-Wood Forest Products*, F.A.O., Rome.
9. R.M. Mallik (2000) : "Sustainable Management of Non-Timber Forest Products in Orissa : Some Issues and Options", *Indian Journal of Agricultural Economics*, Vol. 55, No. 3, July-Sept., pp. 384–397.
10. De Beer and McDermott (1989) : *Economic Value of Non-Timber Forest Products in South West Asia*. Council for the International Union of Conservation of Nature, Netherlands.
11. Campbell J.Y. (1993) : *Changing Objectives, New Products and Management Challenges Making the Shift Major* versus *Minor to Many Forest Products*. Paper presented at the Seminar on Forest Produce, Coimbatore.
12. Malhotra *et al.* (1992) : *Role of Non-Timber Forest Produce in the Village Economy*, IBRAD, Calcutta.
13. R.M. Mallik (2000) : *Op. cit.*
14. Gupta, T. and Guleria. A (1982) : *Non-Wood Forest Products in India*. Oxford & IBH Publishing Co. Pvt. Ltd., New Delhi.
15. Tewari, D.D. and Campbell J.Y. (1995) : "Sustainable Management of NTFP in India." *Journal of Sustainable Forestry*, pp. 53-79.
16. Mallik, R.M. (1994) : Study of Some Minor Forest Produce in Orissa : An Empirical Investigation, N.C.D.S., Bhubaneswar, Orissa.
17. Mallik, R.M. (1996) : *Procurement and Marketing of Kendu Leaves in Orissa : A Study of Economic Deprivation and Benefits to Primary Collectors*, NCDS, Bhubaneswar, Orissa.
18. (i) Mallik R.M. and Panigrahi. N. (1998), *Study of Domestic and Commercial Use including Marketing of NTFP*. NCDS, Bhubaneswar, Orissa.
    (ii) Malhotra K.C., *et al.* (1992), *op. cit.*
    (iii) Fernandes, W. *et al.* (1988), *Forests, Environment and Tribal Economy*. Indian Social Institute, New Delhi.
19. Mallik, R.M. (1994), *op. cit.*
20. (i) Mallik, R.M. (1996), *op. cit.*
    (ii) Mallik, R.M. (1998), *op. cit.*
21. Campbell J.Y. (1988), *Putting People's Products First : Multiple Use Management for Non-Wood Forest Products in India*. Mimeograph.
22. Mallik, R.M. (1998), *op. cit.*

23. (i) Muraleedharan, P.K. *et al.* (1997), *Bio-diversity in Tropical Moist Forests : A Study of Sustainable Use of NTFP in the Western Ghats, Kenal.* Kenal Forest Research Institute, Trichur, Kerala.
    (ii) Sankar, S.K. (1998), *Sustainability of JFM in South-West Bengal : Case Study from Midnapur District*, Paper presented in Rama Krishna Mission Lokasikshya Parishad, West Bengal, March 24.
24. For the data on area under forests, there are three basic sources, viz., Statistical Abstracts of India (ASI), CMIE, and Ministry of Environment and Forests. While the ASI data show a decline in 'area under forests' between 1970–71 and 1990–91, the CMIE data reveals an increasing trend from 1950–51 to 1995–96. On the other hand, Ministry's data between 1989 and 1999, give a stable picture of area under forests. The other source of data is NRSA, which is assessed through satellite mapping and it is more reliable. However, it is available only for a short period.
25. Ratna Reddy V. *et al.* (2001), Forest Degradation in India : Extent and Determinants, *Indian Journal of Agricultural Economics.* Vol. 56, No. 4, Oct.-Dec., pp. 631–651.
26. Saxena, N.C. (1995), "Forest Policy and the Rural Poor in Orissa", *Wasteland News* (Oct.-Dec.) Society for Promotion of Wasteland Development, New Delhi.
27 (i) Andhra Pradesh Abnus Leaves Act 1956, (ii) Andhra Pradesh Forest Act 1967, (iii) Andhra Pradesh Forest Produce Transit Rules 1970, (iv) The Andhra Pradesh NTFP Act 1971, (v) The Andhra Pradesh NTFP Rules 1970, (vi) The Andhra Pradesh Forest Contract Rules 1977, (vii) The Scheduled Areas NTFP Act 1979, (viii) The Andhra Pradesh Forest Produce Rules 1989, (ix) The Andhra Pradesh Scheduled Areas NTFP Rules 1990.
28. Mandal is a Unit of Administration in Andhra Pradesh equivalent to a Tehsil in other States of India.

2

Profile of the Tribal Areas of North Coastal Andhra (NCA)

Introduction

In this chapter an attempt has been made to present the socio-economic and cultural characteristics of the NTFP collectors, i.e., tribals in the tribal areas of North Coastal Andhra (NCA), using the recently available statistical data, drawn from secondary sources. More specifically, it describes the geographical location of the area, its size, the existing flora and fauna, the tribal communities of the area, their population size, sex ratio, literacy rates, infrastructural facilities, and economic activities. It provides the backdrop for the study.

Geographical Location of NCA

The North Coastal Andhra Pradesh region comprises of the revenue districts of Visakhapatnam, Vizianagaram, and Srikakulam. Visàkhapatnam district is situated between the geographic coordinates of 10°-15′and 189°-32′ of the northern latitude and between 81°-54′ and 83°-30′ of eastern longitude. The district is bounded by Vizianagaram district in the north, East Godavari district in the south, Koraput of Orissa State in the west, and Bay of Bengal in the east. Vizianagaram district lies between 17°-15′ and 19°-15′ of the Northern latitude and between 83°-0′ and 89°-45′ of Eastern longitude. Srikakulam district lies between 80°-21′ and 19°-10′ of northern latitudes and between 83°-5′ and 84°-50′ of the Eastern longitude. It is bounded in the North and West by Koraput and Ganjam districts of Orissa in the East by the Bay of Bengal and on the South by Vizianagaram district.

The Tribal Areas of NCA

Article 366 (25) defines Scheduled Tribes as : "such tribes or tribal communities or parts of or groups within such tribes or tribal communities as are deemed under article 342 to be Scheduled Tribes (STs) for the purpose of this Constitution"[1] The Scheduled Tribes live in contiguous areas unlike other communities. In order to protect the interests of the Scheduled Tribes with regard to land alienation and other social factors, provisions of "Fifth Schedule" and "Sixth Schedule" have been enshrined in the Constitution. The Fifth Schedule under Article 244(1) of Constitution defines "Scheduled Areas" as : such areas as the President may by order declare to be Scheduled Areas after consultation with the Governor of the State. The Sixth Schedule under Article 244(2) of the Constitution relates to those areas in the north-east which have been declared as "tribal areas" and provides for a District or Regional Autonomous Councils for such areas.[2] Basing on these definitions, data on the tribals and tribal areas are generated and published by the Tribal Welfare Department, Government of Andhra Pradesh, which have been used in the analysis. The tribals live mostly in the forests, and the proportion of those living in the plains is very small. Therefore, the 'Scheduled Areas' largely fall under forests. In this study forest area is considered as the tribal area.

As per 2002–03 statistics, the NCA region has a forest area of 6,60,600 hectares, which accounts for 10.65 per cent of the total forest area of the State. In the total geographical area, the proportion of the forest area in the NCA is 28.12 per cent while it is only 22.59 per cent at the State level. The distribution of the forests is quite uneven among the districts in NCA. Visakhapatnam district has a share of 72.32 per cent, while the shares of Vizianagaram and Srikakulam are 16.94 per cent and 10.72 per cent respectively. In the total geographical area, the proportion of forest area in these districts is 42.12 per cent in

Visakhapatnam, 17.77 per cent in Vizianagaram and 12.12 per cent in Srikakulam. From these statistics, it is very clear that NCA and in particular Visakhapatnam district have considerable forest area for studying the tribal problems.

Flora and Fauna of the Forests of NCA

As the tribals meet their life sustenance to a large extent by gathering the natural produce available in the forests, the study of the flora and fauna of the forests assumes much importance. Since the available flora and fauna vary across the districts in the region, district-wise presentation is made in this section.

Visakhapatnam District

The forest types found in the district are : Southern tropical moist mixed deciduous forests; Northern tropical dry deciduous forests; Southern tropical dry mixed deciduous forests; Dry deciduous green forests; and Dry evergreen forests. These are endowed with a variety of flora and fauna.

Flora

The common wood species available in the forests of Visakhapatnam are : Guggilam (*Robusta*), Tangedu/Konda Tangedu/Billu, Chiramanu, Yegisa, Maddi, and Somidi. Apart from these, there are a number of fruit-bearing, flower-bearing, bark-bearing, gum-yielding, leaf-bearing trees, medicinal plants, and grasses found in these forests, which are the sources of many commercially exploitable non-wood products. The most prominent among them are: Gum Karaya, Myrobalans, Honey, Tamarind, Pungam seed, Marking nuts, Sheekakai, Hill brooms, Naramamidi bark, and Adda leaf.

Fauna

The common species found in these forests are Tiger and Wild Jackal among carnivores and Snow Bear, Wild Bear, Sambar, Spotted Deer, Wild Buffaloes and Monkeys among herbivores.

The birds spotted include : Peafowl, Pigeon, Myna, and Grey Patridge. Besides migratory birds like Ducks, and Keels are also seen all over the forest area. Reptiles and snakes are also found in the thick forests of the district.

Vizianagaram District

The common forest types found in Vizianagaram district are the same as those found in Visakhapatnam district, a mention of which has already been made.

Flora

The flora found in these forests are same as those found in the forests of Visakhapatnam. The prominent non-wood forest products available in these forests are: Gum Karaya, Myrobalans, Tamarind, Pungam seed, Mohua seed, Marking nuts, Sheekakai, Hill brooms, Soapnuts, and Naramamidi bark.

Fauna

The fauna in these forests is fairly high in the interior hill regions, but is heavily threatened with extinction. The reasons for the depletion are mainly shrinkage of habitat and uncontrolled poaching. The common varieties found are : Fount-horned Antelope, Yellow bat, Sloth bear, Indian bison, Wild buffalo, Jungle cat, Civet, Mouse deer, Barking deer, Fox, Hare, Hyena, Jackal, Langoor, Leapest, Mangoose, and Sambar. The common bird varieties are Ashy Long Tail Warbles, Black Iibis, and Blue Rock Pigeon, House Crow, House Sparrow, and Common Myna.

Srikakulam District

The various types of forest found in Srikakulam district are : South Indian moist deciduous which includes mixed forests, sal forests, and savannah; the South Indian dry deciduous which includes mixed forests and thorn forests; and the South

Indian dry evergreen miscellaneous forests. These forests are endowed with a rich variety of flora and fauna.

Flora

The flora variety found in the forests of Srikakulam is more or less the same as those found in the forests of Vizianagaram. These are amenable for extraction of a number of non-wood products and have commercial value. The most prominent among them are: Myrobalans, Tamarind, Pungam seed, Marking nuts, Sheekakai, Hill brooms, and Naramamidi bark.

Fauna

The land fauna in Srikakulam district is very small. Human habitations and destruction of the forests resulted in the disappearance of many species. The tiger is almost extinct in these forests. However, Leopard, Hyena, and Wolf are occasionally seen in the forests. The Jackal, Fox, Wild cat, and Wild dog are the other carnivorous animals found in the district. The herbivorous class is represented by Sambar, Spotted deer, Wild goat, Bear, and Wild bear. The Black buck, Blue bull, and Bison are conspicuously absent in these forests. Among the birds; the Peafowl, Peacock, Jungle fowl, Pigeon, Parrot, Myna, Partridges geese, and doves are common.

Size and Composition of Tribal Population in NCA

As per the 2001 census, the total scheduled tribes population in NCA was 9,23,660; which constituted 18.38 per cent of the total Scheduled Tribes population of the State. The proportion of ST population in the region is 10.72 per cent while this proportion is only 6.59 at the State level. Thus, the concentration of the tribal population is relatively more in NCA. It is also supported by the fact that with a tribal area of 10.65 per cent in the State's total, the region has a total tribal population of 18.38 per cent.

The distribution of the tribal population across the districts in the region follows more or less, the same pattern as the distribution of area of the total population of the region. About 60.37 per cent is located in Visakhapatnam, 23.26 per cent is located in Vizianagaram district, and 16.37 per cent is located in Srikakulam. The proportion of tribal population in the total population of the district is 14.55 per cent in Visakhapatnam, 9.55 per cent in Vizianagaram, and 5.96 per cent in Srikakulam. Thus in the districts of Visakhapatnam and Vizianagaram, the proportion of the tribal population is higher than the State average, while it is closer to the State average in the Srikakulam district.

A significant feature of the tribal population of the NCA is that the proportion of the tribal people to the urban population is very small at 2.99 per cent while it is 7.51 per cent at the State level. Within the districts in the region, it is 3.40 per cent in Visakhapatnam, 2.89 per cent in Vizianagaram, and 1.65 per cent in Srikakulam. Thus, tribals are mainly confined to either forests or rural areas. The sex ratio defined by number of females per 1000 males in NCA is 1008. While it is 972 at the State level, within the districts of the region: it is 1002 in Visakhapatnam, 1025 in Vizianagaram and 1009 in Srikakulam. Thus among the tribals in NCA, females outnumber the males contrary to most of the other tribal areas.

Tribal Communities in NCA

The tribals way of life, their religious and social customs, and their economic activities depend on the tribal community to which they belong in the NCA, which is home to as many as 33 tribal communities. The district-wise population of these communities is presented in Table 2.1. In Visakhapatnam the numerically dominant tribal communities are: Bhagatha, Konda dora, Valmiki, Khondu, Konda kapu, Kotia, Yerukula, and Mooka dora. In Vizianagaram district the dominant tribes are: Jathapu, Konda dora, Savara, Yerukula, Manne dora, and Mooka dora. In Srikakulam, the dominant tribes are: Savara, Jathapu, Kotia, Konda dora, and Yerukula.

The Bhagathas occupy the highest rung in the local social hierarchical ladder. They are divided into a number of

Table 2.1 : District-wise Population of the Tribal Groups in NCA—2001*

Name of the Tribe	*Visakhapatnam district*	*Vizianagaram district*	*Srikakulam district*	*NCA*
Ahdhra	463 (0.08)	55 (0.03)	31 (0.019)	549 (0.057)
Bhagatha	114185 (19.72)	1530 (0.72)	773 (0.49)	116488 (12.26)
Bhil	17(0.003)	21 (0.009)	5 (0.003)	43 (0.0045)
Chenchu	99 (0.02)	222 (0.104)	173 (0.108)	494 (0.052)
Gadaba	19019 (3.28)	947 (0.45)	1275 (0.802)	21241 (2.24)
Gondulu	38 (0.006)	6210 (0.029)	107 (0.067)	207 (0.0217)
Govudu	5273 (0.91)	859 (0.405)	118 (0.074)	6250 (0.66)
Hill reddy	5273 (0.91)	70 (0.033)	4 (0.0025)	5347 (0.56)
Jathapu	241 (0.04)	97021 (45.76)	27137 (17.08)	124399 (13.09)
Kammdra	28876 (4.99)	405 (0.19)	252 (0.16)	29533 (3.11)
Kattunayakam	46 (0.008)	—	5 (0.003)	51 (0.005)
Kolam	352 (0.061)	62 (0.029)	14 (0.008)	428 (0.045)
Konda dora	90989 (15.72)	55073 (25.97)	6035 (3.79)	152097 (16.01)
Konda kapu	55710 (9.62)	1733 (0.817)	1719 (1.08)	59162 (6.23)
Konda reddi	3043 (0.53)	51 (0.024)	44 (0.028)	3138 (0.33)
Kondu	58340 (10.08)	415 (0.195)	2857 (1.79)	61612 (6.49)
Kotia	40371 (6.97)	829 (0.39)	18432 (11.60)	59632 (6.28)
Koya	164 (0.03)	392 (0.18)	254 (0.16)	810 (0.085)
Kulia	222 (0.04)	53 (0.025)	26 (0.016)	301 (0.032)
Malia	2543 (0.44)	276 (0.130)	318 (0.20)	3137 (0.33)
Manne dora	6658 (1.15)	4096 (1.93)	39 (0.025)	10793 (1.136)
Mukha dora	14267 (2.16)	4718 (2.23)	39 (0.025)	19024 (2.003)
Nayak /Naiks	1765 (0.30)	55 (0.025)	45 (0.028)	1865 (0.196)
Pradhan	4 (0.007)	22 (0.010)	23 (0.014)	49 (0.005)
Porja	8811 (1.52)	32 (0.015)	33 (0.021)	8876 (0.93)
Reddi dora	5047 (0.87)	37 (0.017)	19 (0.0011)	5103 (0.54)
Rona	85 (0.015)	22 (0.010)	6 (0.0037)	113 (0.012)
Savara	176 (0.030)	33804 (15.94)	94782 (59.66)	128762 (13.56)
Sugali/ Lambada Toti	635 (0.11)	350 (0.17)	255 (0.161)	1240 (0.131)
Valmiki	78249 (13.52)	829 (0.391)	99 (0.062)	79177(8.34)
Yanadi	216 (0.04)	356 (0.17)	598 (0.376)	1170 (0.12)
Yerukula	37793 (6.53)	7635 (3.60)	3247 (2.04)	48675 (5.12)
Total no. of Tribals	**578970 (100.00)**	**212032 (100.00)**	**158862 (100.00)**	**949864 (100.00)**

Source: *Census of India 2001 series; 2004 Statistical data on Tribes and Tribal areas; Tribal Cultural Research & Training Institute, Hyderabad, Andhra Pradesh.

unilateral agnatic king groups called *gothrams* such as: Korra, Killo, Gollari, Pangi, etc. They prohibit eating of beef and pork. Nuclear families are more predominant compared to joint families in this community. Agriculture is the mainstay of their livelihood, while agricultural labour and collection of NTFP are subsidiary occupations. The Konda Dora tribe has a number of clans such as: Korra, Killo, Swabi, Contalu, Kimuel, Pargi, Paralek, Bidaka, Somelunger, Surrek, Gooligune, Olijukulu, etc. They are basically shifting cultivators. They also collect and sell NTFP. They eat beef and pork. The most important festival for them is Koda Pandri and this festival is followed by hunting festival.

The Valmiki tribe claims that its people are descendants of the famous sage Valmiki—The author of *Ramayana*. This tribe is divided into a number of *gotrams* in order to regulate marriage institutions among them such as: Naga bowse, Matsya Bowse, Pangi Bowse, Jilla Bowse, Bantala Bowse, Korra Bowse, Bhallu Bowse, Poolu Bowse, and Chilli Bowse. They are basically agriculturists and forest labourers. Some of them became traders and petty money lenders. They sell the earthen pots also in the shandies. They practice *podu*, i.e., shifting cultivation on the slopes of hills.

The Khond tribe, also known as Samantha, Kondakodu, Jathapu, Jatapudorta, Kodi, Kodhu, Kondu, and Kuniga, live on the densely wooded hill slopes. They are divided into sub-tribes such as: Dongria Khond, Desya Khond, Kuttiya Khond, Tikiria Khond, and Yeneti Khond. Each sub-tribe is again divided into a number of clans. Each clan has a distinct name and matrimonial alliances are permitted based on clan names. Monogamy is the rule and polygamy is very rare. Eating of beef and pork is not traditionally prohibited in this tribe. These tribes mainly subsist on cultivation. They grow millets like: Ragi, Sama, and Korra; oil seeds like niger, castor; and pulses like redgram in *podu* fields. They are also adept in hunting and fishing. They are well versed in handicrafts like baskets and mat weaving, oil extraction, etc.

The Konda Kapus are synonymous with Konda Doras. Some of the Bhagatas are also styling themselves as Konda

Kapus whenever they interact with non-tribal population. The Kotia tribe members are also called Doras claiming equal status with Bhagata. They are divided into four sub-groups namely: Bodo Kotia, Sano Kotia, Putia Poika, and Dhulia. Each sub-tribe is again divided into various clans. Kotias are basically agriculturists and cultivate food crops like: ragi, jowar, maize, and paddy; and vegetables like cabbage, brinjal, tomato, potato, etc. They collect and sell NTFP items like: adda leaves, tamarind, sheekakai, broom sticks, mohua flower, etc.

The Yerukula tribe members call themselves as Kurru. It is divided into a number of functional and endogamous sub-divisions and each sub-division is named after the commodity which they trade in and occupation they adopt. The sub-divisions are: Dobba Yerukula, Yeetha Pullala, Yerukula, Kunchapuri Yerukula, Parika, Muggula Yerukula, Karivepaku Yerukula, and Uppu Yerukula. Each sub-division is further divided into four groups namely: Sathupadi, Kavidi, Mampati, and Mendraguthi. The traditional occupation of these tribes are basket-making, mat weaving, pig rearing, rope making, etc. The Yerukula women are specialised in sooth saying and fortune telling. Some of them also participate in economic activities like basket making, mat weaving, etc.

The Mooka Dora are also known as Nooka Dora, Racha Reddy, Mooka raja, and Sabarlu. They are divided into various clans such as: Korra, Gammela, Kakara, Sugra, Kinchoyi, etc. Most of these tribes are settled with agriculture as their primary occupation, and supplement their incomes by the collection and sale of NTFP. They claim a social status just below the Bagathas in social hierarchy. The Savaras usually live in exclusive settlements of their own. They build their settlements on hill slopes and near hill streams. The most significant feature of this tribe is absence of clan system. Agriculture is their main occupation. They practice Podu and terrace cultivation on hill slopes as dry and wet farming. Their subsidiary occupations are collection and sale of NTFP, fishing and hunting. The Manne Dora tribe is divided into various *gothrams* namely: Killo, Matya, Gollari, Rambi, Pongi, Korra, and Naga. Their main occupation is agriculture, while collection and sale of

NTFP is their subsidiary occupation. The Jatapus are an acculturated tribe and belong to the same section as that of Konda tribe. Therefore, Jatapus and Khonds are one and the same tribe.

Literacy Level of Tribals in NCA

Education is one of the basic factors influencing the tribal livelihoods. For studying the educational levels of the tribals, access to the published sources of data is very limited. Only the data on the number of literates is available for 1991. Although it is very old, the same is used in the analysis here in order to have some idea. Illiteracy is relatively more among the tribals in NCA. Only 15.04 per cent are literate in this region while at the State level 17.16 are literate. At the district level, in this region, the literacy rate is the highest in Srikakulam and lowest in Vizianagaram. In all the districts, the female literacy rate is lower than the male literacy rate (Table 2.2).

Table 2.2 : District-wise Number of Literates and Literacy Rate by Sex of Tribals in NCA—1991*

District/Region	*No. of Literates*			*% of Literates to total population*		
	Male	*Female*	*Total*	*Male*	*Female*	*Total*
Srikakulam	15532	5577	21109	28.97	10.41	19.70
Vizianagaram	17437	6761	24198	22.52	8.79	15.68
Visakhapatnam	47458	14491	61947	25.14	7.83	16.58
North Coastal Andhra	80427	26829	107256	25.17	8.51	16.89
Andhra Pradesh	**430931**	**141480**	**572411**	**25.25**	**8.68**	**17.15**

Source : * Director, Census Corporation, Hyderabad; District and State level data on Demographic Diversity of India, 1991 Census.

It is observed that the literacy rate is varying significantly across the tribal communities. As per the 1991 census, it was 22.18 per cent in the case of Bagatas, 17.68 per cent in Chenchus, 17.51 per cent in Jatapus, 14.96 per cent in Konda Doras, 17.92 per cent in Konda Reddis, 5.19 per cent in Kondas, 17.83 per cent in Kotias, 19.02 per cent in Manne Doras, 9.86 per cent in

Mooka Doras, 13.68 per cent in Savaras, 39.87 per cent in Valmikis, and 25.74 per cent in Yerukalas. Thus among the prominent tribes of NCA, the educationally advanced include : Valmikis, Yerukalas, and Jatapus, while Khonds and Mooka doras are the most backward.

Occupational Distribution of Tribals in NCA

The major source of livelihood for the tribals in the NCA is agriculture. As per the 1991 census the latest year for which the data on occupational classification is available, cultivators account for 58.77 per cent, agricultural labourers account for 28.05 per cent and others which include NTFP gatherers, account for 11.50 per cent in NCA (Table 2.3). Among the total number of workers, the highest proportion of cultivators is found only in Visakhapatnam, whereas in Vizianagaram, large proportion is engaged in agricultural labour activities. Contrary to these two districts, in Srikakulam, the highest proportion is found under the "others" category. A peculiar feature in the tribal areas is that the females outnumber the males under "agricultural labour" category.

Distribution of Landholdings and Average Size of Holdings of Tribals in NCA

As observed in the previous section, agriculture is the mainstay of tribals in NCA. Its ability to meet the livelihood requirements of the tribals depends on the size of holding, crops grown, and productivity. As per the 1995–96 agricultural census data, the latest year for which published data are available, about three-fourths of the tribal holdings in NCA are small and marginal. The average size of the holdings is 1.46 hectares. Within the districts of the region, the proportion of the small and marginal holdings is relatively more in Srikakulam and Vizianagaram. The average size of the holding is 0.77 hectare in Srikakulam, 1.03 hectares in Vizianagaram, and 1.86 hectares in Visakhapatnam (Table 2.4). Therefore, it may be difficult for the tribals to subsist on agriculture alone.

Table 2.3 : District-wise Occupational Distribution of Tribals in NCA—1991*

District	Cultivators			Agriculture Labour			Household Industry			Other Workers			Total		
	Male	Female	Total	Male	Female	Total	Male	Female	Total	Male	Female	Total	Male	Female	Total
Srikakulam	10619	6195	16814	2117	20171	22288	1013	1269	2282	25412	4490	29902	39161	32125	71286
			(23.58)			(31.26)			(3.22)			(41.94)			(100.00)
Vizianagaram	25349	12923	38272	26662	26175	52837	1777	1061	2838	4804	1872	66.76	58592	42031	100623
			(38.03)			(52.52)			(2.82)			(6.63)			(100.00)
Visakhapatnam	113397	73884	187281	9620	20926	40546	1236	574	1810	8261	2627	10888	142514	98011	240525
			(77.86)			(16.86)			(0.75)			(4.53)			(100.00)
NCA	149365	93002	242367	48399	67276	115675	4026	2904	6930	38477	8989	47466	240267	172167	412434
			(58.77)			(28.05)			(1.68)			(11.50)			(100.00)
Andhra Pradesh	**584051**	**893755**	**1477806**	**453019**	**539338**	**992357**	**30176**	**25610**	**55786**	**130982**	**542731**	**673713**	**1198228**	**2001434**	**319962**
			(46.19)			**(31.01)**			**(1.74)**			**(21.06)**			**(100.00)**

* *Source* : 1991 Census; India Horticulture Data Base 2001.

Table 2.4 : District-wise Number of Operational Holdings held by Size Group and Average Size of Holding of Scheduled Tribes in NCA—1995-96*

District	Operational Holdings						Ope-rated Area (Hect-ares)	Average size of Hold-ing (Hect-ares)
	Below 1 Hect.	1-2 Hect.	3-4 Hect.	4-10 Hect.	10 Hect. and above	Total Hold-ings		
Srikakulam	20254 *(76.38)	4444 (16.76)	1560 (5.88)	242 (0.91)	17 (0.06)	26517	20490	0.7727
Vizia-nagaram	22985 (67.45)	6989 (20.51)	3099 (9.09)	937 (2.75)	65 (0.19)	34075	34994	1.0269
Visakha-patnam	35326 (43.37)	19631 (24.10)	17432 (21.40)	8282 (10.17)	785 (0.96)	81456	151311	1.8576
NCA	**78565 (55.31)**	**31064 (21.87)**	**22091 (15.55)**	**9461 (6.66)**	**867 (0.61)**	**142048**	**206795**	**1.4558**

* Figures in brackets indicate percentage of hectare-wise operational holdings to that of total holdings in each district

Source : Agricultural Census Data 1995–96; ITDA Annual Action Plans, Tribal Welfare Commissionerate, Andhra Pradesh.

Area Irrigated by Source

The types of crops grown and the crop yields are determined to a large extent by the irrigation coverage and quality of irrigation. In the tribal areas of NCA agriculture is mostly rain-fed and only 15.88 per cent of the cropped area has assured irrigation facilities. The major source of irrigation is tanks. Only 20 per cent of the area irrigated is covered by canals. A large part of the area under tanks and other sources prompt us to draw an inference that, the quality of irrigation in the region is poor. At the district level, irrigation coverage is relatively more in Vizianagaram and Srikakulam (Table 2.5).

Crop Pattern

For assessing the incomes from agriculture, secondary data on the total area under crops, crop yields, and cost of cultivation in the tribal areas are not available. As the main focus of this study is not the analysis of crop incomes, attempt has not been made to collect the primary data. For analysing the crop pattern, the only available information is the type of crops grown. The major crops grown in the tribal areas of NCA are : paddy, jowar, bazra, small millets, pulses, oil seeds, sugarcane, spices and cardamom, fruits and vegetables, turmeric, and ginger. The major plantation crops in the region are cashew and mango.

Table 2.5 : District-wise Area Irrigated by Source in the Tribal Areas of NCA

(In Hectares)

District	*Canals*	*Tanks*	*Wells*	*Tube wells*	*Other sources*	*Total Irri-gated Areas*	*Net area sown*	*% of Irrigated area to net area sown*
Srikakulam	1229 *(34.82)	1584 (44.87)	33 (0.93)	4 (0.11)	680 (19.26)	3530	16929	20.85
Vizia-nagaram	544 (11.56)	3698 (78.56)	22 (0.47)	2 (0.04)	441 (9.37)	4707	19685	23.91
Visakha-patnam	1340 (19.26)	898 (12.90)	23 (0.33)	4 (0.05)	4694 (67.45)	6959	59055	11.78
NCA	**3113 (20.49)**	**6180 (40.67)**	**78 (0.51)**	**10 (0.07)**	**5815 (38.27)**	**15196**	**95669**	**15.88**

* Figures in brackets indicate percentage of Source of Irrigation to that of Total Irrigated Area in each district.\

Source : ITDA Annual Action Plans, Tribal Welfare Commissionerate, Andhra Pradesh; Benchmark Surveys of Tribal Cultural Research & Training Institute, Hyderabad, Andhra Pradesh

Infrastructure Facilities

In improving the livelihoods of tribals, infrastructure facilities like : health care services, educational institutes, transport and power, play a key role. Generally, the tribals access to these facilities is limited.

Medical Care

The number of medical institutions which include : dispensaries, primary health centres, community health centres, mobile medical units (M.M.U.s), and sub-health centres are only 37.68 per one lakh population in NCA. This number is 35.15 in Visakhapatnam and 31.07 in Srikakulam. The number of community health workers per one lakh population in these districts is 574, 218, and 230 respectively, while this number is 435 at the regional level (Table 2.6).

Table 2.6 : District-wise Infrastructural Facilities in NCA*

Infrastructural Facilities	*Srikakulam*	*Vizia-nagaram*	*Visakha-patnam*	*NCA*
Health Care facilities :				
1. No. of Medical Institutions per 1 lakh population.	31.07	48.87	35.15	37.68
2. No. of Community Health Workers per 1 lakh population	230	218	574	435
Educational Institutions per 1 lakh population	197	209	153	173
Percentage of Villages and Habitations connected by Roads	52.22	32.99	29.92	33.36
Percentage of electrified villages	98.56	79.27	82.95	83.82
Shandy Points	12	21	40	73

* *Source* : IDTA Reports.

Educational Institutions

The types of educational institutions established in the tribal areas are : *Girijan Vidya Vikas Kendra* Schools (G.V.V.K. Schools), *Ashram* schools, *Gurukulam* residential institutions, residential junior colleges, and polytechnic colleges. For each one lakh of population, these institutions number at 197 in Srikakulam district, 209 in Vizianagaram, 153 in Visakhapatnam, and 173 at the regional level.

Table 2.7 : List of NTFP Available in NCA Districts, their Potential and Period of Collection*

(Quantity in quintals)

Name of the Commodity	*Season*	*Visakha-patnam*	*Vizia-nagaram*	*Srika-kulam*	*NCA Total*
Gum Karaya	Throughout the year	60-75	40-50	30-50	150-200
Myrabolans	Nov-March	10000-12000	4000-5000	600-500	15000-20000
Nux vomica	Oct-Feb	75-100	75-100	30-50	150-250
Seeded Tamarind	Jan-April	40000-50000	40000-50000	5000-6000	Upto 1 lakh
Deseeded Tamarind	March-May	300-500	3500-4000	—	3500-4000
Tamarind Seed	March-June	400-500	600-750	—	1000-1250
Pungam Seed	April-June	2500-3000	2000-2500	8000-1000	12500-15000
Cleaning Nuts	Nov-March	100-200	350-400	10-15	450-650
Mohwa Seed	May-August	25-50	1300-1500	5-10	1400-1500
Marking nuts	Jan-April	2500-3000	3000-3500	2000-2500	7500-9000
Honey	Mar-July Oct-Jan	400-450	—	—	400-450
Sheekakai	Feb-April	2000-2500	500-600	50-75	3000-3500
Hill Brooms	Feb-April	1.40-2.0 lakh	1.50-2.0 lakh	Upto 1 lakh	3.00-5.00 lakh
Soapnuts	Feb-May	180-250	500-550	300-350	1000-1200
Naramamidi Bark	Jan-June	1400-2000	700-750	1000-1250	3000-4000
Adda Leaf	April-June	80000-100000	200-300	—	80000-100000

* *Source* : GCC, Visakhapatnam.

Road Connectivity

The percentage of villages and habitations connected by roads in these districts is respectively, 52.22; 32.99; and 29.92, while it is 33.36 at the regional level.

Electricity

For providing power, tribal villages are connected by conventional power lines and solar lines. The percentage of villages electrified by these two sources is 98.56 in Srikakulam, 79.27 in Vizianagaram, 82.95 in Visakhapatnam, while it is 83.82 at the regional level. Among the conventional lines and solar lines, the major source is solar.

Marketing

The major sources of marketing in the tribal areas are the shandies. In the NCA region, there are 73 shandy points. At the district level, there are 40 in Visakhapatnam, 21 in Vizianagaram, and 12 in Srikakulam.

Summing Up

The NCA region, comprising the districts of Visakhapatnam, Vizianagaram, and Srikakulam has a scheduled area of 6,60,600 hectares, which accounts for 10.65 per cent of the tribal area in the State. This area is covered by the forests rich in flora and fauna, which are the sources of NTFP. Nearly one-fifth of the tribal population of the State is living in this region. Within this region the concentration in terms of area and population is much higher in Visakhapatnam, and much lower in Srikakulam.

The major tribes of this region are : Bhagatha, Konda dora, Valmiki, Kondu, Konda kapu, Kotia, Yerukala, Mooka Dora, Jathapu, Savara, and Manne Dora. The literacy levels are generally low, and vary across these tribal groups. The major occupation of these tribes is agriculture, followed by agricultural labour. Many tribals also take up collection and sale of non-timber forest produce as an economic activity. Some are also engaged in activities such as: pottery, making of agricultural implements, baskets, etc.

Agriculture in the tribal areas is subsistence agriculture, and income derived from it is hardly sufficient to meet their requirements. Therefore, promoting the income from the other activities like collection and sale of NTFP play a key role. But due to the population pressure, the incomes from NTFP may also be low in this region. For promoting incomes, access to infrastructural facilities like transport, and power is essential. But access to such facilities in this region is limited. Given the income, the other two prominent factors promoting tribal development are access to health care facilities and education. Access to health care facilities is very poor in this region. However, in the case of educational infrastructure the situation is marginally better.

NOTES

1. Tribal Cultural Research & Training Institute (2004), *Tribes and Tribal Areas of Andhra Pradesh (Basic Statistics)* Tribal Welfare Department, Government of Andhra Pradesh, p. 7.
2. *Ibid.*, p. 8.

3

Forest and NTFP Policies and Tribals Access to NTFP

Introduction

The Forest Policy in general and NTFP policy in particular are subjected to many changes in the Indian States. These changes may have differential effect on the sustainability of NTFP, the access of the tribals to NTFP, and the tribal livelihoods. In this chapter an attempt has been made to document the major changes in the forest policy and in particular, those that took place during the last century in the NTFP; policies relating to regulation and marketing of NTFP, and provision of NTFP to the industries and assess their impact on tribals access to NTFP in Andhra Pradesh, on the basis of information drawn from secondary sources, i.e., both published and unpublished.

National Policies on Forests and Panchayats Extension to Scheduled Areas (PESA)

From times immemorial until recently, the tribal people had the freedom to enjoy the forests and this has given them a conviction which remains even today, deep in their hearts, that forests belong to them. This state of affairs continued happily until about the middle of the nineteenth century. Thereafter, people from outside began to move into the forests and conditions began to change. The gradual extension of the authority of the government and the natural desire of the forest officials to exercise even greater control over the use of forest products, deeply disturbed the entire tribal economy and introduced a psychological conflict.

The Gist of 1894 Forest Policy

> *"The sole object with which State forests are administered is the public benefit. In some cases the public to be benefited is the body of tax payers and the people of track within which the forests are situated. But in almost all cases the constitution and preservation of a forest involved, in greater or lesser degree, the regulation of rights and restriction of privileges of users in the forest area which may have been previously enjoyed by inhabitants of its immediate neighbourhood. These regulations and restrictions are justified only when the advantage to be gained by public is great; and the cardinal principle to be observed is that the rights and privileges of the individuals must be limited, otherwise than for their own benefit. Only in such degree as is absolutely necessary to secure that advantage."*

This passage illustrates that the 1894 policy was mostly concerned with the tribal people and they had complete rights over the forests in which they lived.

The following are the major policy issues[1] in the larger interests of tribals :

(a) The 1894 policy is mostly concerned with tribal people. They had complete rights on forests in which they lived.
(b) This policy envisaged release of forest and for cultivation of tribal people subject to certain safeguards.
(c) The principle laid down for the object of utilization of forest area was to secure the greatest good of the tribal community.
(d) No restrictions were placed upon local demands merely in order to increase the revenue. The principle laid down in the Resolution was that income to the State should be made a secondary goal to the full satisfaction of the local needs.

(e) In the case of Minor Forests, the object was the supply of forest produce to the greatest advantage and convenience of the community.

(f) Under Chapter 4, rights were recorded. The rights to which the area was subject were extensive and the forest had to be managed mainly in the interest of local community.

The Gist of 1952 Forest Policy

The new forest policy of 1952 introduced great changes. They are epitomized in the following official statement :

"Village communities in the neighbourhood of a forest will naturally make greater use of its products for the satisfaction of their domestic and agricultural needs. Such use, however, should in no event be permitted at the cost of National interest. The accident of a village being situated close to a forest does not prejudice the right of the country as a whole to receive the benefits of a national asset. The scientific conservation of a Forest inevitably involved the Regulation of Rights and the restriction of privileges of user depending upon the value and importance of the forest. However, irksome such restraints may be to the neighbouring areas... while, therefore, the needs of the local population must be met to a reasonable extent, National interest should not be sacrificed because they are not directly discernable, nor should the rights of interest of future generations be subordinated to the improvidence of the present generation."

(a) Departure of 1952 Policy from the 1894 Policy Affecting the Tribals

Although it is claimed that the policy of 1952 was a continuation of the old policy of 1894, it was in fact different in at least in the following aspects which are of great concern to the tribals :

(i) The 1894 policy envisaged the release of forest land for cultivation subject to certain safeguards. The 1952 policy withdrew this concession.

(ii) The 1894 policy had left a margin for the supply of tribals needs from the outlying areas in the reserve forest. The new policy decided that there should be village forest for this purpose.

(iii) The old policy (1894) did not touch the private forest of the tribals. The new policy applied the controls on them.

(iv) The 1894 policy did not touch the issue of free grazing in forests. The 1952 policy sought to bring it under control. Fees were introduced and grazing was to be kept to the minimum.

(v) The 1952 policy made one important concession. It admitted that while it was emphatically opposed to shifting cultivation, persuasive and not coercive measures should be used rather than in an authoritarian manner, to attempt to wean the tribals from their traditional methods.

(b) The Impact of the 1952 Policy

The tribal who formerly regarded himself as the lord of the forests, was through a deliberate process, turned into a subject and placed under the Forest Department. The tribal villages were no longer an essential part of the forest but were there nearly on sufferance. The traditional rights of the tribals were no longer recognized as rights. In 1894, they became 'Rights and Privileges' but in 1952, they became 'Rights and Concessions,' and were later regarded as 'Concessions'.

(i) It was only after the 1894 policy that the forest officials appeared on the scene in huge numbers and claimed authority to limit and regulate tribal rights in favour of the rights of the government. This new conception affected the tribal people very deeply and was the root cause of delicate relations between them and the Forest Department, which continues even to the present time.

(ii) *Reaction of Officials* : This new emphasis has a definite impact on the personnel of forest departments all over

India. The immediate effect of the 1952 policy has been to restrict the Rights of the Tribals on a very large scale.

(iii) *Forest Department's Claims on Forests* : There are many cases where the forest departments have had claims on a given forest. Forest departments would not agree to construction of a canal in the forest, simply because they were afraid that people would come to repair it and in the process cut the trees.

(iv) *System of Permits* : The system of permits, licenses, and passes has grown up because of this 'man-shyness'. While the permit fees are not very high, the inconvenience caused, however, is tremendous.

(v) *Exploitation by Contractors* : Apart from the policy and psychological reactions upon the service personnel in the forest department, its implications have produced other complications. The emphasis on realization of maximum annual revenue has increased the importance of a contractor. The tribal who seldom knows the rules, is at his mercy. It is the common practice of the contractor, to purchase NTFP that is leased out to him from tribals and subsequently sell at higher rates.

(vi) *Reactions of the Tribal People* : There is a constant propaganda that the tribals are destroying the forest. But the simple honest tribals countered the complaint by asking, how they could destroy the forest since they owned no trucks. They did not have even bullock carts. At the most, they could carry away a head-load of produce for the sale, to maintain their families and that too against a licence. Their fuel needs for cooking were not much because they had not much to cook.

There is a feeling among tribals, that all the arguments in support of preservation and development of forests are intended to deny them their rightful share. Vast tracks are placed at the disposal of outsiders for developing industry or a project, who mercilessly destroy the forest wealth owing or not owing to necessity.

The Gist of 1988 Forest Policy

In view of the social, economic, and ecological importance of forests, considerable thought has been given to the multifarious implications of the forest policy. Although the 1952 forest policy aimed at one-third forest coverage of the total land in the country, due to various constraints, this goal could not be attained. Rather, extensive diversion of forest land has taken place for non-forest use. The general diversity has also been considerably affected for the restriction of flora and fauna. The government has increasingly realized the tremendous importance of forests in contributing to the ecological stability of the country. This has necessitated re-examination of the forest policy, and in giving emphasis to the conservation and ecological aspects.

(a) Salient Features of 1988 Forest Policy

The major cause of degradation of forests is attributed to forest contractors and their labour. In order to put an end to this, emphasis is made to replace contractors and establish Tribal Co-operatives, Government Corporations, etc. The salient features are as follows :

- (i) Maintenance of environmental stability, preservation of land, restoration of ecological balance;
- (ii) Conservation of natural heritage of the country by preserving and retaining natural forest and protecting the vast genetic resources of the country;
- (iii) Emphasises on creating massive people's movement through the involvement of village communities living in and close to forest, for protection and development of the forest;
- (iv) Having symbiotic relations between tribal people and forest, necessitated that, all the agencies responsible for forest management, including the Forest Development Co-operatives and Corporations should associate with the tribal people closely with regard to protection, regeneration, and development of forest as well to

provide gainful employment to people living in and around the forests.

(b) Joint Forest Management (JFM) in the Country

In pursuing this policy, the GoI issued notification in June 1990 requesting State governments to involve local communities in the management of forests. It was envisaged that, the communities in view of their participation in protection and development of forest areas will be entitled to sharing usufructs, in a manner specified by the concerned State forest departments. This has led to the development of Joint Forest Management programme. Twenty-two State governments which have issued resolutions in this regard have evolved their own mechanisms of involving local communities in conformity to proclaimed Policy. In all, 36,130 Forest Protection Committees are managing a total of 10.25 million hectares of forest area.

Areas under JFM in Andhra Pradesh and Southern/Adjacent States*

State	*Date of notification*	*No. of JFM committees*	*Areas under JFM. '000 hectares*
Andhra Pradesh	28.09.1992	6575	1632.19
Orissa	03.08.1988	3704	419.31
Madhya Pradesh	10.12.1991	12038	5088.00
Tamilnadu	08.08.1997	599	224.38
Karnataka	12.04.1993	1212	12.80
Kerala	16.01.1998	21	4.00
Total (including other States)		**36130**	**10248.64**

* *Source* : Project Implementation Plan (Volumes I to V), A.P. Community Forest Management Project, Andhra Pradesh Forest Department

(c) Implementation of 1988 Forest Policy with reference to JFM in Andhra Pradesh

The Government of Andhra Pradesh came out with a State Forest Policy during 1993 that focussed on participatory management of forests. The focal theme of forest sector vision includes sustainable management of resources, and the protection and regeneration of the forests, and forest management. The role of the forester, at least in respect of participatory management of forests is that of a facilitator, a social mobilizer, and an extension worker.

(i) Under Joint Forest Management programme in Andhra Pradesh a total of 6,575 *Vana Samrakshana Samithis* (VSSs) comprising nearly 1.3 million members who are managing 1.63 million hectares out of which nearly 4.15 lakh belongs to tribal communities, and 2.45 lakh to *dalits*. Others include the BCs and small portion of OCs.

(ii) Only degraded forests have been included under this programme.

(iii) Individual members of the committee shall be entitled to get 50 per cent of the net benefits from forest produce and 50 per cent will be ploughed backed for the development of the area.

(d) The Community Forest Management (CFM) Programme

The Community Forest Management approach of the Government of A.P. (Andhra Pradesh) is being implemented with the World Bank's financial assistance to the tune of Rs. 654 crore by the forest department in 14 districts which include : Adilabad, Khammam, Warangal, Kareemnagar, Nizamabad, Mahaboobnagar, Srikakulam, Vizianagaram, Visakhapatnam, East Godavari, Nellore, Chittoor, and Cuddapah.

The project aims at 50,000 selected villages with high poverty incidence in these regions, to consolidate and expand the benefits of joint forest management involving local forest communities through VSSs. The VSSs participation is estimated to benefit approximately 3.26 lakh households or 1.8 million people. Tribal communities constitute the 5,000 VSS villages that have been targeted under this project.

(e) The Sustainability of Vana Samarakshana Samiti (VSS) and its Limitations

(i) The sustainability of VSS has to be looked at in terms of :

1. Sustainability of VSS as an institution;
2. Sustainability of the management of forest that has been allotted to VSS; and
3. Sustainability of the livelihoods of the VSS concerned (i.e. VSS members).

While the institutional sustainability is dependent on the way the equity and equality issues are addressed and the way the enthusiasm of the members sustained, the sustainability of the management of forests depends on the practices which incorporate the conservation of bio-diversity, sustainable harvest practices, and such other matters. In the long run, the income beyond the forest resources has to be used for both forest development as well as the development of VSS members. It is all the more important to look into the livelihood status of each member and how that can be sustained and improved. This would be possible only when, there is a correct estimate of how much return can be exactly expected from the forest produce and to what extent that can contribute to the livelihoods of the members, and what additional measures have to be taken to fill the gap.

(ii) In the Scheduled Areas, the GCC clientele includes only the tribals. However, the VSS provides membership to all communities.

(iii) The marketing of NTFP in non-scheduled areas is not organized and the VSS is not equipped to market it either.

(iv) The NTFP can contribute substantially to the livelihoods of VSS members by certain intervention measures such as : improved techniques of value addition, storage, and marketing arrangements. However, the forest department does not have perfect inventory of the NTFP items and quantities so as to assess the exact needs.

(v) The forest department does not have any past experience in marketing NTFP and, therefore, should focus on active convergence among the other related institutions like the GCC and *Velugu* programme (SERP) of the Government of Andhra Pradesh.

(vi) Now with the formation of the VSS and the provision of 100 per cent benefits out of the NTFP to the members; the primary stakeholders in respect of NTFP constitute two categories i.e., the tribal members and other non-tribal VSS members. These issues of sharing the benefits between the two categories have to be examined more carefully, in view of the tribal laws as per details given in the following, according to which usufruct rights lie with the tribals.

(f) Legal and Political Framework for Tribals

The governments both at the Centre as well as at the State have formulated a number of policies to safeguard the interests of tribals and have initiated a number of development schemes for the welfare and upliftment of tribal communities. They can be broadly categorized as follows :

(i) Constitutional Safeguards

Administrative : Clause (1) of Article 244, applies to the administration and control of scheduled areas in a State.

Tribal Development : Article 275 (1) provides grant-in-aid to the State to implement the various developmental schemes for the welfare of the Scheduled Tribes.

Others include : Article 15(4): Promotion of Education.

Article 330 and 332 : Political safeguards provide reservation for the SCs, STs in Parliament and State Legislative Assemblies.

Article 16(4) : Employment: Reservation of the Posts.

(ii) Social Safeguards

Article 338A : The National Commission for Scheduled Tribes is to investigate, monitor, and evaluate all matters relating to the constitutional safeguards provided for the Scheduled Tribes.

Article 339 : Appointment of a Commission to report about the administration of the scheduled areas and the welfare of the Scheduled Tribes in the State.

(iii) Economic Safeguards

Article 275(I) : Grants-in-aid from the Consolidated Fund of India will be provided each year for promoting the welfare of the Scheduled Tribes and administration of Scheduled Areas.

(iv) Political Safeguards

Article 244(1) : The Fifth Schedule provides for the establishment of a Tribes Advisory Council, for the administration and control of Scheduled Areas and the Scheduled Tribes in any State (other than the States of Assam, Meghalaya, Tripura and Mizoram) to advise on matters pertaining to welfare and advancement of the Scheduled Tribes. Extension of the 73rd and 74th Amendments of the Constitution to the Scheduled Areas through the Panchayats (Panchayat Extension to the Scheduled Areas) Act 1996 (PESA), has been made to ensure effective participation of the tribals in the process of planning and decision-making.

(v) Five Year Plans

The First and Second Five Year Plans emphasized additional financial resources through a community development approach, to address the problems of tribal people. The Third and Fourth Five Year Plans emphasized on converting those Community Development Blocks where the concentration of tribal population was 66 per cent and above, into Tribal

Development Blocks (TDBs). In the Fifth Five Year Plan, an area-specific strategy was evolved, based on the recommendations of an expert committee for the rapid socio-economic development of tribal people inhabiting the Scheduled Areas. The Tribal Sub Plan (TSP) strategy had the two main objectives of socio-economic development of Scheduled Tribes and protection of tribals against exploitation.

The salient features of TSP are :

(a) To identify the resources for TSP areas;
(b) To prepare a broad policy framework for the development; and
(c) To define a suitable administrative strategy for its implementation; and
(d) To ensure flow of funds for TSP areas, at least in equal proportion to the Scheduled Tribes population of the State.

(vi) Policy Regulations with regard to Tribals and Tribal Tracts

(a) *The Agency Tracts Interests and Land Transfer Act 1917*: It safeguards the interest of hill tribes of the area and protects them from exploitation by non-tribals and money lenders.
(b) *The Andhra Pradesh Estate Act 1948/ Andhra Pradesh Mahals Regulation 1969, and the Andhra Pradesh Mutta Regulation 1969* : These are landmark enactments that facilitated State ownership of private estates and lands in the scheduled areas, and paved the way for settlement of land tenure.

Issues related to NTFP and Policies on Panchayats Extension to Scheduled Areas (PESA) and Joint Forest Management (JFM)

The management of NTFP in the States is in the hands of TDCCs, Forest Department, and FDCs. Certain NTFP are nationalized in certain States and are listed in the private trade category in some States. The policies related to NTFP framed for the benefit of tribals, come into conflict with Joint Forest Management on the one hand and with PESA (Panchayat Law applicable to the V Scheduled Areas) on the other. The Joint Forest Management / Community Forest Management is based on the concept of people being co-managers. The PESA bestows ownership rights on the entire Gram Sabha / Panchayat with no condition that people need to protect forest before they enjoy the usufruct, whereas Joint Forest Management is based on the principle of care and share. According to PESA, people are the owners of NTFP but most important NTFP are still owned by government and PESA is riddled with ambiguities. The PESA is popularly known as Tribal Self Rule Law aimed at empowering the village community by vesting it with powers over the issues having a bearing on their life and livelihood like: development, planning, natural resources, customary and traditional practices, and dispute resolution in accordance with such practices, etc. According to PESA, panchayats and government are both owners of NTFP. But the forest department contends that villages do not have control over reserve forests as they are situated outside village boundaries and, therefore, PESA is not applicable to reserve forests. The two ministries of the GoI, Rural Development and Environment and Forests have different views about the applicability of PESA over reserve forests.

There is a contradiction between JFM and PESA, as JFM encourages small community based informal groups, whereas PESA recognizes formal panchayats and Gram Sabhas. Even the revised JFM guidelines issued by the Ministry of Environment and Forests in 2002 do not mention PESA, indicating the low importance given to its provisions and their potential bearing on the JFM framework in Schedule-V areas by the Central Ministry. The other set of problems that have arisen in the States such as Orissa, and have tried to dilute the provisions of PESA, though they had no legal jurisdiction to do so as PESA is a Central Act. Jharkhand has not conducted Panchayati Raj elections and is the only State without Panchayats.

In Andhra Pradesh too, there is a clear contradiction between PESA and G.O.Ms. No. 173 of Environment, Forests, Science and Technology Department of Andhra Pradesh. The usufructory rights of VSS prescribed therein include all NTFP except those for which GCC holds monopoly rights. However, the right to collection shall remain with VSS members if they so desire and the members shall be paid collection charges for the delivery of the produce, as per rates fixed by the government. There is a contradiction between the ownership rights vesting in Gram Panchayats/Sabhas clause and monopoly rights vested in the GCC. Such indifference to PESA can be seen in many other States too. The irony is that while PESA remains unimplemented, the GoI has proposed amending Schedule-V of Constitution itself, to open up tribal areas for commercial exploitation by national and multinational corporate interests.

NTFP Policies of States and Need for a Uniform Policy

Forests in Tribal Lives

In India there are about 100 million forest dwellers, of which half are tribals living in and around forest lands and another 275 million for whom forests have continued to be an important source for their livelihood and means of survival. Forests are not spread evenly in India. More than 50 per cent of the forests are located in the Central Plateau, which is the major forest region in India (but is characterized by low agricultural productivity and poor soils, and heavy concentration. A perusal of the districts in five States which have more than 30 per cent of the geographical area are declared as forests and these are also the districts with heavy concentration of tribal population.

In the tropical forests, the quantities of NTFP are incredibly large and provide subsistence and income especially during the slack season. Moreover the collection of NTFP is a source of cash income, especially because of their increasing commercial value. However, the different NTFP policies of the States and the degree of control over NTFP have been affecting the economy of tribals. This situation has been described in the following section.

Institutional Structure in the States Controlling NTFP

(a) Andhra Pradesh

In Andhra Pradesh, the Girijan Co-operative Corporation Ltd. is functioning under the administrative control of the Tribal Welfare Department. This TDCC is headquartered at Visakhapatnam, and has a two-tier structure with Girijan Primary Co-operative Marketing Societies (GPCMS) constituting the primary level. The GCC was formed in 1956 to procure and market NTFP, provide credit facilities to its members, and supply essential commodities by acting as PDS outlets in the tribal areas. Procurement of NTFP is one of the core functions of the GCC. Fifty per cent of the administrative costs of the Corporation are borne by the State government, as it has the staff strength that is as large as 1600. The Forest Department in Andhra Pradesh primarily performs a monitoring role in the case of tendu leaves sold in advance to private traders. The Andhra Pradesh Forest Development Corporation (APFDC) arranges the necessary finance for procurement of tendu leaves.

(b) Chhattisgarh

The Chattisgarh Minor Forest Produce Federation (CMFPF) is at the apex of a three-tier co-operative structure that has Primary Forest Produce Co-operative Societies (PCS) at the primary level and District Forest Produce Co-operative Unions at intermediary level. The Primary Co-operative Societies and District Unions have elected members and chairmen. While the DFO is the *ex officio* Managing Director of the district union, the Forest Department manages the apex federation with a political representative as its chairperson. The Federation comes under the administrative control of the Forest Department and conducts all its operations with the help of the latter.

(c) Jharkhand

Though it is the Jharkhand Forest Development Corporation (JFDC) that plays a major role in collection and procurement of nationalised produce, this is a State that has more than one agency dealing with NTFP. They come under different departments. Even after the nationalisation and passing of the legislation in response to PESA, it is the private agents/ contractors who still rule the roost in the collection and trading of NTFP.

(d) Orissa

Orissa is another State which is characterised by multiple actors in the NTFP trading scenario. Even in the case of nationalised and non-nationalised produce, more than one State or State-promoted agencies are engaged in procuring and marketing of NTFP. While the Panchayat has been provided with the responsibility and authority of managing non-nationalised NTFP, it does not have the capacity to exercise them. While the Orissa Forest Development Corporation (OFDC) comes under the administrative control of the Forest Department, the TDCC comes under the Tribal Welfare Department and Orissa Rural & Marketing Agricultural Society (ORMAS) under the Panchayati Raj Department. Unlike Andhra Pradesh and Chattisgarh, the TDCC does not have a primary level of co-operatives. The TDCC, OFDC, and Kendu Leaves division have their own staff and infrastructure, whose expenditure is borne from the operations of NTFP.

Status of Procurement of MFP by Federations in Different States

(a) Andhra Pradesh

A trade wing of the Forest Department deals in tendu leaf. The Girijan Co-operative Corporation (GCC) holds monopoly rights of specified NTFP. The number of items under monopoly rights can change depending on sustainable harvesting criteria and as per the recommendations of the government in the Department of Environment, Forests, Science and Technology. It is down to 24 items this year from 37 in the initial years. The agency fixes procurement price based on the sale prices prevailing in the nearest wholesale market duly deducting 15 per cent costs towards trade charges, primary and secondary transport, and permissible driages.

(b) Chhattisgarh

The State has a Minor Forest Produce (Trading and Development) Co-operative Federation (CMFPF) that deals in trading of nationalised produce. In the case of non-nationalised produce, the State does not charge any royalty since 1986. There are no restrictions on primary gatherers regarding collection, movement, or storing. However, during the transport of the produce from one place to another by the trader, a transit pass (TP) is required from the forest authorities even within the State.

(c) Jharkhand

The Jharkhand Forest Development Corporation (JFDC) deals with nationalized forest produce in the State. There is one more agency named Tribal Co-operative Development Corporation (TCDC) that deals with nationalized items in some areas as well as with non-nationalized produce. Then there are some produce-specific State agencies dealing with lac and tassar, as the State is a market leader in the above produce. Apart from the usual restrictions on nationalised produce, the traders have to get a transit permit from the State Forest Department to transport produce from one place to another.

(d) Orissa

While the OFDC is responsible for financing and marketing of Kendu leaves (KL). In the case of Sal seed, areas have been distributed between the TDCC and the OFDC. As far as the non-nationalised produce is concerned, the panchayats have been granted ownership rights over NTFP in their areas of jurisdiction. In operational terms, it means that traders who want to operate in any area have to get them registered with the respective panchayats by paying a fee. The traders have to stick to an MPP fixed by a district level committee. The Minimum Purchase Price (MPP) fixed by the district level committee is to be ratified by the Gram Sabha and the Gram Panchayats have been empowered to modify the MPP, if needed. There is no restriction on the movement of produce inside the State.

Functional Arrangement in the States Trading in NTFP

Sl. No.	*State*	*Monopoly Agency for NTFP*	*Nationalized Commodity*	*Collecting Agency*	*Price fixation method*
1.	Gujarat	GSFDC	Tendu leaves, Mahua flower, Mahua seeds and Doll, Gum Karaya	Village Panchayat	—
2.	M.P.	MP MFP Federation	Tendu leaves, Gum Karaya, Myrobalan, Sal seed	District Forest Union/District MFP Union	Price Fixation Committee constituted by the Federation
3.	Chattisgarh	CGMFP (T&D) Co-op. Federation Chattisgarh	Tendu Sal, Bamboo	Primary Forest Produce Co-op. Unions	District Union
4.	Orissa	Gram Panchayats (Presently challenged in the High Court of Orissa)	Tamarind, Hill brooms, Myrobalan, Nux vomica, Sal leaves, Harda, Amla, Marking nuts, Soapnut, Gendigulum, Charagum, Dhwara gum, Arrowroot, Honey, Cleaning nuts, Kusumlac, Mahuwa flower, Kera seed.	—	—

(contd.)

(contd.)

Sl. No.	State	Monopoly Agency for NTFP	Nationalized Commodity	Collecting Agency	Price fixation method
			Mahua seed, Bantulsi seed, Chakunda seed, Neem seed, Kusum seed, Karanj seed, Char seed, Benachar, Bankulthi seed, Gillo seed, Gaba seed, Indrozob, Shikakai, Babul seed, Banhaldi, Baidak, Saili leaves. Sal Seed, Tendu leaves, Sal seed	—	—
		M/s.Tribal Development Cooperative Corporation Ltd.	—	—	By High Power Committee.
		M/s Orissa Forest Development Corporation	—	—	—
5	Andhra Pradesh	M/s Girijan Cooperative Corporation Ltd.	Adda leaf, Wild broom, Hill broom, Shikakai, Amla fruit, Cleaning nuts, Chiranjee, Rock bee Honey, Apiary Honey, Kusum oil seed, Myrobalan, Mahua seed.		1. Centralized commodities rates fixed by VC & MD of GCC.
			Mahua Flower, Marking nuts, Nux vomica, Nara mamaidi bark, Pongam seeds, Sarphagandha roots (*Raulfia Serpentina*), Soapnuts, Honey wax, Gum Karaya, Tamarind (a) Shell, (b) Seeded,	Forest Department	2. Decentralized commodities rates fixed by the Divisional Manager of GCC.

(contd.)

(contd.)

Sl. No.	State	Monopoly Agency for NTFP	Nationalized Commodity	Collecting Agency	Price fixation method
			(c) Deseeded, (d) Green, (e) Seed, Teriods, Maredu geddalu, Sugandhi-pala, Tendu leaves and Bamboo		
6	Rajas-than	Rajasthan Tribal Area Cooperative Development Federation	Gum Karaya (all kinds), Malkangani, Mahuwa seed, Bichu Kanta, Dolma, Karanj seed, Sal seed, Musli, Amala, Soapnuts, Palas seed, honey, Chiranji, Gilloy, Ratanjot, Dhaluni, Lal Arandi, Neem seed, Baheda chaal, Amla chaal, Chitak chaal, Shatavan, Puwad seed, Bhivan-guda Chatvor, Marodfall, Choti Kateri. Tendu leaves.	Lamps and own bran-ches of RTADCF	By RTADC-EF on the basis of recommen-dation of District Collector, D.C. fixed the price on the basis of last years sales and prevailing market rates in nearby mandies.
		Territorial Circles of Forest Department			
7	Bihar	M/s Bihar State Forest Development Corporation	Sal seed, Mahua seed, Tendu leaves and Myrobalan	M/s Hanu-man Minor Oil Pvt. Ltd. for Sal seed	By High Power Com-mittee at Patna for sal seed. Tendu leaves, Ma-hua seed, Myrobalan.
8	West Bengal	M/s West Bengal Tribal Development Cooperative Corporation	Sal seed and Tendu leaves	LAMP	—

(contd.)

(contd.)

Sl. No.	*State*	*Monopoly Agency for NTFP*	*Nationalized Commodity*	*Collecting Agency*	*Price fixation method*
9	Maharashtra	M/s Maharashtra State Cooperative Tribal Corpn. Ltd.	Mahua Flower, Mahua fruits, Gum, Hirda (Terminalia Chebula), Char, Awala, Baheda, Neem seed, Karanj seed, Palas lac, Kusum lac, Vanerand seeds, Takada, Nirmali/kapi, Guggul, Bapchi seed, Kunchla kari, Shikakai Ritha, Biba, Gunj seed, Broom grass, Mango seed, Wauding, Baphali, Grass and fodder (excluding bamboo), Honey,Palas leaves, Sitaphal, Cashew nuts (except those grown by FDMC)	Through the network of its own office.	The price are fixed at least once or twice in a week. The cost on four items viz., APMC cess, weighment charge, Hundi and Adivasi Co-operative Society commission are deducted from the basic price of APMC.
10	Tamil Nadu	Forest Department	None	Lease holder	—
11	Karnataka	Forest Department LAMP Federation	No MFP is nationalized but the produce has to be traded in the regulated mandies.	LAMP	—
12	Himachal Pradesh	H.P. State Forest Co-operative Corporation Ltd.	—	Resin, Bamboo and Kahir	—
13	North Eastern States	State Govt./ District Council	All MFP items	—	**Mahul System on yearly basis.**

Source : Proceedings of the Regional Workshop on NTFP, Chhattisgarh State Minor Forest Produce (Training & Development) Cooperative Federation, Raipur, Chhattisgarh;
Proceedings of the Non-Wood Forest Produce (NWFP) Policy, NIRD, Hyderabad.

Payment of Taxes by Traders

Particulars	*Andhra Pradesh*	*Orissa*	*Chattisgarh*	*MP*	*Jharkhand*
Forest Dev tax/ Market Cess	—	—	3%	3%	—
Commercial taxes	—	—	4% (20% in case of Tendu)	4% (20% in case of Tendu)	—
Surcharge on commercial taxes	—	—	15%	15%	—

Privileges to Tribals through Insurance

Group Insurance Scheme for MFP Gatherers

(Value in Rupees)

Particulars	*AP*	*Orissa*	*Chattisgarh*	*MP*	*Jharkhand*
Normal death	30,000	—	35,000	35,000	—
Partial disability	—	—	12,500	12,500	—
Accidental death/ Permanent disability	30,000	—	25,000	25,000	—
Medical assistance	5,000	—	—	—	—

Benefit Sharing

The NTFP forms an integral part of the livelihood of the forest dependent communities. Since the people dependent on the forest, generally are part of socially and economically backward communities, it goes without saying that the welfare State has definite responsibilities towards them. The minimum that the primary collectors deserve is a share in the profit from the operations of NTFP, as the State generates significant revenue from its trade that is based on the hard labour of the former.

Procedures adopted by Federations in Benefiting the Primary Collectors

(i) In Chattisgarh, the CMFPF distributes incentive wages to primary collectors from operations of tendu leaf. A system of incentive distribution was evolved only in the year 1998, in response to PESA. While 70 per cent of the net profit is distributed as cash to registered collectors, the rest is kept aside for infrastructure development and forest management. In case of other notified items, the profit is shared among the gatherers and invested in the development of forests and in infrastructure development in Gram Sabhas. For other NTFP, the federation just allows primary gatherers to sell in *haats*.

(ii) Orissa was the first State to have a provision for channelising of profits from Kendu Leaf (*beedi* leaf) operations. A provision exists that at least 50 per cent of the profit earned from Kendu Leaf operations has to be distributed to panchayat bodies in the Kendu Leaf growing subdivisions. But so far, only *ad hoc* grants have been given.

(iii) The situation has been reversed in Jharkhand after the nationalisation of NTFP. Earlier, the agents used to pay a registration fee to the panchayats every season. The present system, where the forest department plays a dominant role in the trade, has no such provision.

(iv) In Andhra Pradesh the forest department has shown its inclination to share benefits from Kendu Leaf operations from 1999 onwards. It intends to give 50 per cent of the net revenue from Kendu Leaf operations to respective JFM committees.

The GCC tries to pass on the profits in terms of high sale value realization for the traded NTFP, by enhancing the purchase prices of different NTFP or by ensuring a minimum price line of the previous years.

Implications of Implementing the NTFP Trade Policies—Nationalised Produce

Except for tendu leaf and bamboo, the list of nationalized items (or items under monopoly rights) of neighbouring States is not the same. This has implications in terms of restrictions on the movement of produce and the buying obligation of the State agencies. While the FD and the GCC hold monopoly rights of all significant produce available in Andhra Pradesh, the number of nationalized or monopoly items are four in Chattisgarh, five in Jharkhand, and only two in Orissa. A common trend seen across all the five neighbouring States (except Andhra Pradesh) is that, State agencies having monopoly procure their stocks, only when the markets are favourable. The major differentiating factor between the States is the access of primary gatherers to the market or to the State appointed agents.

In Andhra Pradesh the GCC enjoys certan basic infrastructure facilities in the tribal areas including pooling centres, and godown facilities. The stocks reach the central warehouses for transhipment by the GCC. In Chattisgarh, Raipur, Dhamtari, and Jagdalpur play a predominant role in NTFP trading. However, in other district headquarters, the presence of traders or other intermediaries plays a predominant role. The opposite situation prevails in Orissa till recently, i.e., as long as the royalty system was in vogue. The forest bureaucracy and the agents appointed by it were comparatively stricter in imposing the then prevalent rules. This system led to depressed market conditions and poor prices. This, in turn, ensured that different types of produce that had market demand were not procured and hence not collected. This hit the communities hard, as they lost a potential source of income. The State is thus at a disadvantage *vis-à-vis* other States.

Conditions are very similar to those of Orissa were prevalent in Jharkhand. The State has an advantage, Ranchi being the centre of trading for most important produce. The above two factors have ensured market penetration but not to the extent of Chattisgarh. Through monopoly rights over most of the produce, it could harness the NTFP potential, which enabled it to control a major share in the market.

In addition to cross-border transactions of produce under State control, the differing policy scenario in neighbouring States promotes clandestine dealing in all the produce. The biggest missing link is market information. The only ones with the latest market information appear to be few big traders, while the State agencies as well as the primary collectors are all at sea as to information on the availability of the produce—their quantity, quality, and crucially, the price. This results in all the stakeholders losing in the final bargain, except for the risk-taking big traders with money and muscle power.

Summing Up

An attempt has been made in this chapter to document national forest policies and their impact on tribals access to NTFP. Since the tribals are deprived due to different State NTFP policies, there is need for a uniform national NTFP policy. The first National Forest Policy saw light in the year 1894 and was mostly concerned with tribals and their rights over forests. The subsequent Forest Policies of 1952 and 1984, departed from 1894 forest policy causing a great concern to the tribals. These forest policies in the name of national interest have deviated from the traditional rights of the tribals over forests. Their privileges have now been treated merely as laws and concessions.

The 1988 National Forest Policy gave much emphasis to creating massive people's movement involving the village communities living in and close to forests. This movement has been popularized as Joint Forest Management programme which came into existence through the GoI notification in June 1990 and 22 States evolved their own mechanisms for involving the local communities. In all 36,130 Forest Protection Committees are managing a total of 10.25 million hectares of the forest area and Andhra Pradesh contributes 1.63 million hectares of forest area with 6,575 JFM Committees. However, in the light of legal and political framework for tribals in

Andhra Pradesh and JFM (*Vana Samrakshana Samithis*) including the tribal and non-tribal communities, the issue of sharing the benefits between the two categories has been discussed with a mention of tribal laws and their usufruct rights for careful examination.

The policies related to NTFP of the different States are also caught between JFM and PESA. The JFM concept is based on the principle of care and share whereas PESA bestows ownership rights on the entire Gram Sabha/Panchayat without any conditions, that people need to protect forests before they enjoy the usufruct. The JFMs encourage small community based informal groups whereas PESA recognizes formal Panchayats and Gram Sabhas. This chapter has also discussed the institutional structure in different States, the role of TDCCs, forest department, and other government agencies controlling NTFP, the price fixation methods, and benefit sharing by these agencies in the interest of the tribals.

The general trend observed is that there is no synchronisation in policies or trading of NTFP and the nationalized commodities for any agency is not more than four in any State except in Andhra Pradesh where the GCC has been given monopoly on the procurement of 25 NTFPs from tribals. The conflicting approach of the State agencies in procurement and trading, benefit sharing, tax structure, etc., for NTFP is resulting in deprived and differing opportunities for tribals living in each State, criss-cross border transactions for price advantage, influx, erratic market situation with upswing and downswing trends, etc.

4

Production and Extraction of NTFP in North Coastal Andhra

Introduction

As pointed out in the introductory chapter, NTFPs are a major source of livelihood for a large number of people living in the forests. About one-third of the income of tribals in India comes from the collection of unprocessed NTFP. In addition to the generation of income, it creates opportunities for employment. According to the National Commission on Agriculture[1] (1976), NTFP collection had the potential to create 1000 million man days of employment per year in India by 2000 A.D. The studies conducted by research institutes and individual scholars supported that this activity has immense employment and income earning potential.[2]

The NTFP also provide food security for the poor particularly during the periods of drought and famine. Therefore, in the context of improving the tribal livelihoods, management of sustainable production and extraction of NTFP assume greater significance. Most of the NTFPs are tree based and their production depends on the stock of the NTFP bearing trees in the forests. These trees are generated in the natural process with very little man-made efforts.

Since NTFPs are extracted from these trees, the method of extraction may sometimes damage the trees, and affect the available stocks. As the data on the stocks of trees are not available, it is difficult to estimate the production potential of NTFP, including the unexploited potential if any. Also it is very difficult to analyse systematically, whether the production of

NTFP is sustainable in this area. In this chapter, an attempt has been made to analyse the following: the trends and growth in the collection of NTFP, instability in the collection of NTFP, the method of extraction of NTFP, whether the methods adopted for extraction cause any damage to the tree, whether the method of extraction has a bearing on the quality of the product, distance travelled and time spent for the collection, and quantity collected per person engaged in the collection, etc. Such an understanding is useful in planning for improving the tribal livelihoods through sustained production of NTFP.

Sources of Data and the Techniques used in the Analysis

The analysis in this chapter is based on both primary and secondary data. In Andhra Pradesh, the GCC is the authorised institution for procurement and sale of NTFP. As the marketing of NTFP is to be done only through the GCC, the quantities procured by the GCC are assumed as the quantities collected. Such an assumption does not cause much bias in the results as the quantities retained for home consumption are either minimal, or nothing at all in respect of many NTFP. The time series data on the quantities of NTFP procured, quantities sold, the purchase price, sale price, and the value of the products procured are available with the GCC.

The data on the procurement of prominent NTFP both in terms of quantity and value obtained from the records of GCC for the period 1991 to 2003, have been used in studying the trends in growth and fluctuations in the collection of NTFP. The trends in growth are analysed in terms of trend growth rates, and the fluctuations are analyzed in terms of annual percentage variations and instability index. For computing the growth rates, the linear and exponential trend curves are estimated by the method of least squares, and the best fitted form is chosen by the maximum value of R^2 and the significance levels of the parameters. The growth rates based on the best fitted form is used in the analysis. The instability index is computed by using the formula.

$$I = (I - R^2) * 100$$

where I *is the index of instability and* R^2 *is the coefficient of multiple determination of the best fitted trend equation.*

Studies show that NTFP production and consequently collection is subjected to cyclical variations. An attempt has also been made in this study to analyse the cyclical fluctuations in the collection of NTFP. For estimating the cyclical component from the annual time series data, there are two popular methods namely Moving Average Method, and Linear Trend Method. Here, by using Linear Trend Method, Cyclical components are estimated under both Multiplicative hypothesis and Additive hypothesis of time series. The data on the other aspects like: methods/techniques adopted for the extraction of NTFP, distance travelled for collection, time spent on collection, quantities collected, quantities sold, sale price, incomes earned through NTFP collection, etc., are obtained from sample of NTFP gatherers. Information relating to the selection of the sample and method of collecting the data has been dealt with in the introductory chapter.

About the Trees Providing Prominent NTFP in NCA and the Methods of Collection and Uses

The prominent NTFP collected in the NCA are : Adda Leaf, Cleaning Nuts, Tamarind, Gum Dikamali, Gum Karaya, Gum Kondagogu, Gum Tiruman, Gum Olibanum, Hill Brooms, Honey, Maredugaddalu, Marking Nuts, Mohua Flower, Mohua Seed, Myrobalans, Naramamidi Bark, Nux vomica, Pungam Seed, Sheekakai, Soapnuts, and Wild Brooms. The characteristics of the trees from which these NTFP are collected, the conditions under which these trees grow, the methods of extraction, and the uses of NTFP are briefly explained here.

Adda Leaf **(Bauhania valhi)**

Adda leaf is a climber plant, which germinates naturally in the forest areas. People also grow this climber plant in their own land in rural areas. Generally leaves of the plant go up with the support of the tree and also spread on open places in the forest. Within one year after germination, its leaves mature for collection. The size of the leaf ranges from 12 cm to 25 cm depending upon the climber plant. This plant is found in valleys and wetter parts of tropical and sub-tropical forests. The life of this plant depends on the climatic conditions and collection techniques. On an average this plant is reported to survive for more than 50 years. Adda leaf is extracted by way of cutting vines or leaves from the plant. Generally cutting is done with a sharp big size sickle. These leaves are also extracted by way of gathering fallen leaves from the ground.

The major uses of Adda leaf are for making platters and cups, which are used for eating food particularly in hotels, places of worship, and parties. Adda leaf plant also gives fruit after 2 or 3 years of age, which is very tasty and nutritious. The inner bark of its vines are the source of fibre which are very strong and are used for making ropes for domestic purpose. Its bark is also used as tanning material.

Gum Karaya (Sterculia urens)

Gum Karaya tree is a moderate sized tree found in tropical deciduous forests mostly in dry and rocky areas. It is the source of an important gum known as "Gum Karaya." For extracting the gum, the trees are usually tapped or blazed, and the hardened sap oozed out in the lumps is collected. The gum exudes from the bark throughout the year, but most of it is generally produced by blazing or by stripping of the bark. The gum begins to exude after tapping or blazing and exudation continues for several days, but the maximum amount of gum is produced within the first 24 hours after blazing. The gum is allowed to thicken and the collection is made every third or fourth day. The yield of the gum from a matured tree is estimated at 1 to 4.5 kg per tree per season.[3]

Gum Karaya tree is having wider applications in: (1) pharmaceutical and medicinal preparations; (2) bulking agent in laxatives; (3) stabilizer in ice-creaming, Meringues, Toppings, and in cream products; (4) Gelling agent in cosmetics; (5) Emulsifier in the processed meats and cheese spreads; and (6) strong adhesive material, and thickening agent for drilling muds.

Cleaning Nuts (Strychnos potatorum)

Cleaning nut tree is a tall tree of size 13 metres and it is found in deciduous forests. Its seeds are small in size, circular, and hard to break. They are covered with pulp (the seed covered with pulp). The tribals collect the fruit by shaking the branches and the fruit gathered thus is cleaned thoroughly in a stream or river till the seeds are separated from the fruit.

The ripened seeds are used for cleaning muddy water. They are reported to be very effective as coagulant aids. Alum aided by these seeds has been found to be very effective in removing the suspended impurities from coal washery wastes. These seeds possess tonic, stomachic, demulcent and emetic properties and are used in acute diarrhoea, diabetes, gonorrhoea, etc. They play a key role in the treatment of eye diseases, particularly conjuctivitis.[4] Its fruit is used in the treatment of dysentery and bronchitis. Leaves are used as poultice over maggot-infested ulcers. Powdered bark, mixed with lime juice is used for treating cholera.[5]

Rock Bee Honey (Apis dorsata)

Rock bees are migrant inhabitants, and ferocious by nature with their painful string. These bees are generally not amenable for domestication. However, once hived, they are reported to be harmless. These bees collect nectar of flowers and other plant exudations, convert it into honey, and keep it in sealed comb cells. These bees are found all over India, mostly in forests. On the basis of their location, the honey hives are classified as those on the trees and rock cliffs and those that are in the tree trunk burrows. The tree trunk comb does not yield much honey. This honey is also not of best quality. However, its collection is relatively easy. Even one man can collect it. On the other hand, Rock honey is collected in groups. A skilled person climbs the tree with a smoke torch, which is made of dry sticks enveloped by fresh leaves. This smoke disturbs the bees and they fly away. He also carries with him a vessel to collect honey and a sickle to cut the comb.

Honey is a good sweetening agent and highly nutritious food. It is considered as panacea for several common body ailments and serves both as tonic and a medicine. It has mild laxative, bactericidal, sedative, antiseptic, and alkaline characteristics. Honey also constitutes an important ingredient of certain lotions, cosmetics, soaps, creams, balms, toilet waters, and inhalations.[6]

Myrobalans **(terminalia chebula)**

Myrobalans tree is 15 to 24 m in height and 1.5 to 2.4 m in girth with a cylindrical bole of 4 to 9 m, a rounded crown, and spreading branches. It is not subjected to serious pest menace. It is found in deciduous forests. This species is a strong light demander. It requires direct-overhead light and cannot tolerate shade. It is frost-hardy and drought-resistant to a considerable extent.[7]

Myrobalans are collected by shaking the branches of the tree or striking with a long sharp stick and fruits are gathered from the ground. The dried fruits constitute one of the most important vegetable tanning materials. The dried flesh surrounding the seed is rich in tannin. In addition to its use in tanning industry, the Myrobalans are used on an extensive scale for the internal treatment of locomotive feed-waters and as an additive in oil-drilling compositions. The Myrobalan fruits are also credited with laxative, and stomatic tonic properties. The fruit-pulp is used as a dentifrice to cure bleeding and ulceration of gums and also used as one of the ingredients in *triphala.*

Mohua Seed **(Madhuca latifolia)**

Mohua tree is a medium to large sized tree, with a short bole and large rounded crown. It is drought and frost hardy but suffers under severe climatic conditions. It is found in water logged or low lying land under favourable soil and climatic conditions. Mohua trees begin to bear fruits at the age of 8 to 10 years and continue to yield fruits till 60 years. When the fruits are ripe, they fall from the tree. The fruits of this tree are also collected by shaking the trees. For obtaining the seed, fruits are broken to procure the cotyledons and seed is separated from cotyledons. Mohua seeds yield fatty oil, known commonly as Mohua butter. It is used in the manufacture of soaps, particularly in detergents. It is also used in the manufacture of lubricating greases and fatty alcohols. Mohua seed oil is also used for making candles, and in the treatment of skin related diseases, rheumatism, and headache. It is also a laxatic and considered useful in cases of habitual constipation, piles, and haemorrhoids.

Tribals use this oil for cooking. Ripe fruit has cream coloured pericarp which is edible. Mohua berries are also eaten raw or cooked. They are also eaten by cattle, sheep, and goats. Mohua flowers are a rich source of sugar, vitamins, and calcium. They offer wholesome nourishment. They are eaten raw or cooked. These flowers are also used in the preparation of distilled liquors. Mohua spirit prepared by distillation is the most important alcoholic drink in most of the tribal areas. Mohua flowers are also used for the preparation of vinegar.

Naramamidi Bark **(Litsa glutinosa)**

Naramamidi bark is a large tree like a mango tree, and its branches are round in shape with green leaves. It is found all over the tropical and subtropical deciduous forests. Generally its trees are found on roadside and interior parts of forest areas. Moist climate is generally more suitable for the growth of the tree. Tribals peel out the bark from the trunk/ branches or dry the branches for some days to remove the bark.

The bark yields about 15 per cent tannin and about 6.5 per cent soluble non-tannin on zero moisture.[8] It can be used alone to form the tanning liquor. Its bark is also used as dye stuff, particularly for drying fishing nets, making *agarbatti* and plastic bangles. Its leaves are eaten by cattle, and wood is used in making wooden furnitures as well as fuel wood.

Nux vomica (Strychnus Nux vomica)

Nux vomica is fairly vertical tree with a cylindrical bole. It is an evergreen or deciduous tree, usually 13 m high and 0.9 to 1.8 m in girth, with a 3.6–6.0 m long. Its leaves are 8–15 cm long, broadly elliptic and obtuse or acute.[9] It is found growing in forests where the absolute maximum shade temperature varies from 35–45 degrees and minimum from 4–18 degrees. It grows at an altitude of 360 metres.

Tribals collect its fruit either by shaking the branches of the tree or by striking with a stick. After that they break the fruit by pressing with their hands and separate the seeds. The seeds are rubbed with dust so that pulp around the seeds is removed. Then the seeds are washed in a stream or river. The wet seeds are spread on the open ground for drying.

Nux vomica is also used as a tonic and stimulant for nervous disorders. It is also used in the preparation of medicated products for the hair and scalp. The leaves are applied as a poultice on sloughing wounds and maggot infested ulcers. Roots and bark are used in the treatment of fevers; an infusion of the latter is prescribed for epilepsy. Commercially, Nux vomica is used in the extraction of *strychnine* and *brucine* from its seed powder. It has a reputation for acting as a cardiovascular and respiratory stimulant and a bitter tonic, stimulating all parts of the central nervous system.

Seeded Tamarind (Tamarindus indica)

Seeded Tamarind tree has a short and thick trunk, which is seldom straight.[10] It is a moderate-sized to large-sized tree with a height up to 24 m and girth of 7 m. It is found in tropical deciduous forests. It is grown by the farmers in their own fields and on the wasteland lying on the roadside. Seeded tamarind is collected by shaking the branches of the tree or by hitting the fruits with a stick and gathering from the ground. A fully grown Tamarind tree yields 180–250 kg of fruit per season. On an average, the pod is composed of 55 per cent pulp, 34 per cent seed, and 11 per cent shell and fibre.[11] The tree begins to bear fruit at the age of 13–14 years, and continues to yield abundant crops for more than 60 years.

Tamarind pulp is used in the manufacture of medicine as a refrigerant, carminative, and laxative. It is also a commonly prescribed in febrile diseases and bilious disorders. The pulp is also reported to possess antiseptic properties and is applied as a poultice on inflammatory swellings. It is also used as an auxiliary in dying and tanning, and for polishing and cleaning metal-ware. Seed is used as a valuable raw material for the preparation of sizing powder for textiles. Kernel powder is used as a sizing material in the textile industry.[12] Oils are useful in the preparation of paints and varnishes, and for burning in lamps.[13] The tender leaves, flowers, and the young seedlings are eaten as vegetables.

Hill Brooms

Hill broom is a kind of wild grass. Its height varies from 2 to 5 ft. It is available in the lowland near the river banks, inside the agriculture fields, and interior part of forest areas. It comes up automatically and needs moist climate for growing fast. Flowers come at the top after one year. Tribals locate the broom bushes in the forest and cut the grass with a sickle and bundle them in consumer-convenient packs.

Wild Brooms

Wild brooms plants also come up in the form of bushes and have sticks that are comparatively stronger than Hill brooms. They are available in the barren land of forest areas. Tribals locate the broom bushes in the forest, cut the sticks with a sickle, and move from one bush to other in collection, and on to another bush for more gathering. Wild brooms are used for cleaning the rough surfaces, fields, tar roads, etc.

Gum Olibanum **(Boswellia serrata)**

Gum Olibanum is a moderate sized tree found in the dry and rocky areas of tropical deciduous forests. The bark of a mature tree is fairly thick, which is about 1 cm. The resin obtained from the tree is known as *Gugul* gum or Indian Myrrh. The gum collection of Olibanum from the tree is almost the same as that of Gum Karaya.

The Gum olibanum tree looks transparent with a golden yellow tinge. It is a semi-fluid substance having aromatic properties. The maximum yield of the gum portion is obtained from the bark portion. Deep blazing adversely affects the growth of the tree. Therefore, the depth of the blaze should not be more than 0.5 to 0.6 cm. Middle aged trees yield more gum and trees of lower girth class should not be tapped, as it may adversely affect their growth. Gum Olibanum is used as incense and as fixture in the preparation of perfumes, medicines, ointments, and drugs for rheumatism. It burns readily due to which it is used as an incense in religious ceremonies and its odour is balsamic.

Sheekakai (Acacia concinna)

Sheekakai is a climber plant found in the moist deciduous and evergreen forests, except in the arid and dry regions. The pods are collected either by plucking green fruit by hand or shaking vines of plant that have climbed onto the trees. The fruits falling on the ground are also to be gathered. Sometimes fire burns the fruits scattered on the ground. The pods are eaten by monkeys and other wild animals. Thus most of the collection is being done directly from the vines of the plant.

Sheekakai is used as a detergent and it is preserved for its pods, which make an excellent substitute for soap. The pods are also good for cleaning/shining the old and dirty brassware. Presently the dry pods are being powdered and often scented and marketed as Sheekakai powder or in combination with other herbs. The powder is also used for washing linen, silk, and gold ornaments. The tender leaves are used as a substitute of culinary preparations for tamarind pulp or lemon juice, and the bark is used for tanning.

Marking Nuts **(Semicarpus anacardium)**

Marking nut is a moderate sized deciduous tree found particularly throughout the tropical forests. The marking nuts are collected either by felling of the nuts or striking with a stick, and gathering the nuts from the ground. The pericarp of the fruits yields black dye, which is used for primary, redox painting. The extract of the pericarp is also used for manufacture of varnishes, lacquer, enamels, moulding compositions, and water proofing, and insulating materials. Its nuts are used locally as a tan.

Pungam Seed **(Pungamia glabra)**

Pungam seed is a small to medium sized glabrous tree with spreading crown. It is found throughout tropical India up to 1200 m in the Himalayas, Central, Western, and Southern and moisture-rich places, particularly along river banks. Pungam seeds are collected by felling seeds of the tree and gathering them from the ground. The seeds yield 30 to 35 per cent yellowish brown oil.[14] The experiments reveal that Pungam oil is an excellent bio-diesel and can be used as a substitute for fossil fuels. It is also used in skin diseases. The twigs and leaves are widely used as green manure particularly in paddy, coffee, and sugarcane fields. Its wood is useful for paper making in admixture with other hard woods.

Seasonality in the Collection of NTFP in NCA

As the NTFP are plant-based products, in many cases, their production is subjected to seasonality. Therefore, their collection is confined to particular months in a year. The data relating to the period of availability or collection of the prominent NTFP in NCA and their production potential are presented in Table 4.1. The data on production potential is drawn from the office of the GCC and it should be read with a note of caution. As accurate data on the stock of NTFP are not available, it is difficult to arrive at reliable estimates of the total

Table 4.1 : The Period of Availability and the Production Potential of Procurement of Prominent NTFP in NCA

(Quantity in quintal)

Name of the Commodity	*Period*	*Visakha-patnam (Qtls.)*	*Vizia-nagaram (Qtls.)*	*Srika-kulam (Qtls.)*	*North Coastal Total (Qtls.)*
Gum Karaya	Through-out the year	600-750	400-500	30-50	1000-1300
Myrabolans	Nov-Mar	10000-12000	4000-5000	600-500	15000-20000
Nux vomica	Oct-Feb	75-100	75-100	30-50	150-250
Seeded Tamarind	Jan-April	40000-50000	40000-50000	5000-6000	Upto 1 lakh
Deseeded Tamarind	March-May	100-200	3500-4000	—	3500-4000
Tamarind Seed	March-June	400-500	600-750	—	1000-1250
Pungam Seed	April-June	2500-3000	2000-2500	8000-10000	12500-15000
Cleaning nuts	Nov-March	100-200	350-400	10-15	450-650
Mohwa Seed	May-Aug	25-50	1300-1500	5-10	1400-1500
Marking nuts	Jan-April	2500-3000	3000-3500	2000-2500	7500-9000
Honey	Mar-July Oct-Jan	400-450	—	—	400-450
Sheekakai	Feb-May	10-20	500-600	50-75	600-700
Hill Brooms	Feb-April	1.40-2.0 lakh	1.50-2.0 lakh	Upto 1 lakh	3.00-5.00 lakh
Soapnuts	Feb-May	1800-2500	500-550	300-350	1000-1200
Narama-midi Bark	Jan-June	1400-2000	700-750	1000-1250	3000-4000
Adda leaf	Apr-June	80000-100000	200-300	—	80000-100000

Source : Marketing Department, GCC Corporate Office, Visakhapatnam

stock of NTFP. Except Gum Karaya, all the other products are available only during particular months in a year. Myrobalans and Cleaning nuts are available from November to March. The collection of Sheekakai, Hill brooms, and Soapnuts starts in February and continues up to May, whereas the collection of Tamarind and Marking nuts starts in January and ends in April. Nux vomica is available from October to February, while

Naramamidi bark is available from January to June, Mohua seed is available from May to August, and Adda leaf is available from April to June. Honey is collected during two periods in a year, viz., March to July and October to January.

Trends in the Growth and Instability in the Collection of NTFP in NCA

The data on the quantities of NTFP collected (procured by GCC) and their values are presented in Appendix Table 4.1. The trend growth rates, linear and exponential trend equations are estimated and the results are presented in Appendix Tables 4.2 to 4.5. In most of the cases, linear form gave a good fit. Therefore, the growth rates based on the linear form are used in the analysis here. They are presented in Table 4.2 along with instability indices.

The collection of Gum Karaya secures the first position in terms of value. In the total value of the NTFP procured by GCC in 2002–03, it accounted for 25.67 per cent. However, its collection recorded a significant declining trend during the study period from 1990–91 to 2002–03. The value of the product on the contrary showed an upward trend, although the rate of growth was not statistically significant. The collection of Gum Karaya was also subject to some fluctuations. The extent of instability was 60 per cent in quantity and 97 per cent in value. The larger instability in the value may be due to wider price fluctuations.

Among the various NTFP collected in NCA, tamarind stands first in quantitative terms. The GCC procures tamarind in the form of seeded tamarind and deseeded tamarind. It also procures tamarind seed. The values of deseeded tamarind, seeded tamarind, and tamarind seed accounted for 13.26 per cent of the total value of NTFP collected in 2002–03. The procurement of both seeded tamarind and deseeded tamarind recorded a positive trend during the period from 1990–91 to 2002–03, but the rates of growth were not statistically significant. However, their value recorded a significant positive rate of growth. Among the seeded and deseeded tamarind varieties, the procurement of seeded tamarind grew at a relatively faster rate. This is well reflected in the collection of tamarind seed. It recorded a significant negative growth. However, the value of tamarind seed collected showed a positive trend, although the rate of growth is not statistically significant. The collections (procurement) of seeded tamarind, deseeded tamarind, and tamarind seed were subject to wider fluctuations. The extent of instability was more than 90 per cent. However, the extents of instability in terms of their values are relatively lower. It prompts us to believe that the tamarind prices are relatively more stable.

Table 4.2 : Trend Growth Rates and Instability Indices of Quantity and Value of Prominent NTFP in North Coastal Andhra Pradesh : 1990-91 to 2002-03

Commodities	*Quantity*		*Value*	
	Growth Rate	*Instability Index*	*Growth Rate*	*Instability Index*
Adda leaf	7.33*	60.32	1.78	97.03
Cleaning nuts	-25.14*	55.43	-23.97	51.77
Deseeded tamarind	2.24	95.93	8.66**	71.38
Gum Dikamali	6.28	88.94	23.35*	52.19
Gum Karaya	-13.43*	55.29	-0.17	99.9
Gum Kondagogu	25.08*	7.51	27.63*	7.14
Gum Olibanum	0.93	99.31	8.89	82.42
Gum Thiruman	17.03	81.31	-16.14	83.25
Hill brooms	4.56	92.87	15.06*	56.69
Honey	3.88	99.19	10.15*	52.46
Marедugeddalu	31.07	56.92	38.70	43.81
Marking nuts	10.56*	59.13	15.48**	70.46
Mohua flower	-5.25	91.05	3.67	95.37
Mohua seed	0.28	99.94	2.03	97.40
Myrobalans	0.25	99.95	7.17	97.40
Naramamidi bark	4.42	94.23	14.89**	59.32
Nux vomica	0.84	99.74	0.87	99.90
Pungam seed	0.58	99.86	2.79	97.03
Seeded tamarind	4.36	84.52	10.10*	51.59
Sheekakai	9.06*	46.17	9.51**	73.44
Soapnuts	-4.58	79.89	2.27	95.83
Tamarind	-2.50	93.69	5.68	80.84
Wild brooms	-8.81	74.47	-7.93	77.22

* Significant at the 1% level.

** Significant at the 5% level.

The collection of Gum Kondagogu gained prominence after 2000. During 2002–03, its value accounted for 5.07 per cent in the total value of NTFP procured. The collection of this product recorded a significant upward trend during the period of study. It increased at the rate of 25 per cent per annum. In value terms, the collection increased at the rate of 27 per cent per annum. The extent of instability in the collection of this product is only 7 per cent. The same extent of instability for its value indicates stability in the prices of this product. The collections of other gum products Gum Dikamali and Gum Olibanum, and Gum Thiruman are relatively low. Their contributions in terms of value are also low. Both Gum Thikamali and Gum Olibanum recorded a positive trend while Gum Tiruman recorded negative trend during the period of study. The collections of these products were also subject to wider fluctuations. In all cases, the extent of instability was more than 80 per cent with the only exception being the value of Gum Dikamali.

In terms of the larger collection in quantity and value, Mohua seed and Mohua flower are also prominent in NCA. In 2002–03, the value of Mohua seed and Mohua flower together accounted for 4.73 per cent of the total value of NTFP. Both these products recorded a positive trend during the research period. However, the rate of growth was not statistically significant. This may be due to the wider fluctuations in collection. The extent of instability of these products ranged between 95 per cent and 100 per cent.

Naramamidi bark is another product, which became very prominent in this region after 1995. In 2002–03, its contribution to the total value of NTFP was 8.15 per cent. The collection of this product increased significantly during the study period. Although the growth rate of the quantity collected was not statistically significant, the growth rate of its value was statistically significant. It may be due to the fluctuations in collection. The extent of instability of the quantity is estimated to be 94 per cent. While it is 59 per cent for value.

Honey is another popular product in the NCA and its contribution to the total value of NTFP in 2002–03 was 4.37 per cent. The pattern of growth of the collection of this product during the study period was more or less same as that of Naramamidi bark. The collection of this product in quantity terms recorded a positive growth, but the rate of growth was not statistically significant. This may be due to wider fluctuations in collection. The extent of instability was observed to be 99 per cent. However, its value recorded a significant positive growth of 10.15 per cent with an instability index of 52 per cent.

The individual contributions of the other products to the total value of the NTFP were relatively low. Among these, the collection of Marking nuts and Sheekakai increased significantly with relatively lower fluctuations, during the study period. The collection of Maredugaddalu, Pungam seed, and Hill brooms also recorded a positive trend during this period. But the rate of growth was not statistically significant. It may be due to the wider fluctuations in collection. The extent of instability of these products was observed to be more than 90 per cent, with the exception being Maredugaddalu. However, the value of the Hill brooms collected, recorded a statistically significant positive growth, with a lower size of instability. On the other hand, the collection of Adda leaf and Cleaning nuts showed a significant negative trend. Although the value of the Adda leaf exhibited a positive trend, it was not statistically significant. The extent of instability in the collection of these products was also relatively low. The collection of the remaining products, viz., Nux vomica, Soap-nuts, and Wild brooms recorded a downward trend. But their rates of growth are not static. However, the value of the collections of Nux vomica and Soapnuts was on an upward trend during the study period though it was statistically not significant. For these products the extent of instability was also relatively high.

Thus, the collection of all kinds of NTFP except in the case of Cleaning nuts, Gum Karaya, Gum Thiruman, Mohua flower, Nux vomica, Soapnuts, Tamarind seed, and Wild brooms was on an upward swing in NCA during the period from 1991–92 to 2002–03. But the trend rates of growth were not statistically significant. It may be due to wider fluctuations in the collection that these products are usually subjected to.

The extent of instability for most of these products exceeded 90 per cent. However, in value terms, all products except Cleaning nuts, Gum Karaya, Gum Thiruman, and Wild brooms showed an upward trend. Their sizes of instability were also relatively lower.

Cyclical Variations in the Collection of NTFP in NCA

In the previous section it was observed that the extent of instability in the collection of NTFP in the NCA was very high. It may be due to the cyclical fluctuations in the production. In this section, an attempt has been made to analyse the cyclical fluctuations in the collection of NTFP in the NCA region during the period from 1990–91 to 2002–03. Here, cyclical component of the time series data of the collection of NTFP is estimated by Moving Average Method using both additive hypothesis and multiplicative hypothesis. Under the additive hypothesis, cyclical component for the tth year $C_t = Y_t - MA_{t'}$* where Y_t is the collection of NTFP in the tth year and $MA_{t'}$ is the moving average** of the collection of NTFP. Under the multiplicative hypothesis, $C_t = Y_t / MA_t^{*}$. The estimated values of the cyclical components of the 23 prominent NTFP collected in the NCA are presented in the Appendix Tables 4.6 to 4.27.

For all the commodities, the cyclical components based on both the Additive hypothesis and Multiplicative hypothesis showed the same type of cyclical movements. Also for all products, quantities collected and their values showed more or less the same type of cyclical movements. Gum Karaya registered cyclical fluctuations with an amplitude of 4 to 5 years. The expansion phase of the cycle is 2 years and the contraction phase of the cycle is two to three years. More or less a similar pattern of the cyclical movements was observed for Gum Tiruman and Gum Olibanum, while for Gum Kondagogu, data are inadequate to analyse the cyclical fluctuations.

Tamarind (Seeded, Deseeded, and Tamarind seed) exhibited cycles of 2 years amplitude, with an expansion phase of one year and contraction phase of one year. Some other such products are: as Nux vomica, Myrobalans, Pungam seed,

Cleaning nuts, Mohua flower, Mohua seed and Soapnuts. The collection of Honey recorded cycles of four years amplitude with an expansion and contraction phase of two years. On the other hand, the products such as: Marking nuts, Sheekakai, Adda leaf, and Naramamidi bark exhibited cycles of three years amplitude with expansion phase of one year and contraction phase of two years. More or less opposite type cycles are exhibited by Hill brooms. In this case, the contraction phase of the cycle is only one year, while the expansion phase constitutes 2 to 3 years.

Thus the collection of all NTFP in NCA was subjected to cyclical fluctuations. Some products have cycles of 4 years amplitude and some have cycles of 2 years amplitude with an equal expansionary and contractionary phases. There are also products with one year expansion phase and 2 or 3 years contraction phase. Exactly opposite type of cycles are also exhibited by some products.

Analysis of Primary Data

In the previous section, it is observed that there was no significant growth in the total collection of NTFP in NCA during the period from 1990–91 to 2002–03. In fact, there was significant downward trend in the case of some NTFP. The collection of these NTFP was also subjected to cyclical fluctuations. Therefore, if there was an increase in the NTFP gatherers with the increase in tribal population, the quantity collected per household declined especially during the downward phase of the cycle. If the major source of income to these NTFP gatherers was the collection of NTFP, there was a threat to the sustainability of their livelihoods. In order to protect the interests of such tribals, there is a need to know the dependence of tribals on NTFP as a source of income, the change in the per capita collection, and factors causing the changes. The required data for analysing these aspects are collected through a sample survey.* In this section, an attempt has been made to analyse these data. More specifically, this section examines the changes in the families engaged in NTFP

* Explanation relating to the sample design and the method of collection of data, and the method of analysis is provided in the introductory chapter.

collection, NTFP species available, time taken for collection, distance travelled for collection, quantities collected, income earned through NTFP collection, during the last five years ending with 2004. Based on these observations, an attempt has also been made to assess whether the tribal livelihoods are sustainable through NTFP collection, if the same trend in the parameters relating to NTFP collection, and disposal is continued in the future.

Dependence of Tribals on NTFP

In this section, the dependence of tribals on NTFP as a source of livelihood is assessed in terms of the proportion of households with NTFP activity as a major source of income and the proportion of the workers engaged in NTFP activity, as main activity in the total work force. The main economic activities in the tribal areas are: agriculture, NTFP collection, activities relating to household industry, and the service activities. These activities are classified under three heads namely: agriculture, which includes cultivation and agricultural labour activity, NTFP activity, and others. The distribution of sample households by the main economic activity and location of households presented in Table 4.3 shows that, about 25 per cent of the tribal households depend on the collection of NTFP as a major source of livelihood.

Table 4.3 : Distribution of Sample Households by Main Source of Income and Region

Source of Income→ Region ↓	*Agriculture*		*NTFP*		*Others*		*Total*	
Interior	28 (13.73)	(44.44)	35 (52.24)	(55.56)	— (0.00)	(0.00)	63 (23.95)	(100.00)
Semi-Interior	110 (53.92)	(89.43)	12 (17.91)	(9.76)	1 (50.00)	(0.81)	123 (46.77)	(100.00)
Close to Plains	66 (32.35)	(75.86)	20 (29.85)	(22.99)	1 (50.00)	(1.15)	87 (33.08)	(100.00)
Total	**204 (100.00)**	**(74.57)**	**67 (100.00)**	**(25.48)**	**2 (100.00)**	**(0.76)**	**263 (100.00)**	**(100.00)**

Source : Primary data collected from field survey.

The sample data reveals that in 2004, about 40 per cent of the tribals are engaged in NTFP collection (Table 4.4), and for 25 per cent of the tribals, it is a major source of livelihood. The proportion is more in the case of interior areas and in the areas close to plains. Nevertheless, there has been a decline in the proportion of the tribal households engaged in NTFP collection, indicating either a decline in the quantities of NTFP available or availability of better opportunities in other activities. In respect of most of the NTFP in the three regions, there has been a decline in the number of days engaged in collection, increase in the time spent, and distance travelled for collection, the decline in the stock of NTFP and decline in the quantities collected, during the period 2000–2004. The magnitude of these changes is relatively higher in the areas close to plains and lower in the interior areas as expected. These changes indicate that NTFP production/ collection is not sustainable in NCA.

Table 4.4 : Distribution of Sample Household Members participating in Economic Activities by Region

Activity→ Region ↓	*Agriculture*	*NTFP*	*Others*	*Total*
Interior	94 (43.32) (23.80)	122 (56.22) (40.53)	1 (0.46) (14.29)	217 (100.00) (31.31)
Semi-Interior	172 (64.66) (43.54)	91 (34.21) (30.23)	3 (1.13) (42.86)	266 (100.00) (38.05)
Close to Plains	129 (58.64) (32.66)	88 (40.00) (29.24)	3 (1.36) (42.86)	220 (100.00) (31.75)
Total	**395 (56.99) (100.00)**	**301 (43.43) (100.00)**	**7 (1.01) (100.00)**	**693 (100.00) (100.00)**

Source : Primary data collected from field survey.

Sustainability of NTFP Collection as a Source of Livelihood for Tribals

In the previous section, it was observed that NTFP was a major source of livelihood for nearly one-fourth of the tribal population in Andhra Pradesh. Therefore, sustaining the collection of NTFP assumes importance in the context of improving the tribal livelihoods. In this connection, knowledge of the change in the value of parameters relating to NTFP collection is helpful in designing the required policy interventions. This section examines changes in the important parameters like: number of families engaged in the collection of NTFP; number of days engaged in collection; number of species available; quantities collected; time spent in collection; distance travelled for collection; over the last five years, i.e., from 2000 to 2004; and attempts to assess the sustainability of collection of NTFP.

(a) Variation in the Number of Families engaged in Collection of NTFP

With the increase in the size of population, the families engaged in various economic activities generally increases. However, the proportion engaged varies from activity to activity. More people are engaged in more promising areas and *vice versa.* In the less promising areas, there may be even withdrawal of the people, who were previously engaged. The data on the families engaged in the collection of various types of NTFP in the years 2000 and 2004, as shown in Table 4.5 indicates that, there has been a decline the number of families engaged in the collection of all prominent types of NTFP in the three regions with the exception of tamarind, in the interior and semi-interior regions and marking nuts in interior region, where there is no change. The rate of decline is found to be much faster in the areas closer to plains. In the interior areas, the rate of decline in the families engaged in NTFP collection is relatively low. This decline in the families engaged in NTFP collection over time, may be due to the decline in the quantities of the products available, or availability of better opportunities to engage in other activities.

(b) Variation in the Number of Days engaged per Year in NTFP Collection

The number of days engaged per year in the collection of NTFP, may also be an indicator for the quantities of NTFP available for collection. A decline in the number of days engaged in

Table 4.5 : Product-wise and Region-wise Change in the Number of Families engaged in the Collection of NTFP in the Tribal Areas of NCA during the years 2000 and 2004*

Type of Product	Interior			Semi-Interior			Close to Plains		
	Families engaged in Collection		% Change	Families engaged in Collection		% Change	Families engaged in Collection		% Change
	2000	2004		2000	2004		2000	2004	
Gum Karaya	13	11	-15.38	09	07	-22.22	04	01	-75.00
Amla	42	37	-11.90	48	42	-12.50	15	11	-26.67
NM Bark	40	31	-22.50	30	23	-23.33	09	05	-44.44
Tamarind	42	42	No change	46	46	No change	65	60	-7.69
Soapnut	06	05	-16.66	15	12	-20.00	50	39	-22.00
Myro-balan	42	40	-4.76	46	40	-13.04	25	20	-20.00
Pungam	42	40	-4.76	46	42	-8.70	12	10	-16.66
Marking-nuts	20	20	No change	33	30	-9.09	08	07	-12.50
Nux vomica	11	10	-9.09	09	08	-11.11	13	11	-15.38
Hill Brooms	21	20	-4.76	22	20	-9.09	11	09	-18.18

Source : Primary data collected from field survey.

collection over time, may indicate the decline in the quantities available. The data on the number of days engaged per year in the collection of prominent NTFP presented in Table 4.6 shows that, there has been a decline in the number of days engaged in the collection of all types of NTFP in all the three regions. During the period from 2000–2004: the rate of decline varied from 10 per cent in the case of Naramamidi bark, Gum Karaya and Hill brooms to 28.57 per cent in the case of Myrobalans in the interior areas; while it varied from 13.04 per cent in the case of Gum Karaya to 31.58 per cent in case of *amla* in the semi-interior areas; and from 13.33 per cent for Naramamidi bark to 57.14 per cent for Nux vomica in the areas closer to plains. These statistics also support the fact that there has been a decline in the opportunities for the collection of NTFP

Table 4.6 : Product-wise and Region-wise Change in the Number of Days engaged per year in the collection of NTFP's in the Tribal Areas of NCA during the years 2000 and 2004*

Type of Product	Interior: No. of days engaged in Collection 2000	Interior: 2004	Interior: % Change	Semi-Interior: No. of days engaged in Collection 2000	Semi-Interior: 2004	Semi-Interior: % Change	Close to Plains: No. of days engaged in Collection 2000	Close to Plains: 2004	Close to Plains: % Change
Gum Karaya	100	90	-10.00	92	80	-13.04	73	60	-17.81
Amla	20	15	-25.00	19	13	-31.58	18	10	-44.45
NM Bark	20	18	-10.00	18	15	-16.67	15	13	-13.33
Tamarind	35	30	-14.29	33	28	-15.15	27	21	-22.22
Soapnut	20	17	-15.00	18	15	-16.67	15	11	-26.67
Myrobalan	21	15	-28.57	20	14	-30.00	17	10	-41.18
Pungam Seed	19	17	-10.53	16	13	-18.75	14	10	-28.57
Marking nuts	25	20	-20.00	23	17	-26.09	17	10	-41.18
Nux vomica	13	11	-15.38	12	9	-25.00	7	3	-57.14
Hill Brooms	20	18	-10.00	18	15	-16.67	9	5	-44.44

Source : Primary data collected from field survey.

(c) Variation in the Stock of NTFP

Change in the stock of NTFP, i.e., the trees which produce NTFP is a good indicator for assessing the sustainability of production of NTFP. The stock may change as a result of change in the rate of regeneration and destruction due to the adoption of unscientific ways of collection of NTFP. The data on the stock of NTFP presented in Table 4.7 show that, there had been a decline in the stock of all types of NTFP in the three regions, with the exception of tamarind in the interior region and in the areas closer to plains, during the period from 2000–2004. The rate of decline varied from 0 per cent to 2.5 per cent in the interior region, from 1.64 per cent to 40 per cent in semi-interior, and from 0 per cent to 73.77 per cent in the regions close to plains. Thus the degeneration of the NTFP stock is found to be much faster in the areas closer to plains and in the semi-interior areas. From the focussed group discussions, it is observed that the degeneration is mainly due to unscientific methods of collection of produce from the spices like Gum Karaya and Naramamidi bark. In the case of other species like Amla, Nux vomica, Soapnuts, cutting of branches for collection of pods is the main reason for degeneration. The degeneration of the NTFP stock in the NCA also supports the phenomena of the unsustainable nature of its collection in the area. The decline in the stock may have a bearing on the time spent in collection, distances travelled for collection, and on the quantities collected. The decline in the stock may lead to increase in the time spent and distance travelled on collection and decline in the quantities collected. These aspects are examined in the following sections.

Table 4.7 : Product-wise and Region-wise Change in the Stock of NTFP in the Tribal Areas of NCA during the Years 2000 and 2004*

Type of Product	*Interior*			*Semi-Interior*			*Close to Plains*		
	The stock of NTFP (in Nos)		*%*	*The stock of NTFP (in Nos)*		*%*	*The stock of NTFP (in Nos)*		*% Change*
	2000	*2004*		*2000*	*2004*		*2000*	*2004*	
Gum Karaya	200	150	-25.00	100	60	-40.00	60	15	-73.77
Amla	1515	1200	-20.79	1290	1000	-22.48	140	100	-28.57
NM Bark	100	75	-25.00	85	60	-29.41	20	10	-50.00
Tamarind	1000	1000	No change	610	600	-1.64	700	700	No change
Soapnut	22	20	-9.09	58	50	-13.79	260	220	-15.38
Myrobalan	670	600	-10.45	455	400	-12.09	165	140	-15.15
Pungam Seed	850	800	-5.88	550	500	-9.09	115	100	-13.04
Marking nuts	250	240	-4.00	215	200	-6.98	80	70	-12.50
Nux vomica	80	70	-12.50	73	60	-17.81	65	50	-23.08
Hill Brooms	1600	1500	-6.25	1100	1000	-9.09	1000	900	-10.00

Source : Primary data collected from field survey.

(d) Variation in the Quantities of NTFP Collected

As expected, the quantity of all types of NTFP collected per household is the highest in the interior areas and lowest in the areas close to plains. However, in the three regions, there had been a decline in the quantities collected during the period 2000–2004. Across the products, the rate of decline varied from 0 per cent to 25 per cent in interior areas, from 1.64 per cent to 40 per cent in semi-interior areas, and from 0 per cent to 75 per cent in the areas closer to plains (Table 4.8).

Table 4.8 : Product-wise and Region-wise Change in the Quantities (Kg.) of the Collection of NTFP Per Family in the Tribal Areas of NCA during the years 2000 and 2004*

Type of Product	Interior			Semi-Interior			Close to Plains		
	Qty. collected per year (in kgs)		% Change	Qty. collected per year (in kgs)		% Change	Qty. collected per year (in kgs)		% Change
	2000	2004		2000	2004		2000	2004	
Gum Karaya	600	450	-25.00	300	180	-40.00	180	45	-75.00
Amla	4545	3600	-20.79	3870	3000	-22.48	420	300	-28.57
NM Bark	100	75	-25.00	85	60	-29.41	20	10	-50.00
Tamarind	15000	15000	No Change	9150	9000	-1.64	10500	10500	No change
Soapnut	88	80	-9.09	232	200	-13.79	1040	880	-15.38
Myrobalans	2480	2400	-3.23	1820	1600	-12.09	660	560	-15.15
Pungam Seed	2550	2400	-5.88	1650	1500	-9.09	345	300	-13.04
Marking nuts	2520	2400	-4.76	2139	2000	-6.49	800	700	-12.50
Nux vomica	410	350	-14.63	365	300	-17.81	325	250	-23.08
Hill Brooms	1600	1500	-6.25	1100	1000	-9.09	1045	900	-13.88

Source : Primary data collected from field survey.

(e) Variation in the Average Time Spent per day in the Collection of NTFP

On an average, a family spends 3 hours to 5 hours per day in the collection of various types of NTFP in the interior and semi-interior areas and from 4 hours to 7 hours in the areas close to plains. During the period 2000–2004, there had been an increase in the time spent on the collection in all the regions. The rate of increase varied from 0 per cent to 26 per cent in the interior areas, from 5 per cent to 40 per cent in the semi-interior areas, and from 10 per cent to 44 per cent in the areas closer to plains (Table 4.9). This increase in the time spent on collection may be due to the decline in the production of NTFP.

Table 4.9 : Product-wise and Region-wise Change in Average Time Spent Per Day in the Collection of NTFP in the Tribal Areas of NCA during the Years 2000 and 2004

Type of Product	*Interior*			*Semi-Interior*			*Close to Plains*		
	Average time spent for collection (in hrs)		*% Change*	*Average time spent for collection (in hrs)*		*% Change*	*Average time spent for collection (in hrs)*		*% Change*
	2000	*2004*		*2000*	*2004*		*2000*	*2004*	
Gum Karaya	5.50	6.40	16.36	5.50	7.15	30.00	5.50	7.30	32.73
Amla	4.00	4.30	7.50	4.00	5.00	25.00	4.00	5.15	28.75
NM Bark	5.00	6.30	26.00	5.00	7.00	40.00	5.00	7.20	44.00
Tamarind	3.30	3.50	16.67	3.30	4.00	21.21	3.30	4.10	24.24
Soapnut	4.00	4.15	3.75	4.00	4.30	7.50	4.00	4.40	10.00
Myrobalan Seed	4.00	4.10	2.50	4.00	4.20	5.00	4.00	4.40	10.00
Pungam Seed	6.00	6.30	5.00	6.00	6.45	7.50	6.00	7.00	16.67
Marking nuts	4.00	4.20	5.00	4.00	4.30	7.50	4.00	5.00	25.00
Nux vomica	5.00	5.30	6.00	5.00	6.00	20.00	5.00	6.15	23.00
Hill Brooms	4.50	4.50	No change	4.50	5.00	11.11	4.50	5.15	14.44

Source : Primary data collected from field survey.

(f) Variation in the Distance Travelled for the Collection of NTFP

The distance travelled per day for collection of NTFP is an indicator of the proximity of the availability of the products to the place of living. An increase in the distance travelled over time, may be an indicator of the destruction of the stock of NTFP around the dwellings. For collection of various types of products, an NTFP collector travels from 8 km to 12 km per day in the interior areas, from 8 km to 18 km in the semi-interior areas, and from 8 km to 19 km in the areas nearer to plains. It is observed that the distance travelled per day for collection increased significantly in respect of most of the NTFP during the period 2002–2004, in all the three regions. The rate of increase is found to be much higher in the areas close to plains as expected. It varied from 0 per cent to 60 per cent in the interior areas, from 0 per cent to 80 per cent in the semi-interior areas, and from 0 per cent to 90 per cent in the areas closer to plains (Table 4.10). This increase in the distance travelled for collection supports the results of the decline in the stock of NTFP, and increase in the time spent for collection.

Table 4.10 : Product-wise and Region-wise Change in Average Distance Travelled Per Day in the Collection of NTFP in the Tribal Areas of NCA during the Years 2000 and 2004*

Type of Product	*Interior* Average time spent for collection (in kms)		*Interior* % Change	*Semi-Interior* Average time spent for collection (in kms)		*Semi-Interior* % Change	*Close to Plains* Average time spent for collection (in kms)		*Close to Plains* % Change
	2000	*2004*		*2000*	*2004*		*2000*	*2004*	
Gum Karaya	8	11	37.50	8	13	62.50	8	15	87.50
Amla	8	10	25.00	8	12	50.00	8	13	62.50
NM Bark	10	16	60.00	10	18	80.00	10	19	90.00
Tamarind	7	8	14.29	7	9	28.57	7	10	42.86
Soapnut	8	9	12.50	8	10	25.00	8	11	37.50
Myrobalan	8	8	No change	8	8.5	6.25	8	9	12.50
Pungam seed	12	12	No change	12	12	No change	12	12	No change
Marking nuts	8	8	No change	8	8	No change	8	8	No change
Nux vomica	10	12	20.00	10	14	40.00	10	15	50.00
Hill Brooms	9	9	No change	9	9	No change	9	9.5	5.56

* *Source* : Primary data collected from field survey.

Summing Up

In the NCA region, 23 kinds of NTFP, which have high commercial and nutritional value are available in considerable quantities. The sources of some of these products are trees and the others are climbers, which have a life span of 50 to 60 years. The production of all NTFP except Gum Karaya, is seasonal in nature and it varies from product to product, falling in the period from October to June. The products are generallly collected by shaking the branches of trees and in some cases, by cutting or blazing the bark of the trees, without causing any damage to the tree. In terms of the value realised through sales, the most prominent product in this region is Gum Karaya. It is followed by Tamarind, Naramamidi bark, Gum Kondagogu, Mohua seed and flower, Honey, Nux vomica, Hill brooms, Adda leaf, Maredugaddalu, Sheekakai, Myrobalans, Marking nuts, Gum Dikamali, Cleaning nuts, and Pungam seed.

During the period from 1990–91 to 2002–03, the collection of only Adda leaf, Gum Kondagogu, and Marking nuts, which are not much popular in terms of value realized, recorded significant positive growth. The most popular products Gum Karaya and Cleaning nuts recorded significant negative rate of growth. The rates of growth of collection of all other products are not statistically significant, although some have shown positive signs. However, collection measured in terms of value realised recorded positive rate of growth in respect of many products. This may be due to increase in the prices of these products. Only four products namely: Cleaning nuts, Gum Karaya, Gum Thiruman, and Wild brooms recorded negative growth rates. But these rates of growth are not statistically significant. The collection of all these products over time, except Gum Kondagogu, is quite unstable and they are subject to cyclical fluctuations with cycles of amplitude ranging from 2 to 5 years.

NOTES

1. Government of India, (1976), *Report on the National Commission on Agriculture*, Part IX, Forestry, Ministry of Agriculture and Irrigation, New Delhi.
2. (i) Gaikwad, John, S. (1988), *Role of Minor Forest Produce in Tribal Economy*. Workshop on Integrated Tribal Development, Administrative Staff College, Hyderabad.
   (ii) Goel, C.L. (1990), *Improving Tribal Economy from Minor Forest Products through Government Efforts*. M.F.P. Division, Forest Research Institute, Dehradun.
   (iii) Tewari, K.M. (1989), *A Plan for Creation of Employment Opportunities to Increase the Income of People Living Below the Grinding Poverty*. Forest Research Institute, Dehradun.
3. M.S. Ramanujam *et al.* (1998), *Pricing of Minor Forest Products procured by GCC*, Govt. of Andhra Pradesh, IAMR Report No. 9/1997, IAMR, New Delhi, pp.36–39.
4. Chopra, R.N. *et al.* (1956), *Glossary of Indian Medicinal Plants*, ICSSR, New Delhi, p. 236.
5. Dastur, J.F. (1951), *Medicinal Plants of India and Pakistan*, Taraporevala & Sons Co. Ltd., Bombay, p. 221.
6. M.S. Ramanujam *et al.*, (1998), *op. cit.*, pp. 56 –59.
7. Troup, R.S. (1921) , *The Silviculture of Indian Trees*, Oxford University Press, Oxford, p. 513.
8. Krisna Murthy, T. (1933), *Minor Forest Products of India*, New Delhi, Oxford & IBH Publishing, p. 331.
9. Troup, R.S. (1921), *The Sericulture of Indian Trees, Vol. II*, Oxford University Press, Oxford, p. 674.
10. Watt G., *A Dictionary of the Economic Products of India, Vol. VI (3)*, Government Press, Calcutta, 1889-1893 p. 404; Watt G., *The Commercial Products of India*, John Murray, London, 1908, p.1066; Hooker, J.D., *Flora of British India, Vol. II, 1872–97*, p. 237.
11. Lewis and Neelakantan, *Journal of Scientific and Industrial Research*, New Delhi, 1964, pp. 23, 204.
12. Srinivasan and Agarwal, *Bulletin of the Botanical Survey of India*, Calcutta, 1968, pp. 10, 381.
13. Bhat, *Indian Oil and Soap Journal*, Calcutta, 1966-67, pp. 32, 53.
14. Krishna Murthy, (1993), *op. cit.*, p. 304.

5

Pricing and Marketing of NTFP in North Coastal Andhra

Introduction

In the previous chapter it has been observed that if the past trends are continued, production of NTFP in the North Coastal Andhra (NCA) is not sustainable. The collection of various products are also subjected to wider fluctuations due to the production cycles. Also there has been an increase in the efforts made by the tribals for collection in terms of time spent and the distance travelled. Under these conditions, for improving the livelihoods of the tribals, the competitive markets in which the prices respond well to the changes in the demand and supply for the NTFP assume importance. In a competitive market, the difference between the sale price and purchase price is just exhausted by the operational costs of procurement, storage, transport, processing costs, if any, along with the normal profit margins. However, such markets do not exist for the NTFP in the NCA region. For certain kinds of NTFP, marketing is to be done only through the GCC. For others there are open markets which are operated mainly through a chain of middlemen. In this chapter an attempt has been made to examine how the markets for NTFP in the NCA region, viz., open markets, and marketing by the GCC, have been operating and identify the inefficiencies, if any. Against this background, an attempt has also been made, to suggest a suitable strategy for marketing and pricing policy.

Methodology

When the markets are operating competitively, the tribals will have a higher share in the prices that the consumers pay for their products and presumably they will be higher than their labour costs. However, a higher share need not necessarily mean that markets are operating competitively. As the competitive markets do not exist in the case of NTFP, the aspects relating to: nature of marketing of NTFP, the sale prices in relation to procurement prices, the prices paid to the commodities in relation to the labour costs incurred in procurement, and variations in the procurement and sale prices are analysed in this chapter, using the secondary sources of information.

The marketing of certain varieties of NTFPs is done through open markets under different marketing channels. The aspects relating to the operation of these markets are analysed drawing information from the earlier studies, both published and unpublished. The study of the procurement prices in relation to the labour costs involved in the collection process is also based on the information drawn from the secondary sources. The marketing of all prominent NTFP is done only through the GCC. For these commodities, the share of NTFP gatherers in consumer's rupee, trends in the growth instability, and cyclical variations in the procurement and sale prices are analysed for the period from 1990–91 to 2002–03, drawing the data from the records of GCC. The cyclical variations are estimated by using the techniques specified in chapter IV under "Sources of Data and the Technique used in the Analysis". The analysis of the price determination of NTFP in the open market and the price fixation by the GCC is also based on the information drawn from the earlier studies and from the various Government of India Acts. Finally based on the inferences drawn from the pricing analysis, an attempt has been made to suggest a more appropriate pricing policy.

Marketing of NTFP

As pointed out earlier, the prominent NTFP available in the NCA region are: Tamarind, Adda leaf, Cleaning nuts, Marking nuts, Mohua seed, Ungam seed, Naramamidi, Hill brooms, Sheekakai, Wild brooms, Beedi leaf, etc. Of these, marketing of all NTFP except tendu products has been done under aegis of GCC. For the remaining products there is an open market. Thus there are two effective channels now to deal with the marketing of NTFP namely, open market and the GCC.

Marketing of NTFP through Open Markets

Traditionally, the forests have provided the tribals: food, material for building houses, fuel for lighting up and warmth, and cooking, and fodder for their cattle. Until monetisation crept into the tribal areas, the vast majority of tribal population used to survive on tubers, fruits, and leaves of various trees. Gradually, the tribal lifestyle had undergone change and the process of exchange of products available in the forests with salt, kerosene, etc., which were supplied by non-tribals.

With monetisation and settling down of non-tribals in tribal areas, the trade grew to a considerable extent. The main market places in the tribal areas were the traditional weekly shandies. Private traders from the plains visit the shandies and purchase NTFP, and the agricultural products from the tribals. The traders established long standing relations with the tribals and also advanced money as loans. The tribals in turn invariably sold their produce to the traders, who established relations with them. The intimacy and fidelity among some traders and their clients was so intense that, the tribals were very much satisfied with the fringe benefits they got like cigars and other petty things, from the traders, and did not bother about the underweighment and low prices offered by traders. The business tact and the personal touch of the trader used to override the other considerations in the transaction and paved the way for exploitation of the tribals, by way of offering low prices for the products and underweighment. The demand and supply factors play very little role in determining the prices of the tribal products. After purchasing the products at prices dictated by them, the traders transported those products to the plain areas and sold to the wholesale traders in the open market for huge profits.

A number of studies were conducted which examined the issues related to the marketing of NTFP through private traders, and money lenders by various research institutes, individual researchers, and voluntary organizations.[1]

In all the studies, a major observation was that, the prices paid to the tribals were much lower than the wholesale prices in the open market. Prices paid to the tribals hardly covered the cost of labour involved in the collection and the tribals are thus, ruthlessly exploited. The Malayappan Committee appointed to suggest the ways of improving the conditions of tribals observed that, exploitation by traders and money lenders was responsible for the misery of the tribals and unless these unscrupulous middlemen are eliminated, the socio-economic advancement of the tribals is not possible.

Marketing of NTFP through GCC

For protecting the tribals from the exploitation by private traders and money lenders the government had set up a specialized corporation to market the NTFP, on the lines suggested by Malayappan Committee. Its name was re-designated as "Girijan Cooperative Corporation" (GCC) in 1970. The details of its origin, functions, administrative structure, and activities are discussed in the following chapter. One of the major functions of the Corporation is to market the NTFP, to pass on the maximum possible price advantage to the tribals, not merely to enable them to earn wages, but also to secure proper money equivalent to the produce collected by them. Though the corporation was granted monopoly rights over the purchase of NTFP, the operations of the private traders continue ceaselessly. Some tribals prefer to sell their products to the private trader. In an attempt to find out the shares of private traders and, the GCC and reason behind the tribals entertaining the private traders, several studies were conducted. A brief review of some of the prominent studies are discussed as below.

A study conducted by Raghava Rao[2] revealed that of the total value of the NTFP marketed by the sample households in the Chintapalli Block of Visakhapatnam district, about 15 per cent was purchased by private traders, middlemen, and money lenders and the remaining 85 per cent is procured by the corporation. In this study, it was observed that the tribals prefer to sell the produce to the traders because of their long standing contact and intimacy. A study conducted by Suryanarayana[3] in the Srikakulam district showed that, of the total marketed items of NTFP by the sample tribal households: 13.88 per cent of Adda leaf, 49.18 per cent of Adda leaf plates, 22.92 per cent of Soapnuts, 25.01 per cent of Nux vomica, 18.17 per cent of Myrobalans, 28.14 per cent of tamarind, 20.54 per cent of Pungam seed, 29.55 per cent of Mohua seed, 97.31 per cent of Mohua flower were purchased by private traders, while the rest of it was procured by the corporation.

A study[4] made by the Consulting and Applied Research Division (CARD) of the Administrative Staff College of India revealed that, of the total NTFP collected by different tribal groups in Andhra Pradesh 21 per cent of the Mohua seed, 38 per cent of the Mohua flower, 4 per cent of Adda leaf, 48.1 per cent of Hill brooms, 49.1 per cent of Gum Karaya, 45.7 per cent of tamarind, 19.80 per cent of Nux vomica, 92 per cent of Soapnuts and 6.3 per cent of Myrobalans were purchased by private traders, while 21 per cent, 4 per cent, 78.2 per cent, 9.7 per cent, 44.4 per cent, 37.12 per cent, 80.20 per cent, 2 per cent, and 82.7 per cent respectively of them were purchased by the corporation.

According to the study conducted by Bapuji[5] in Srikakulam district: of the total marketed NTFP of the sample tribal households, about 69.57 per cent of the Seeded tamarind, 66.67 per cent of the Myrobalans, 50 per cent of the Mohua seed, 16.167 per cent of Mohua flower, 61 per cent of Soapnuts, 70 per cent of Pungam seed, 60 per cent of the Cleaning nuts, and 58.33 per cent of the Marking nuts were purchased by the corporation, while the rest was purchased by private traders.

The corporation, being a welfare organization was established and organised by the government for the benefit of the tribals, with the main objective, i.e., to purchase NTFP at reasonable prices and eliminate the profit seeking trader and merchant class from tribal areas. The studies reviewed nonetheless indicate that, private traders are active in the NTFP trade in tribal areas and some of the tribals are entertaining them. It appears that the prices offered and the procurement mechanisms adopted by the corporation are not satisfactory to the tribals. In this section an attempt has been made to examine in depth, the price related aspects such as: the share of tribals in the consumers' rupee, the trends in the growth and instability of procurement prices, and sale prices, and the cyclical variations in the procurement and sale prices of NTFP.

Procurement Prices *Vs.* Sale Prices

The corporation is said to be performing well, if it sells the procured products at higher prices and passes on a large part to the tribals. To assess the performance of GCC in this angle, an attempt has been made here to study the procurement prices in relation to sale prices, and sale prices in relation to the wholesale prices in the nearest market, drawing the data on whole procurement and sale prices of GCC from the office of the GCC, Visakhapatnam and wholesale prices in the nearest market from the Study Report of G. Parthasarathy. He had collected the data on the wholesale prices of eight prominent NTFP from the wholesale traders at Visakhapatnam in March 1998. This data, along with the data on sale prices of GCC in the same year, are presented in Table 5.1.

Table 5.1 : Sale Price of GCC as a Percentage of Wholesale Price in the Open Market*

Sl. No.	*Commodity*	*Sale price** per quintal (in Rs.)*	*Wholesale price in open market per quintal*	*Sale price as a percentage of wholesale price*
1.	Myrobalans	586	800.00	73.25
2.	Nux vomica	459	600.00	76.50
3.	Marking nuts	406	800.00	50.75
4.	Shikakai	983	1000.00	98.30
5.	Soapnuts	780	1600.00	48.75
6.	Seeded Tamarind	602	750.00	80.27
7.	Deseeded Tamarind	883	1400.00	63.07
8.	Adda leaf	501	500.00	100.20

Source : * Collected from the Girijan Cooperative Corporation Visakhapatnam, Andhra Pradesh.

** G. Partha Sarathy, and K. Uma Shankar Patnaik (2003), Procurement and Marketing of Minor Forest Produce in Tribal Area, Atlantic Publications, New Delhi, p. 104.

It shows that the corporation sells its products at prices that are much lower than the wholesale prices in the open market. Only Adda leaf and Sheekakai were sold at prices almost equivalent to the wholesale prices. In certain other cases, the percentage of sale price of the corporation on the wholesale price varied from 48.75 per cent to 80.27 per cent. Thus it appears that the corporation is not efficient in marketing the products procured. However, the inference drawn should be read with a word of caution as it is based only on one year data. The estimates of the percentage of sale prices passed on to the tribals for various NTFP during the period from 1991–92 to 2003–04 presented in Table 5.2 shows that, the tribals share in the sale price of the corporation varied from product to product. It is also subjected to variation over time. In general more than 75 per cent of the sale price was passed on to the NTFP gatherers, especially during 2000–01 and in the following years. The processing, transport, storage and establishment charges of the corporation constitute less than 25 per cent. Thus, the performance of the corporation in respect of offering a higher share to the tribals in the sale price, through minimizing its expenditure is appreciable.

However, the prices received by the tribals may or may not cover their labour costs, as the sale prices of the corporation are much lower than the wholesale prices in the open market. Parthasarathy and Uma Shankar Patnaik[6] conducted a sample survey in Andhra Pradesh to examine whether the prices received by the tribals meet at least the labour cost. Each household was asked about number of members engaged in the collection of NTFP, total days spent, and total quantity procured. From that data, average quantity procured per person per day was estimated. Labour required for collection and processing of 1 kg of MFP was also estimated. It is assumed that the Tribals engaged in the collection of NTFP must obtain at least the market wage prevailing in the village. At the time of conducting the survey, the market wage rate per manday was Rs. 25. The price that needs to be paid for 1 kg of NTFP was derived by applying the wage rate to the labour required for one kg. Finally, the actual prices received by the tribals are compared with the prices based on labour cost. The study concluded that in all sample villages, the prices received are less than the labour costs and the tribals are being exploited (Table 5.3).

Table 5.2 : Percentage of Procurement Price* in the Sale Price** of Prominent NTFP in NCA : 1991-92 to 2002-03

Sl. No.	*Commodity*	*1991-1992*	*1992-1993*	*1993-1994*	*1994-1995*	*1995-1996*	*1996-1997*	*1997-1998*	*1998-1999*	*1999-2000*	*2000-2001*	*2001-2002*	*2002-2003*
1.	Gum Karaya	69.72	75.80	75.80	76.40	67.24	69.37	71.57	72.53	71.82	92.63	90.18	93.34
2.	Gum Thiruman	87.66	107.90	67.02	115.00	66.28	40.18	54.88	53.13	86.64	40.48	58.58	70.33
3.	Gum Olibanum	87.75	86.57	59.33	69.23	67.60	70.06	62.69	79.50	65.16	88.27	80.45	87.30
4.	Gum Kondagogu	—	—	—	—	48.76	63.10	63.65	67.35	59.04	78.74	68.05	85.92
5.	Gum Dikamali	58.64	71.12	96.50	50.71	67.00	69.72	74.21	—*	—**	71.38	76.19	82.60
6.	Myrobalans	70.06	61.34	96.15	76.92	89.46	74.54	68.26	126.05	78.39	75.76	65.00	107.33
7.	Nux vomica	86.33	81.48	94.93	94.67	78.97	71.63	79.74	79.50	79.31	87.14	75.07	60.43
8.	Seeded Tamarind	90.22	78.95	98.68	86.96	86.36	81.23	87.21	91.91	74.58	85.75	122.10	87.53
9.	Deseeded Tamarind	99.62	96.24	107.55	88.22	78.62	79.44	125.71	88.90	78.49	122.62	116.34	79.18
10.	Tamarind Seed	80.00	55.63	59.51	55.86	94.44	80.64	55.55	55.55	86.21	74.42	87.80	78.87
11.	Pungam Seed	89.45	80.00	95.75	80.50	76.63	66.04	83.80	79.12	65.69	95.14	81.82	83.01
12.	Cleaning Nuts	88.29	100.40	**	76.92	40.59	42.51	50.12	59.92	73.39	84.12	72.73	85.56
13.	Marking Nuts	66.11	72.11	69.06	83.83	87.42	93.62	61.58	62.36	93.19	46.50	82.08	81.70
14.	Mohua Seed	67.44	77.60	76.20	77.85	75.76	78.21	82.93	93.27	89.06	106.06	83.33	82.24
15.	Mohua Flower	85.22	66.78	70.47	59.37	66.67	67.43	98.98	101.35	63.57	78.63	104.81	74.07
16.	Honey	**	64.53	99.12	98.32	88.98	80.61	82.93	352.00	**	76.92	81.63	82.96
17.	Sheekakai	68.43	117.81	71.27	90.48	80.32	61.58	71.21	57.27	66.70	78.28	78.93	75.32
18.	Soapnuts	83.75	84.24	74.79	94.34	91.84	91.24	96.15	86.15	86.53	78.75	97.32	87.69
19.	Hill Brooms	5.71	1.07	1.50	48.75	75.05	66.38	1.99	—	65.14	74.47	76.12	92.94
20.	Wild Brooms	—	—	—	—	—	**	87.08	**	65.68	65.33	55.78	56.67
21.	Adda leaf	74.37	71.86	91.18	74.51	63.07	61.73	57.88	68.80	63.03	58.90	78.71	68.63
22.	Naramamidi Bark	**	—	**	—	—	—	—	—	—	—	—	—

Source : Marketing Department, GCC Corporate Office, Visakhapatnam.

* Procurement Price is not available. ** Sale Price is not available.

Table 5.3 : Prices as per the Labour Costs vis-à-vis Actual Price: NCA

Village/Item	*Procured Qty. per day per person (in Kg.)*	*Labour required per one Kg.*	*Market Wage per day*	*Price to be paid for Kg. of MFP of Market wage is to be derived by the labour*	*Actual Price paid per Kg.*	*Percentage difference according to labour cost and actual price*
1. Pedduru						
(a) Tamarind	1.6247	0.62	25	15.50	10.00	55.00
(b) Marking Nuts	3.4942	0.29	25	7.25	4.50	61.00
(c) Tentanga seed (Cassiatora)	4.2746	0.23	25	5.75	3.00	91.67
(d) Tamarind Seed	9.9322	0.10	25	2.50	1.50	66.67
(e) Myrobalans	3.3333	0.30	25	7.50	3.20	134.38
2. Cheruvuru						
(a) Tamarind	1.56	0.64	25	16.00	10.00	60.00
(b) Myrobalans	4.00	0.25	25	6.25	3.20	95.31
(c) Marking Nuts	3.33	0.30	25	7.50	4.50	66.67
(d) Pungam Seed	4.00	0.25	25	6.25	4.00	56.25
3. Kovelapalem						
(a) Gum Karaya	0.318	3.14	25	78.50	70.00	12.14
(b) Naramamidi Bark	2.028	0.49	25	12.25	12.00	2.08
(c) Tamarind	1.600	0.625	25	15.63	10.00	56.30
(d) Marking Nuts	3.320	0.30	25	7.50	4.50	66.67
(e) Myrobalans	3.71	0.27	25	6.75	3.20	110.94
4. Veeravaram						
(a) Gum Karaya	0.3084	3.24	25	81.00	70.00	15.71
(b) Naramamidi Bark	1.70	0.59	25	14.75	12.00	22.91
(c) Tamarind	1.55	0.65	25	16.25	10.00	62.50
(d) Marking Nuts	3.36	0.30	25	7.50	4.50	66.70
5. Pothangi						
(a) Adda leaf	10.90	0.09	25	2.25	2.00	12.50
(b) Seeded Tamarind	9.95	0.10	25	2.50	5.00	–50.00

(contd.)

TABLE 5.3—contd.

Village/Item	Procured Qty. per day per person (in Kg.)	Labour required per one Kg.	Market Wage per day	Price to be paid for Kg. of MFP of Market wage is to be derived by the labour	Actual Price paid per Kg.	Percentage difference according to labour cost and actual price
(c) Pungam Seed	7.84	0.13	25	3.25	4.00	–18.75
(d) Hill Brooms	3.64	0.27	25	6.75	10.00	–32.5
6. Besupuram						
(a) Myrobalans	10.57	0.095	30.00	2.85	3.20	–10.94
(b) Adda leaf	10.88	0.092	30.00	2.76	2.00	38.00
(c) Amla Seed	13.63	0.073	30.00	2.19	2.00	9.50
(d) Naramamidi Bark	2.10	0.48	30.00	14.40	12.00	20.00
(e) Hill Brooms	2.50	0.40	30.00	12.00	10.00	20.00
7. Sumpangiput						
(a) Adda leaf	11.93	0.083	30.00	2.49	2.00	24.50
(b) Deseeded Tamarind	12.45	0.080	30.00	2.40	5.00	–52.80
(c) Pungam Seed	4.81	0.210	30.00	6.30	4.00	57.50
8. Kumarithan						
(a) Adda leaf	9.83	0.10	25.00	2.50	2.00	25.00
(b) Seeded Tamarind	12.49	0.08	25.00	2.00	5.00	–60.00
(c) Pungam Seed	5.99	0.17	25.00	4.25	4.00	6.25
(d) Naramamidi Bark	1.68	0.60	25.00	15.00	12.00	25.00
(e) Myrobalans	6.38	0.16	25.00	4.00	3.20	25.00
(f) Hill Brooms	2.86	0.35	25.00	8.75	10.00	–12.50
(g) Marking Nuts	6.28	0.16	25.00	21.00	21.00	0.00
(h) Soapnuts	5.00	0.20	25.00	5.00	5.00	0.00

Source : G. Parthasarathy *et al.* (2003). Procurement and Marketing of Minor Forest Produce in the Tribal Areas; Atlantic Publications, New Delhi, pp. 99-101.

Trends in the Growth and Instability Indices of Procurement and Sale Prices of NTFP in NCA : 1991–92 to 2002–03

The data on the procurement and sale prices of the NTFP are presented in the Appendix Table 5.1, along with the estimates from year to year. For estimating the trend, growth rates linear, and exponential trend equations are estimated and the results are presented in Appendix Tables 5.2 to 5.5. In most cases, linear form gave a good fit. Therefore, the growth rates based on linear form are used in the analysis here. They are presented in Table 5.4. For these prices, instability indices are also estimated using the formula specified in Chapter IV, section 4.2.

Table 5.4 : Trend in Growth Rates and Instability Indices of Procurement and Sale Prices of Prominent NTFP in NCA : 1990-91 to 2002-03

Commodities	*Procurement Price*		*Sale Price*	
	Growth Rate	*Instability Index*	*Growth Rate*	*Instability Index*
Adda leaf	10.14*	16.65	10.84*	30.2
Cleaning nuts	–0.46	99.74	1.00	97.8
Deseeded Tamarind	6.18*	58.56	5.87**	71.2
Gumdikamali	15.41*	15.67	14.01*	22.9
Gum Karaya	8.56*	12.14	6.28*	43.2
Gum Kondagogu	5.25*	48.25	0.42	99.4
Gum Olibanum	4.85*	46.57	3.92	73.8
Gum Thiruman	0.93	79.32	5.06**	71.6
Hill Broom	8.75*	14.59	–16.55	81.9
Honey	4.33*	44.98	5.17	77.4
Maredugeddalu	8.74*	2.38	13.79*	2.3
Marking nuts	6.74**	73.41	7.71*	66.3
Mohwa flower	7.89*	12.83	5.98*	37.9
Mohwa seed	0.98	86.54	–1.22	89.8
Myrobalans	7.60	76.26	7.09	79.4
Naramamidi bark	14.04*	6.63	15.85*	22.1
Nux vomica	7.30*	60.51	10.53*	59.2
Pungam seed	2.39*	45.14	2.79**	64.8
Seeded Tamarind	5.88*	47.78	5.25**	64.8
Sheekakai	2.41	88.69	3.53	76.7
Soapnuts	2.28	89.01	1.90	94.4
Tamarind	8.40*	42.68	6.54**	63
Wild Broom	0.71	94.06	9.13*	16.3

* Significance at 1 per cent level.

** Significance at 5 per cent level.

The procurement prices of all NTFP except cleaning nuts, Gum Thiruman, Mohua seed, Myrobalans, Sheekakai, Soap-nuts, and Wild broom grew significantly during the period from 1991–92 to 2002–03. The rate of growth varied from 2.39 per cent in the case of Pungam seed, 15.41 per cent in the case of Gum Dikamali. The estimates of the instability indices show that these prices are relatively stable. Among these, the prices which showed higher instability are those of Tamarind, Gum Kondagogu, Honey, Gum Olibanum, Honey, Marking nuts, and Nux vomica. However, the prices of the products, which recorded statistically insignificant growth rates were highly unstable. The year to year variations too, are observed to be very high.

However, a similar type of upward trend is not observed in the case of sale prices of many products: for instance, Gum Kondagogu, Gum Olibanum, and Hill brooms, Honey which although recorded significant growth rates in procurement prices, had nevertheless recorded statistically insignificant growth rates in sale prices. Also, for almost all kind of NTFP, the sale prices are more unstable than the procurement prices; the low growth rate of sale prices will have higher instability relative to procurement prices, and may keep the GCC in a precarious condition, financially. Therefore, there is a need to strengthen the marketing strategies of GCC.

Cyclical Variations in the Procurement and Sale Prices of NTFP in NCA

In the previous chapter, it has been observed that there were indeed cyclical fluctuations in the collection of NTFP. These cyclical fluctuations in collection may cause cyclical fluctuations in prices. For examining this aspect, the cyclical components of both procurement and sale prices are estimated by using the methodology specified in Chapter IV (See page 100 under "Cyclical Variations in the Collection of NTFP in NCA") and these estimates are presented in Appendix Tables 5.6 to 5.27. These results show that both the procurement and sale prices of NTFP in the NCA have been subjected to more or less similar type of cyclical fluctuations as their production, but in the opposite direction. It implies that the GCC's price policy for controlling the price risk of NTFP gatherers is rather weak.

From the foregoing analysis it is very clear that the tribals are not certain about the prices that they would receive for their products. In the years of good crop, the prices are reduced leaving the tribals at the same income level, without having any additional benefit. In the years of bad crops, the price rise may not compensate for the decline in production. This calls for the protection of the interests of NTFP collectors through proper price policy.

Price Policy of GCC

The pricing policy of GCC is governed by the broad guidelines recommended by the Government of India and Government of Andhra Pradesh. The GoI, (vide G.O. Ms. No. 63, Education SW(C) Department, dated 18.3.1963), has recommended guidelines for fixing purchase prices by Tribal Development Co-operative Corporations (TDCCs), according to which the purchase prices payable to tribals are to be fixed by taking nearest wholesale market price as a base and to deduct the costs such as: transport, incidentals, trade charges, estimated driages, market fluctuations, component, etc., account for about 40 per cent of the wholesale price. Thus,

Purchase Price = Wholesale Price in the nearest open market — 40 per cent of the wholesale price in the nearest open market.

The Government of Andhra Pradesh, vide G.O. Ms. No.1477, Revenue TW-II (C) Dept., dt. 31.12.1977 has revised the pricing policy, according to which GCC has to pass on the prevailing market price for the NTFP deducting 15 per cent value towards direct overheads like: handling, transport, and permissible driages of respective commodities towards storage losses. The other yardstick that the GCC adopts to arrive at purchase price for NTFP is maintaining the price line of the previous years of at least 4 to 5 years.

The major criticism against this pricing policy is that, the purchase prices arrived by taking the wholesale prices in the nearest open market as a base, may not reflect the labour costs involved in the collection of NTFP. Very often, products from the neighbouring States flow into the nearby open markets and depress the wholesale prices. A part of it is passed on to the tribals may not cover even the labour costs as revealed by Parthasarathy's study. Also there are some data limitations for the wholesale prices in the nearest open market and using them as base for fixing purchase prices will always cause a downward bias. The choice of the nearest open market is also subjective. Therefore, NTFP needs a pricing policy which is free from these limitations.

Need for Minimum Support Prices

On page 124 under "Cyclical Variations in the Procurement and Sale Prices of NTFP in NCA", it is observed that there are high year-to-year variations in the procurement prices of NTFP and there is a kind of price uncertainty that is faced by the tribals. This price uncertainty sometimes leads the tribals to adopt unscientific methods of collection which in turn destroy the NTFP stock. This may pose a threat to the sustainable production of NTFP and consequently to the the tribal livelihoods. Therefore, the pricing policy of the NTFP should be aimed at eliminating the price uncertainties and provide remunerative prices to the tribals. A minimum support price scheme of the type, which is in existence for the agricultural commodities[7] in the country, can stabilize the prices of NTFP and provide remunerative prices to the tribals.

The Minimum Support Price (MSP) scheme for NTFP can be designed exactly on the same lines as the MSP scheme for farm products, operating in the country now. An independent agency like CACP can be established to fix the support prices for the various NTFP based on the cost of collection and processing. The government should announce these prices in every crop season. The TDCCs may be entrusted with the task of purchasing the products from the tribals at the announced prices. The tribals may also be allowed to sell their produce in the open market which may promote a healthy competition between TDCCs and private traders. Although this scheme protects well the interests of the farmers, it has a limitation. When the TDCCs are not efficient in selling the produce, the sale price may not cover the purchase price and the marketing costs. In such cases, the government has to bear the difference by way of providing subsidy, which is against the current policy of the government. Therefore, the MSP scheme for NTFP should go together with the strengthening of the marketing strategies of TDCCs.

Need for a Change in Marketing Strategies

In the previous sections, it is observed that the prices received by the tribals for their products hardly cover their labour costs, and the sale prices of the GCC are less than the wholesale prices in the open market. It appears that the corporation is not efficient in marketing its products. Therefore, there is a need to change the marketing strategy of the corporation by introducing the marketing professionals into the chain, like the Amul of Gujarat. So far the corporation is marketing the NTFP with very little value addition and low professional management. With the change in technology, consumption pattern, and trade liberalization under WTO, markets both domestic and international, are flooded with various types of value-added products, and the synthetic substitutes for natural products. The marketing in the private enterprises are managed by highly skilled professionals. Under these conditions, the corporation can survive only through value addition and professional marketing management. The policy of value addition to the NTFP has an additional advantage of creating employment to the tribals. The professional managers can evolve suitable marketing strategies to compete with their counterparts in the private sector.

Summing Up

In the NCA region, both private traders and the GCC are involved in the marketing of NTFP. Although the GCC has monopoly power over the purchase of most of the products available in the area, clandestine operations of the private traders are still going on. The corporation has failed to curtail the operations of the private traders, and protect the tribals from exploitation by traders, due to the presence of agencies with similar objective like the VSS and SERP. The sale prices received by the tribals bears no direct relationship with the demand and supply of their products. In the case of sale in open market, traders dictate the prices using their long standing connections with the tribals and by giving them petty loans and providing petty consumer articles. The GCC offers the wholesale prices prevailing in the open market after deducting certain percentage towards cost of handling, storage, etc. The prices received by the tribals in the NCA are not even covering the labour costs involved in the collection and processing of NTFP and they are thus exploited. Very often, the sale prices of the GCC are less than the wholesale prices in the open market. However, the GCC is passing on more than 75 per cent of its sale price to the tribals. However, it need not be given credit for passing on a large part of its sale prices to the tribals for the simple reason, that its sale prices are less than the wholesale prices in the open market.

There are wider year-to-year fluctuations in the procurement and sale prices, causing price uncertainty to the tribals. The price uncertainty may cause damage to the stock of NTFP and pose a threat to its sustainability. For stabilizing the prices and for providing remunerative prices to the tribals, the Minimum Support Price scheme like the one existing for the farm products in the country, needs to be introduced for the NTFP. As the introduction of MSP scheme may involve the provision of subsidy, which is against the present economic policy, efforts should be made to make the corporation self-supporting. This requires strengthening of market management through inclusion of professional managers in the marketing chain and introduction of large scale value addition. Such a change in the market management not only creates additional employment to the tribals, but also evolves the strategies suitable to compete with the private sector.

NOTES

1. (i) G. Parthasarathy (1985), *Minor Forest Produce in the Tribal Economy in Andhra Pradesh*, A.E.R. Centre, Waltair. Unpublished Report.
   (ii) G. Parthasarathy and K. Uma Shankar Patnaik (2003), *Procurement and Marketing of Minor Forest Produce in Tribal Areas*, Atlantic Publishers, New Delhi.
   (iii) D.V. Raghava Rao (1973), *Marketing of Produce and Indebtedness among Tribals*, A.E.R. Centre, Waltair. Unpublished Report.
   (iv) B.N. Srivastava, *Exploitation in Tribal Areas*, Bharatiya Adim Jati Sevak Sangh, New Delhi. Unpublished Report.
   (v) C. Suryanarayana, (1979), *An Appraisal of the Working and Evaluation of the Impact of the Government Agencies in the Selected Tribal Villages of Srikakulam*, Andhra University, Waltair. Unpublished Ph.D Thesis.
2. D.V. Raghava Rao (1973), *Marketing of Produce and Indebtedness among the Tribals, op. cit.*
3. C. Suryanarayana (1979), An Appraisal of the Working and Evaluation of the Impact of the Government Agencies in the Selected Tribal Villages of Srikakulam, *op. cit.*
4. CARD (1978), *Management of Tribal Development Programmes : A Study of Minor Forest Produce*, Administrative Staff College of India, Hyderabad. Unpublished Research Report.
5. M. Bapuji (1977), Girijan Cooperative Corporation, *op. cit.*
6. G. Parthasarathy and Uma Shankar Patnaik, (2003), *Procurement and Marketing of Minor Forest Produce in Tribal Areas*. Atlantic Publications, New Delhi.
7. For eliminating the price uncertainties and providing remunerative prices to the farmers, the GoI introduced a scheme called the Minimum Support Price (MSP). Under this scheme, the government announces the prices of various agricultural commodities from time to time and purchases of the commodities from the farmers at these prices, through various authorised agencies. There is an obligation on the part of the government to purchase the entire quantity offered by the farmers. But the farmers are free to sell their products either to State agencies at the minimum support price or in the open market. The minimum support prices are fixed by the Commissioner for Agricultural Costs and Prices (CACP) based on the cost of production. At present the MSP scheme covers 26 commodities.

6

Organization, Objectives, Hierarchy, Government Support and Activities of Girijan Cooperative Corporation (GCC)

Introduction

The GCC is vested with the monopoly power over the collection and marketing of NTFP in Andhra Pradesh. Therefore, the sustainability of the production of NTFP and improving the livelihoods of NTFP gatherers, to a large extent, depends on the performance of GCC. In this chapter, an attempt has been made to present the origin, growth, objectives, organizational structure, and activities of GCC. The study is useful because it aims to identify the limitations if any, and suggest a model for achieving the sustainable production of NTFP and improving tribal livelihoods.

Origin of GCC

The agency areas are rich in NTFP and the forests are the main source of livelihood for the tribals. The forests of Andhra Pradesh are abound in NTFP like: premium gums; tree borne oil seeds like Mohua, Pungam; food items like tamarind, Honey; nuts and seeds like Myrobalans, Nux vomica, Cleaning nuts, Marking nuts; Naramamidi bark, Brooms, and precious medicinal herbs, etc. The collection and sale of these NTFP constitutes both the major economic activity and source of livelihood for the tribals, which provides not merely their requirement for sustenance but also income through trade and barter system. Their agro-based economy suffers from chronic indebtedness and tradition-bound agricultural practices, viz., shifting cultivation. Most of the cultivable land is rain-fed, since there is no proper infrastructure, technical support, and irrigation facilities.

The tribals were exploited by the money lenders and petty traders in the sale of their produce, and purchase of essential commodities. The traders used to collect the loans from tribals in kind and the barter system was the only mode of exchange. In order to mitigate the hardships and to protect the tribals from exploitation by the money lenders, middlemen, and petty traders, and to extend support for the socio-economic upliftment of tribals, the Government of Andhra Pradesh took steps, and passed protective and restrictive legislations.

In the early phase on the recommendations of the Malayappan Committee, the Government of Andhra Pradesh formulated a scheme in the year 1954 for the establishment of a finance and marketing corporation to cater to the needs of tribals particularly in the direction of providing the credit facilities. In pursuance of this policy decision, the government issued orders on 14.2.1955 for the formation of "Andhra Pradesh Scheduled Tribes Finance & Development Corporation" and the corporation was registered on 14.4.1956 as a company under the Indian Companies Act. During the course of its functioning, the corporation encountered many a difficulty in securing finances and it was felt that an institution in the form of a "Co-operative" would have better access to adequate working capital and finances, which are essential for the economic welfare of the tribals.

Subsequently on 26.10.1956, a new organization under the name of "Andhra Pradesh Scheduled Tribes Co-operative Finance & Development Corporation" was registered as a co-operative society under the Madras Co-operative Societies Act 1932 (Madras Act VI of 1932) and came into being. It started its operations from 5.4.1957 in the districts of Srikakulam, Visakhapatnam, East Godavari and West Godavari. In the year 1962, it was renamed as "Andhra Pradesh Scheduled Tribes Co-operative Finance & Development Corporation " and its area of operations was extended to the Scheduled Areas in

Andhra Pradesh and continued to function in its original name until 18.2.1970. Subsequently, the institution has been renamed as Andhra Pradesh Girijan Co-operative Corporation Limited or the GCC.

Expansion of the Activities to all Scheduled Areas of Andhra Pradesh

When the institution was started, it had only two agricultural primary cooperative marketing societies (APCMS); one each in the districts of Visakhapatnam and Srikakulam, with two Daily Requirement Depots (typical fair price shops) and its annual turnover was only Rs. 4.13 lakh. The corporation extended its activities and the area of operation year after year to all the Scheduled Areas of the State to render service to the tribals in all Sub-Plan villages besides Primitive Tribal Groups and MADA pockets. In a span of 49 years, its affiliated Societies and D.R. Depots were increased from 2 each during 1956 to 17 and 187 respectively by 1970, and 44 Girijan Primary Co-operative Marketing Societies and 839 D.R. Depots by 1994.

Year-wise Growth of the Organization by inducting New Societies and Depots

Year	Name of the District	Name of the Primary Society created during the year	Number of DR Depots added during the year
1956-57	Visakhapatnam	1. Downuru/Chintapalli	24
		2. G.L.Puram	35
1957-58	Srikakulam	3. Seethempeta	34
	Visakhapatnam	4. Madugula/Paderu	35
		5. K.D.Peta/Koyyuru	31
1959-60	Srikakulam	6. Salur	26
	Visakhapatnam	7. S. Kota/Araku Valley	24
	East Godavari	8. Yeleswaram/Addateegala	32
1960-61	East Godavari	9. Rampa Chodavaram	30
		10. Gokavaram	5
	West Godavari	11. K.R. Puram	32
1965-66	Khammam	12. Paloncha	19
		13. Bhadrachalam	11

(contd.)

Year	Name of the District	Name of the Primary Society created during the year	Number of DR Depots added during the year
1967-68	Warangal	14. Eturnagaram	23
1968-69	Warangal	15. Gudur @ Narasampeta	24
1969-70	Adilabad	16. Utnoor	34
	Srikakulam	17. Pathapatnam	27
	Nellore	18. Nellore	8
1970-71	Srikakulam	19. Pathapatnam	—
	Adilabad	20. Wankidi @ Asifabad	15
	Mahaboobnagar	21. Mannanur	23
	Karimnagar	22. Mahadevpur	12
1971-72	Visakhapatnam	23. Gajapathinagaram	—
	Chittoor	24. Chittoor	—
	Khammam	25. Yellandu	33
		26. Dammapeta	31
	Adilabad	27. Itchoda	12
1973-74	Kurnool	28. Atmakur	—
	Adilabad	29. Jannaram	9
1974-75	Adilabad	30. Chennur	—
1975-76	Chittoor	31. Tirupati	—
1976-77	Prakasham	32. Pedadornal	10
	Kadapa	33. Kadiri	—
	Guntur	34. Guntur	—
1978	Khammam	35. Venkatapuram	21
1979	Visakhapatnam	36. Munchingput	18
	Nizamabad	37. Kamareddy	—
1989	Nellore	38. Rapur	—
1990	Kadapa	39. Rajampeta	—
1991	East Godavari	40. Gurthedu	—
		41. Pedamallapuram	—
1991-92	Kurnool	42. Nandyal	9
1992-93	Visakhapatnam	43. Kasipatnam	18
		44. GK Veedhi	21
		45. G. Madugula	12
		46. Pedabailu	15
	East Godavari	47. Rajavommangi	29
		48. Maredumilli	21
	Khammam	49. Chinturu	15
	Adilabad	50. SK Nagar	9
		51. Jainoor	—
1993-94	Adilabad	52. Adilabad	10
	Vizianagaram	53. Parvathipuram	15
	Khammam	54. Kukunuru	10
		55. Manuguru	13
	Warangal	56. Mulugu	13

Source : GCC, Corporate Office, Visakhapatnam.

Objectives of GCC

The Government of Andhra Pradesh has laid the following core functions for the GCC to perform in order to safeguard the socio-economic interest of the tribals :

(a) To ensure payment of remunerative prices for the NTFP collected by the tribals, by eliminating the middlemen and private traders, who were indulging in unfair trade practices;
(b) To ensure availability of essential commodities even in the interior agency areas through a network of D.R. Depots; and
(c) To provide support to the tribals in their agricultural activities, through extending credit facilities.

Prior to the entry of GCC, the tribals were in the clutches of the middlemen and traders and were ruthlessly exploited by them. The disposal of their NTFP was secured under the barter system. Valuable gums, honey, and other kinds of NTFP were exchanged even for salt, dry fish, or other day-to-day requirements of tribals. The loaning pattern was also pathetic, in that the petty traders used to advance loans just before the harvest; and tribals due to their illiteracy, and indebtedness, used to deliver the seasonal agricultural produce / NTFP at throw away prices. The entry of GCC changed the scenario to the betterment of tribals. Several initiatives of the GCC over a period of time, have improved the economic condition of tribals. The GCC now performs multifarious activities that includes : collection and marketing of NTFP, value addition, research and development, training programmes, afforestation through regeneration of NTFP species, supply of essential commodities, extending credit for agricultural activities, etc. Today, the GCC serves about 3 million tribals in the scheduled areas of 14 districts, against a total tribal population of 5.2 million in the State. All these activities are geared to achieve the overall objectives of the organization. The details are discussed in the following section :

Share Capital

The corporation's initial authorized share capital of Rs. 3,00,000 (lakh) was made up of 3,000 shares of Rs.100 each. The authorized share capital has increased from time to time. The GCC is collecting 5 per cent shares from borrowers and the credit limit of individual loanee is Rs. 10,000. As on 2005, the corporation's paid-up share capital was Rs. 37.71 lakh (Table 6.1).

Table 6.1 : Society-wise Membership and Share Capital

Sl. No.	*Society*	*No. of Members*	*Share Capital (Million Rs.)*
1.	Seethempeta	17612	268760.25
2.	Pathapatnam	9265	71428.50
3.	G.L.Puram	22192	246746.00
4.	Salur	37120	168214.50
5.	Parvathipuram	3593	57796.00
6.	Paderu	10289	154244.00
7.	Araku	17445	140125.25
8.	Munchingput	7908	60805.50
9.	G. Madugula	1739	8835.00
10.	Pedabailu	371	1855.00
11.	Kasipatnam	581	2905.00
12.	Chintapalli	11589	175380.00
13.	GK Veedhi	1358	7385.00
14.	Koyyuru	8925	91622.50
15.	Rampa Chodavaram	13883	236028.00
16.	Addateegala	20415	153901.00
17.	K.R. Puram	10690	317855.00
18.	Pedamallapuram	1795	17950.00
19.	Rajavommangi	3132	12075.00
20.	Maredumilli	2777	13885.00
21.	Nandyal	853	11859.00
22.	Mannanur	1143	19606.00
23.	Pedadornal	1034	31582.00
24.	Chittoor	2252	34715.00
25.	Nellore	650	21720.00
26.	Cuddapah	633	3350.00
27.	Bhadrachalam	11425	68890.00
28.	Chinturu	1618	172650.00
29.	Venkatapuram	7366	28675.20
30.	Kukunoor	467	8680.00
31.	Paloncha	14152	158865.00
32.	Yellandu	12711	199597.00
33.	Dammapeta	17001	178272.00
34.	Manuguru	1081	18825.00

(contd.)

TABLE 6.1—contd.

Sl. No.	Society	No. of Members	Share Capital (Million Rs.)
35.	Eturnagaram	11020	111040.00
36.	Mahadevpur	4427	22503.62
37.	Narasampeta	11240	254774.85
38.	Mulug	1127	123370.00
39.	Asifabad	6107	15974.00
40.	SPK Nagar	1137	11370.00
41.	Jannaram	992	4082.00
42.	Utnoor	2893	9501.00
43.	Itchoda	5553	22281.00
44.	Adilabad	1714	8570.00
45.	Jainoor	2059	20590.00
	Total	323334	3571000.00

Source : GCC, Corporate Office, Visakhapatnam.

The data showing Share Capital received by the GCC from the Government of Andhra Pradesh during the period from 1957–58 to 2004–05 are presented in Table 6.2. By 2004–05, the share capital received from the government amounted to Rs. 2011.53 lakh.

Table 6.2 : The Share Capital received from the Government of Andhra Pradesh and Government of India

(Rs. in lakh)

S.No.	Year	Share Capital amount received	Repaid	Cumulative balance Share Capital
1.	1957-58	2.00		2.00
2.	1958-59			2.00
3.	1959-60			2.00
4.	1960-61			2.00
5.	1961-62			2.00
6.	1962-63			2.00
7.	1963-64			2.00
8.	1964-65			2.00
9.	1965-66			2.00
10.	1966-67			2.00
11.	1967-68			2.00
12.	1968-69			2.00
13.	1969-70			2.00
14.	1970-71	4.25		6.25

(contd.)

TABLE 6.2 : contd. *(Rs. in lakh)*

S.No.	*Year*	*Share Capital amount received*	*Repaid*	*Cumulative balance Share Capital*
15.	1971-72	8.25	—	14.50
16.	1972-73	—	—	14.50
17.	1973-74	3.00	—	17.50
18.	1974-75	5.00	—	22.50
19.	1975-76	—	—	22.50
20.	1976	(1.7.76 to 31.12.76 = 6 months)		22.50
21.	1977	—	—	
22.	1978	42.71	8.47	56.74
23.	1979	—	—	56.74
24.	1980	1.01	0.07	57.68
25.	1981	—	—	57.68
26.	1982	—	—	57.68
27.	1983	35.00	10.00	82.68
28.	1984	—	—	82.68
29.	1985	—	—	82.68
30.	1986	—	—	82.68
31.	1987	—	—	82.68
32.	1988-89	(1.1.88 to 31.3.89 = 15 months)		82.68
33.	1989-90	—	—	82.68
34.	1990-91	362.38	89.23	355.83
35.	1991-92	238.40	5.72	588.51
36.	1992-93	480	6.67	1061.84
37.	1993-94	19.15	—	1080.99
38.	1994-95	28.80	—	1109.79
39.	1995-96	500.00	—	1609.79
40.	1996-97	56.00	—	1665.79
41.	1997-98	126.00	6.26	1785.53
42.	1998-99	126.00	—	1911.53
43.	1999-2000	—	—	1911.53
44.	2000-01	—	—	1911.53
45.	2001-02	100.00	—	2011.53
46.	2002-03	—	—	2011.53
47.	2003-04	—	—	2011.53
48.	2004-05	—	—	2011.53
	Total	**2137.95**	**126.42**	**2011.53**

Source: GCC, Corporate Office, Visakhapatnam.

Organisational Hierarchy and Flow Chart

The Girijan Co-operative Corporation Ltd. is a State level organisation with its headquarters at Visakhapatnam and governed by a Board of Directors consisting of Chairman, official and non-official directors nominated by the Government of Andhra Pradesh. The affairs of the corporation are administered by the Vice Chairman and Managing Director (VC and MD), a senior I.A.S. officer who is responsible for all operational and financial management decisions. The other wings at corporate office like administration, marketing (bulk and retail), financial, domestic requirements (D.R.s), transport, credit, etc., are headed by General Managers and Deputy General Managers and report to the V.C. and Managing Director on the day-to-day progress. The Project Officers of the Integrated Tribal Development Agencies (ITDAs) headed by I.A.S. officers act as Executive Directors of GCC in the area of their operation and report to the V.C. and M.D.

More than 1,580 employees are engaged in the service of 3 million tribals through a network of : 1 Regional Office at Hyderabad; 10 Divisional Offices coterminous with ITDA Headquarters; 43 Girijan Primary Cooperative Marketing Societies (GPCMS); and 839 D.R. Depots working in close coordination with 10 Integrated Tribal Development Agencies (ITDAs) in Andhra Pradesh. The Organizational Hierarchy flow chart is given in Annexure 6.1.

Institutional Arrangement in the Service of Tribals in Scheduled Areas

Divisional Managers Heading the Divisional Offices in Sub-Plan Mandals

For geographical convenience and effective administration, the GCC has established 10 divisional offices across the State. The Divisional Manager heading each division controls about 4 to 5 Girijan Primary Cooperative Marketing Societies (GPCMs).

Managers heading the Girijan Primary Cooperative Marketing Societies (GPCMS)

The 43 GPCMS are situated in sub-plan mandals of the State and they are in fact the life-line between government and tribals. These societies act as a link between the government and the tribals, and implement the tribal welfare activities through the GCC.

Role of Credit-cum-Purchase Assistants (CCPA) in GPCMS

The CCPA of the GCC plays a predominant role in the tribal economy. The major activity of CCPA is to collect NTFP throughout the year from the tribals. The collection areas of NTFP from the tribals by CCPA are called Shandy Points and D.R. depots. The CCPA also disburses loans to tribals for their agricultural operations and recovers in terms of cash or in kind, i.e., in the form of NTFP.

The Role of Godown Assistant

The GCC has established storage facilities in the form of godowns in the proximity of tribal areas. In all, there are 166 godowns with 29,961 MT (metric tonnes) storage capacity and all of them are located in the tribal areas. The stocks procured from tribals by CCPA are transported to these godowns and handed over to godown assistants who are the custodians of the stocks and safeguard the NTFP till they are disposed.

Salesman and Domestic Requirement Depots in the Proximity of Tribal Areas

The GCC has established about 839 Domestic Requirement Depots (a typical fair price shop) in the tribal habitats, in order to cater to the needs of the tribals by supplying essential commodities like rice and kerosene oil under the public distribution system (PDS), and other daily requirements. These D.R. depots are manned by a salesman and assisted by a measurer-cum-watchman (MCW), who attends to diversified activities making the D.R. depot as centre of all activities like : collection of NTFP throughout the year and disbursing loans during the agricultural operations, alongside the supply of essential commodities.

Role of Self Help Groups

The GCC also encourages self help groups by collecting NTFP through them and handing over 103 D.R. depots in the tribal areas to the SHGs.

Government Support through Monopoly Procurement Rights vested in GCC

For the benefit of tribals, the Government of Andhra Pradesh made required amendments to the relevant acts and rules to overcome the hurdles created by the forest contractors, who were earlier enjoying the right of collection and sale of forest produce. During the year 1961, the government granted lease-hold of Minor Forest Produce or NTFP units to collect seigniorage.

The Andhra Pradesh Minor Forest Produce (Regulation of Trade) Regulation 1979 was made on 26th December, 1978 by the Governor of Andhra Pradesh under paragraph 5(2) of the Schedule V to the Constitution of India after consulting the Andhra Pradesh Tribes Advisory Council. This had received the assent of the President on 28th March, 1980. In exercise of conferred powers, the Governor of Andhra Pradesh, with the assent of President of India made the following regulation in the 30th year of the Republic of India.

This regulation called as 'Andhra Pradesh Scheduled Areas Minor Forest Produce (Regulation of Trade) Regulation 1979'; extends to all the scheduled areas of Andhra Pradesh, and shall enforce and apply to NTFP as notified by the government from time to time. According to Act 1 of the 1979 Regulation of the Government—for the purpose of purchase of and trade in any Minor Forest Produce on their behalf—appointed the Girijan Co-operative Corporation as an Agent in the Scheduled Areas.

(a) The Corporation shall issue a notification under sub-section (3) of Section 1 in respect of the scheduled area and no other person than Corporation shall sell or purchase or cure or otherwise.

(b) The Corporation shall set up a number of purchase centres for the convenience of collectors of respective NTFP, deemed fit. The Corporation, to secure compliance to the provisions shall set up check posts or erect barriers to stop and search all means of transport for unauthorized transport of NTFP.

(c) Under this Regulation, no Court shall take cognizance of any offence punishable under this Regulation except on a complaint made by an Officer of the Corporation duly authorized by the Corporation.

For the purpose of the said Regulation, in exercise of powers conferred by clause (b) of Section (2) of Andhra Pradesh Scheduled Areas Minor Forest Produce (Regulation of Trade), Regulation I of 1979, the Government of Andhra Pradesh had vested rights over NTFP with the GCC.

The Government of Andhra Pradesh (vide G.O.Ms.156 dated 17.09.80), has included 35 Minor Forest Produce (NTFP) commodities in the lease units of GCC. However, over a period of time, the Government as per the recommendations of the forest department has delisted 10 commodities of minor forest produce from GCC. The details are as follows :

List of NTFP and Details of Delisted NTFP by GCC from time to time

As per the AP NTFP (Regulation of Trade) Regulation 1979. (G.O. Ms.No.156, SW, dt.17.9.80).		*List of NTFP being procured by GCC by entering into an Agreement with Forest Department.*	
Sl.No.	*Commodity*	*Sl.No.*	*Commodity*
1.	Adda leaf	1.	Adda leaf
2.	Addanara		Delisted
3.	Peddanara		Delisted
4.	Hill brooms	2.	Hill Brooms
5.	Wild brooms	3.	Wild Brooms
6.	K.T.Bundles		Delisted
7.	Sheekakai	4.	Sheekakai
8.	Koperi grass		Delisted
9.	Thatching grass		Delisted
10.	Gantubarangi		Delisted
11.	Karivepaku		Delisted

(*contd.*)

As per the AP NTFP (Regulation of Trade) Regulation 1979. (G.O. Ms.No.156, SW, dt.17.9.80).		List of NTFP being procured by GCC by entering into an Agreement with Forest Department.	
Sl.No.	*Commodity*	*Sl.No.*	*Commodity*
12.	Nallateega		Delisted
13.	Amla fruit and seed	5.	Amla fruit and seed
14.	Cleaning nuts	6.	Cleaning nuts
15.	Chiranji	7.	Chiranji
16.	Honey Rock Bee	8.	Rock Bee Honey
17.	Honey Apiary	9.	Apiary Honey
18.	Kusum Oil seed	10.	Kusum Oil seed
19.	Myrobalans	11.	Myrobalans
20.	Mohua seed	12.	Mohua seed
21.	Mohua flower	13.	Mohua flower
22.	Marking nuts	14.	Marking nuts
23.	Nux vomica fruit and seed	15.	Nux vomica fruit and seed
24.	Neem seed		Delisted
25.	Pungam fruit and seed	16.	Pungam fruit and seed
26.	Rella bark		Delisted
27.	Tangedu bark		Delisted
28.	Naramamidi bark	24.	Naramamidi bark
29.	Rauwolfia serpentina roots	17.	Rauwolfia serpentina
30.	(a) Shell Tamarind	21.	Tamarind
	(b) Tamarind Seeded		(a) Shell
	(c) Tamarind Deseeded		(b) Seeded
	(d) Tamarind green		(c) Deseeded
	(e) Tamarind seed		(d) Green
			(e) Seed
31.	Soapnuts	18.	Soapnuts
32.	Honey wax	19.	Honey wax
33.	Wood Apples		Delisted
34.	(a) Gum Karaya	20.	(a) Gum Karaya
	(b) Gum Tiruman		(b) Gum Tiruman
	(c) Other Gums		(c) Other Gums
35.	(a) Sal resin		Delisted
	(b) Sal kernal		Delisted
	(c) Sal seed		Delisted
		22.	Teri pods
		23.	Sugandhipala
		25.	Maredugeddalu

Source : A.P. NTFP (Regulation Trade) Regulation 1979. (G.O. Ms. No.156, SW, dt.17.9.80).
MOU between GCC & APFD is renewed annually.

Reasons for Delisting of Certain Items of Minor Forest Produce from Procurement by GCC

(a) Certain items are not in surplus in the forests and hence collection by Tribals for marketing has come down, e.g., Neem Seed.
(b) Certain items are highly perishable such as wood apples, Karivepaku, etc. Hence, they have been withdrawn from the lease units.
(c) Certain items are treated as medicinal herbs. Hence, the forest department wanted to protect them, e.g., Rella bark, Tangedu bark, Nela teega, etc.
(d) Sal resin and its other products are not available in the scheduled areas of the State. Hence, those products have been delisted.

Lease Agreement with Forest Department

As per powers vested on the GCC for procurement of NTFP on monopoly basis, the forest department is extending Lease Units for procurement of NTFP. The Government was also to pay the Forest Rentals at the rate of 15 per cent of the Value of NTFP collected by way of book adjustment. Against settling the accounts of procurement of NTFP to the forest department, the Government is paying the forest rentals to forest department by way of book adjustment.

Lease Agreement between the GCC and Forest Department on yearly basis in the light of amendments to the Andhra Pradesh Panchayat Raj Act

In the light of amendments to the Andhra Pradesh Panchayat Raj Act, pending finalization of the implementation of the PESA, the GCC has been entered into an agreement with the forest department, for extension of lease units to the GCC on an yearly basis. This yearly agreement has come into force against G.O.Ms. Nos. 306 and 337, Environment, Forest, Sciences & Technology Department, according to which the lease agreement will be in force and renewed once in 5 years.

Other Concessions from Government—Reimbursement of Establishment Cost

Against the Establishment Costs (Salary bill) of GCC to the tune of Rs. 21 crore, the Government of Andhra Pradesh is reimbursing about 50 per cent costs, i.e., to an extent of Rs.10 crore and the balance is being met by the GCC through its commercial activities.

Activities of the GCC

The activities of the GCC are broadly categorized as :

(a) NTFP operations through which the GCC tried to introduce different procurement and sales strategies to improve the value of NTFP, establishing *in situ* processing centres to create employment to tribals, secure value addition and brand equity, R & D initiatives, training programmes, etc.;
(b) Domestic Requirements activity; and
(c) Credit related activities.

NTFP Operations—Steps taken by GCC to improve Procurement of NTFP

(a) Concentration on Major NTFP

The major thrust of GCC is to give priority to 10 NTFP commodities having market potential and on which the tribals are highly dependent. The NTFP identified under this category include: Gum Karaya, honey, sheekakai, amla, hill brooms, Mohua, Nux vomica, Naramamidi bark, Maredugaddalu, etc. Emphasis was given to 2–3 items in each GPCM Society and a total of 8 to 10 items from each Division, so as to ensure adequate quantity of procurement.

(b) Steps taken to improve the sale of NTFP

The GCC adopted the following market strategies for marketing of Minor Forest Produce to pass on better returns to NTFP collectors :

(i) Auction-cum-Tenders for Centralized Commodities

The GCC floats tenders on a monthly basis for all varieties of gums and other NTFP and makes efforts to dispose the stocks at highest prices received through tenders. This has enabled the GCC to standardize a system for marketing gums to export houses, and plan procurement and disposal of gums in a systematic way.

(ii) Decentralized NTFP Commodities

In view of perishable nature and seasonal conditions for certain NTFP, the GCC has empowered the divisional managers of GCC to dispose of certain NTFP like: Wet amla, Adda leaf, Wild brooms, Seeded tamarind, etc.

(iii) Forward Sale Tie-up and Joint Venture Agreements with National Level Organizations

Advance sale tie-ups with institutions like: TRIFED, NAFED, A.P. OILFED and MARKFED are pursued for certain NTFP in Andhra Pradesh, so as to ensure procurement in large quantities, and their hassle free disposal. The commodities under this category are: Niger, Soya, Rajmah, Tamarind, etc.

(iv) Value Addition and Brand Equity is the Other Strategy for Marketing the NTFP Under Food and Cosmetics Category

The NTFP/SAP introduced into the consumer market include: Honey, Tamarind, Amla, Sheekakai, Soapnuts, Hill brooms, Rajmah, White beans, Cuttings, Chilli powder, Turmeric powder, etc. The details of the sources of marketing of various products are presented in the following :

The Sources of Marketing of Major NTFP

Sl. No.	*Name of the Commodity*	*Source of Marketing*
1.	Gum Karaya and Other Gums	Bulk Sale to Exporters through auction-cum-tender
2.	Honey	Retail Sales through distribution network
3.	Tamarind	Retail sales through distribution network and through auction-cum-tender
4.	Tamarind Seed	Bulk Sales and User Industry
5.	Hill Brooms	Retail Sales through distribution network
6.	Sheekakai	Bulk and Retail Sales
7	Soapnuts	Retail Sales
8.	Mohwa Flower	User Industry and Bulk Sales
9.	Mohwa Seed	Bulk Sales
10.	Nux vomica	Bulk Sales and User Industry
11	Maredugeddalu	Ayurvedic Firms
12.	Amla	Ayurvedic Firms
13.	Myrobalans	Bulk Sale through auction-cum-tender and to user industry
14.	Cleaning Nuts	Bulk Sale through auction-cum-tender and to user industry in value added form
15.	Adda Leaf (Siali leaf)	Decentralized through auction-cum-tender
16.	Bees Wax	Bulk Sale through auction-cum-tender and to user industry
17.	Naramamidi Bark (*Polyalthia longifolia*)	User Industry and Bulk Sales
18.	Oil Seeds	Bulk Sale through auction-cum-tender

Source : Marketing Department, GCC Corporate Office, Visakhapatnam

(c) Continuous Improvement in Purchase Prices

By concentrating on major NTFP, the GCC could not only tap maximum quantities but also made best efforts to market them through various sources (like advance sale-tie-up with institutional buyers, value addition, and retailing in consumer packs, and sale to user industry etc.). These steps taken by the GCC enabled it to offer higher and higher purchase prices year after year.

Pricing of NTFP

The GCC adopted the pricing method suggested by the Government for a long time. This methód of determination of prices for NTFP was subjected to criticism on several grounds. Recognizing the limitations of this method, the GCC has undertaken revision. The main aim of the GCC in revising its pricing method is to arrive at fair support prices payable to NTFP gatherers, based on the assessment of effort and work load *versus* manhours involved in collection of each NTFP. The revised method of computing the procurement prices is as follows :

The GCC has taken following parameters into cognizance to arrive at the purchase prices. The method of estimation is specified below :

(a) *The Minimum Wage Rate*: Basing on the price index of essential commodities, the minimum wage payable to unskilled worker is estimated as Rs. 29 per eight hours and was fixed by a committee comprising senior officials and the district collector as its chairman.

(b) *Estimation of Labour Inputs :*

(i) Step 1 : Estimation of minimum wage rate for unskilled workers;

(ii) Step 2 : Cost of collecting 1 kg. NTFP when minimum wage is paid ; and

(iii) Step 3 : A notational remuneration @ 10% has been added to the cost of labour inputs taking risk due to hazards into consideration.

(c) *Estimation of Work Load* : For estimating the work load, the following 4 steps have been considered :

(i) Step 1 : Estimation of gross total quantity of NTFP collected;

(ii) Step 2 : Deduction of wastage;

(iii) Step 3 : Estimation of net quantity; and

(iv) Step 4 : Estimation of total time spent.

Following this method, prices are estimated for 12 prominent NTFP and these estimates are presented in Table 6.3.

Table 6.3 : Estimation of Prices for 12 Prominent NTFP basing on Work Load *Vs.* Manhours

Commodity	*Stages of collection*	*Estimated wastage during the process (%)*	*Net Qty. derived per hour (Kg/hr)*	*Cost of collection in case of the minimum wage (Rs. 29.00 per 8 hrs)*	*Collection of 1 Kg of NTFP equivalent to minimum wage (Rs. per Kg)*	*Cost + Notational margin @ 10% (Rs./Kg)*
Gum Karaya	Commuting distance, blazing, gathering, drying, grading, storing and sale	20%	0.06	Rs.3.63	Rs.60.42	Rs.66.50
Honey	Location, smoking, gathering from cliff/Tree segregation, storing and marketing	40%	0.089	Rs.3.63	Rs.40.73	Rs.45.00
Nara-mamidi Bark	Commuting distance, Blazing/ bark gathering, drying, storing and marketing	50%	0.39	Rs.3.63	Rs.9.30	Rs.10.00
Nux vomica	Commuting distance, collection of fruit, separating seeds, washing and cleaning, drying, storing and marketing	33%	0.59	Rs.3.63	Rs.6.15	Rs.7.00
Mohua seed	Commuting distance, collection of fruit and breaking shell/seed collection, drying, storing and marketing	40%	0.44	Rs.3.63	Rs.8.25	Rs.9.00

(Contd.)

TABLE 6.3 (Contd.)

Commodity	Stages of collection	Estimated wastage during the process (%)	Net Qty. derived per hour (Kg/hr)	Cost of collection in case of the minimum wage (Rs. 29.00 per 8 hrs)	Collection of 1 Kg of NTFP equivalent to minimum wage (Rs. per Kg)	Cost + Notational margin @ 10% (Rs./Kg)
Tamarind	Commuting distance, collection, drying, shell removing, storing and marketing	26%	0.84	Rs.3.63	Rs.4.32	Rs.4.75
Sheekakai	Commuting distance, locating, gathering, drying, storing and marketing.	40%	0.42	Rs.3.63	Rs. 8.64	Rs.9.50
Hill Brooms	Commuting distance, collection, drying, cleaning, Broom making, storing and marketing.	50%	0.48	Rs.3.63	Rs.7.55	Rs.8.68
Soapnuts	Commuting distance, locating, gathering, drying, storing and marketing.	40%	0.52	Rs.3.63	Rs.6.98	Rs.7.68
Mohua flower	Commuting distance, collection of flower, drying, storing and marketing	50%	1.02	Rs.3.63	Rs.3.55	Rs.4.00
Marking Nuts	Commuting distance, locating, gathering, sorting out seeds, drying, storing and marketing.	25%	2.10	Rs.3.63	Rs.1.73	Rs.2.00
Myrobalans	Commuting distance, seed collection, drying, storing, marketing.	50%	1.64	Rs.3.63	Rs.2.21	Rs.2.40

Source : Policy Recommendations, Institute of Applied Manpower Research, M.G. Marg, New Delhi.

In situ *Processing Centres to create Employment for Tribal Women*

The long run perspective of GCC is to establish infrastructure facilities by constructing sheds and godowns, processing units in the tribal habitats and equip them with required machinery at various points based on the availability of raw materials. This would generate employment for the tribals, particularly women.

In situ **Processing Centres***

Processing Units	*Location*	*Method of Value Addition*
Tamarind Processing and Packing Units	V. Madugula—Visakhapatnam District. Salur, S. Kota, Kurupam—Vizianagaram Dist. Punganoor—Chittoor Dist. Seethampeta, Pathapatnam, Srikakulam Dist. Narasipatnam—Visakhapatnam District. Power Organisation (SHG) Rajulathallavalasa—Visakhapatnam Dist.	Removal of fibre, seed and other foreign material and reversing the fruit (called as Flower variety) for consumer appeal and packing into 500 gms and 1 Kg. packs.
Rajmah (Red and White), White beans, Cuttings processing Unit	Paderu, Visakhapatnam District	Segregation and packing along with nitrogen gas by automatic filling machines.
Hill Brooms	Paderu, Visakhapatnam District, Salur, Vizianagaram Salur, Vizianagaram district; Seethampeta—Srikakulam district	Segregation and converting into consumer packs with plastic handles.
Soapnut Processing and Packing Units	Srisailam	Removal of seed and other foreign material and packed in retail form

* *Source* : Retail Division, GCC, Corporate Office, Visakhapatnam, Andhra Pradesh.

The GCC has established the following *in situ* processing centres and gave employment to about 10,000 women self help groups.

Value Addition and Brand Equity

In the situation of diminishing NTFP year after year due to depleting forests and the tribals struggling for alternative sources of income, the GCC focussed on giving value addition to raw NTFP. This has ensured that the GCC not only taps commodities like honey to its fullest potential and create unprecedented demand in the market, but also to bring certain other NTFP like Sheekakai, Soapnuts etc., out of their obsolescence by securing value addition.

(a) Central Processing Units

The GCC has set up following processing units to realize better returns for NTFP and provide sustainable employment to tribals.

	Name of the Unit		*Place*
1.	Honey Processing and Packing Units	:	Rajahmundry and Araku
2.	Sheekakai and Soapnut Pulverizing and Packing Unit	:	Rajahmundry
3.	Soap Making Unit	:	Vizianagaram
4.	Rajmah, White Beans, Cuttings Processing and Packing Unit	:	Paderu
5.	Tamarind Processing and Packing Unit	:	V. Madugula, Salur, S.Kota, Rajula Tallavalasa, Aganampudi, Narsipatnam, Anakapalli, Chodavaram, Dhan Foundation (Visakhapatnam)
6.	Hill Broom Processing Units	:	Paderu, Parvathipuram, Salur, Seethempet, Rampa, Chodavaram

Source : Retail Marketing Division, GCC, Corporate Office, Visakhapatnam.

(b) The Range of the Value Added Products Marketed through Retail Activity under Girijan Brand Name

Sl. No.	Brand Name	Pack Sizes
1.	"Girijan" Honey	5 Kg/1Kg/500 gm/200 gm/50 gm
2.	"Ritu" Turmeric Soaps	100 gm/75 gm
3.	"Ritu" Neem Soaps	100 gm/75 gm
4.	"Girijan" Flower Tamarind	1 Kg/500 gm
5.	"Girijan" Pulp Tamarind	1 Kg
6.	"Girijan" Deseeded Tamarind	5 Kg/1 kg
7.	"Girijan" Seeded Tamarind	5 Kg/1 kg
8.	"Girijan" Amla Powder	200 gm/100 gm
9.	"Girijan" Sheekakai Powder	200 gm/100 gm
10.	"Girijan" Soapnut Powder	200 gm/100 gm
11.	"Girijan" Soapnuts	1 Kg/500 gm
12.	"Girijan" Hill Brooms (Gr.I and II)	1 No.
13.	"Girijan" Rajmah (Red)	500 gm
14.	"Girijan" Rajmah (White)	500 gm
15.	"Girijan" Rajmah (Kashmir)	500 gm
16.	"Girijan" Cuttings	500 gm
17.	"Girijan" White beans	500 gm
18.	"Girijan" Turmeric Powder	100 gm

Source : Retail Marketing Division, GCC, Corporate Office, Visakhapatnam, Andhra Pradesh.

(c) Initiatives of GCC to improve the Retail Activity

(i) Channelizing Branded Products through Distribution Network

As many as 175 distributors have been appointed in Andhra Pradesh to cater to the needs of consumers.

(ii) Nurturing Captive Market

By constantly pursuing with the district administration of all the districts in the State, the GCC was able to supply the retail products to Social Welfare and tribal welfare hostels, endowments and jails public sector undertakings (PSUs) co-operatives, etc., and through the Andhra Pradesh Civil Supplies Corporation's Fair Price (F.P.), shops.

(iii) Introduction of New Products

The surplus agricultural produce (SAP) like Rajmah, White beans, Cuttings, Turmeric, Soya, and Chilly powder having household demand are introduced in retail packs under "*Girijan*" brand during the year.

(iv) *Sales Promotion and Campaigning Activity*
For wider geographical coverage of the State, sales officers have been appointed to oversee RMD activities. The RMD efforts are further complimented by campaigning through various media to bring awareness among consumers.

(d) *Improvement in the Retail Sales during 1999–2005 the 5 years period 1999–2005 :*

(*Value Rs. in lakh*)

Sl. No.	*Year*	*Performance*
1.	1999-2000	86.40
2.	2000-2001	150.49
3.	2001-2002	316.31
4.	2002-2003	444.33
5.	2003-2004	581.73
6.	2004-2005	774.62

Source : Retail Marketing Division, GCC, Corporate Office, Visakhapatnam, Andhra Pradesh.

R&D Initiatives of the GCC

The GCC is trying to find new uses and end users for some more NTFP through R&D initiatives and build commercial linkage with the corporate sector, for processed NTFP and introduce them in niche markets.

The GCC has assigned Product Development Activity to consultants to develop the following new products :

Sl. No.	*Trade Name/(Botanical Name)*	*Value Addition/Scope of work.*
1.	Dry Amla (*Emblica officinalis*)	Candies.
2.	Maredugaddalu (*Decalepis hamiltonii*)	Candies/squash concentrates.
3.	Podapathri (*Gymnema sylvestre*)	Diabetic products/other health care products/Herbal tea
4.	Tamarind (*Tamarindus indica*)	Paste, Concentrates and Powders
5.	Sheekakai/Soapnuts	Concentrates, Shampoos, Hair Care products.

(*Contd.*)

(Contd.)

Sl. No.	Trade Name/(Botanical Name)	Value Addition/Scope of work.
6.	Aloevera	Moisturizer creams and soaps.
7.	Gum Karaya (*Streculia urens*)	Laxatives.
8.	Myrobalans (*Terminalia chebula*) Tanikayalu (Terminalia *bellrica*) Dry Amla (*Emblica officinalis*)	Triphala for use by different user Industries.
9.	Bee's wax	Cosmetic products from Bee's wax. (Wax strips for hair removal)
10.	Gum Olibanum	Rheumatic pills, Balms, etc.

Source : Retail Marketing Division, GCC, Corporate Office, Visakhapatnam, Andhra Pradesh.

The following are the major projects in progress :

Project		Scope of Work
(a) CFTRI, Mysore	:	Working on improving the quality of Tamarind and retention of colour thereby enhancing the shelf life of the product
(b) CBRTI, Pune	:	Imparting training to tribals on qualitative aspects of Honey
(c) Kovel Foundation	:	Imparting training to Tribals on Gum tapping, drying, grading and on other quality parameters
(d) Freelance Scientists	:	(a) Quality Control tests for Gum Karaya to comply with the export standards. (b) To find new industrial uses for NTFP.

Some conservative estimates indicate that through the value addition process, the prices realised by the industry for certain NTFP are in the range of 5 to 20 fold. The GCC has made some commendable efforts through market research, complemented with R&D, to bring value to NTFP. The following are the possibilities and expected value realisation through R&D, and the initiatives that have given greater dividends to the GCC (see Table 6.4).

Table 6.4 : NTFP and Value Addition by GCC

Sl. No.	*NTFP/Herbs*	*Uses*	*User Industry*	*Expected Realisation*	GCC's initiatives
1.	Gum Karaya Gum Kondagogu	In farma food cosmetic industry, food, medicine, ice creams	Food industry pharmal	20 fold	The gum powder is marketed (as an ostimy aid) to pharma industry.
2.	Gum Olibanum	Perfume/incense stick/Rheumatism	Cosmetic industry, Ayurvedic and Unani	10 fold	—
3.	Tree borne oil seeds	Extraction of fatty acids	Soap industry	10 fold	—
4.	Hill Brooms/ Wild Brooms	Ready to use consumer products	Households	3 fold	Introduced in consumer pack size
5.	(a) Tamarind	Ready to use consumer Products	Households	2 fold	Tamarind cakes, tamarind concentrate promoted in the consumer market
	(b) Tamarind concentrate	-do-	-do-	3 fold	
	(c) Tamarind powder	-do-	-do-	5 fold	
6..	Tamarind Seed Powder	As sizing material in Jute Industry	Jute Industry	5 fold	—
7.	Naramamidi bark	Incense-stick manufacturers as perfume yielding adhesive	Perfume industry/ Incense-stick industry	5 fold	—
8.	Cleaning nuts	Removes turbidity from potable water. Also binds heavy metals and radioactive elements.	Paper Industry, Municipal Corpns. Jal Samsthans , Nuclear Fuel complexes in treating Radioactive	10 fold	GCC is promoting flocculent out of cleaning nuts to Municipal Corporations for treating potable water. GCC has developed a

TABLE 6.4—*Contd.*

Sl. No.	*NTFP/Herbs*	*Uses*	*User Industry*	*Expected Realisation*	GCC's initiatives
			elements.		biofloculant out of cleaning nuts to remove radioactive wastes. The product is under trial run for its efficacy by GoI
9.	Annato seed	Natural food additive	Food Industry after extracting Bixin from Annato seed	10 fold	—
10.	Aloe vera	Cosmetic Industry. The Gel in facial creams and in soaps	Soap and Ayurvedic Industry	—	GCC launched Aloe vera soaps in consumer market
11.	Nux vomica	Active principal/alkaloids strychnine and brucine in pharma	Chemical and Pharma Industry	20 fold	—
12.	Soapnuts	As a hair care item. For cleaning Jewellery	Household consumers	3 fold	GCC launched powders with other herbal formulations into the consumer market
13.	Sheekakai	Consumer product powder in concentrates	General consumers	3 fold	GCC launched powders with other herbal formulations into the consumer market

TABLE 6.4—*Contd.*

Sl. No.	*NTFP/Herbs*	*Uses*	*User Industry*	*Expected* Realisation	GCC's initiatives
14.	Anatamul/ Maredugeddalu	Food Industry, in squash preparation	Food Industry	5 fold	—
15.	Satavari	As a lactative	Ayurvedic/Veterinary industries	5 fold	—
16.	Myrobalans	Extraction of Tannis from Myrobalans	Tanning industry, leather processing centres	10 fold	—
17.	Neem	As a bio pesticide.The active principle Azardiractin derived from the neem seed fetch very high value in the international market	Bio pesticide industry	100 fold	—
18.	Lemon Grass	Oil out of Lemon Grass by distillation/solvent extraction can be used in perfume industry/mosquito repellant	Perfume Industry	5 fold	—
19.	Adda Leaf	Used as one time use food plates and cups. Biodegradable and eco friendly.	Consumer/Food and Packaging Industry	3-5 fold	Tie-up with NGOs
20.	Brahmi	As a memory booster/ cardiac product	Ayurvedic industry	5 fold	—
21.	(a) Amla (b) Myrobalans (c) Tani	Triphala shoornum	Ayurvedic and Unani Industries as Triphala	5 fold	Amla as Candies under pilot scale trials.

TABLE 6.4—*Contd.*

Sl. No.	*NTFP/Herbs*	*Uses*	*User Industry*	*Expected* Realisation	GCC's initiatives
22.	Senna	In beverages and as a sports drink	Ayurvedic products	5 fold	—
23.	Safed Musli	A rich natural B complex Supplement.	Ayervedic and Farma Industry	10 fold	—
24.	Tulasi	Herbal Hair oil/Rheumatic/ Antibiotic ointments	Pharma and Cosmetic industry	5 fold	—
25.	Gudmar/Podapatri	Active principle Gymnamic acid in treating diabetes	Ayurvedic/Unani industry	5-10 fold	—
26.	Pungam Seed	As a bio-diesel	Transport industry	5 fold	—
27.	RS Roots	Active principle reserpine in treating hypertension	Ayurvedic/Pharma industry	10 fold	—
28.	Marking Nuts	As a redox paint	Automobile industry	5 fold	—
29.	Honey	Instant energizer, mild laxative. Also cures throat irritation/mouth ulcers, etc.	Confectionery industry	2 fold when packed and marketed in consumer packs	GCC introduced diff-erent pack sizes into the consumer market
30.	Honey Centre Spread Toffees	—	Confectionery industry	5 fold	—
31.	Honey Pollen Granules	Rich natural B-complex supplement	Ayurvedic and Pharma industry	5 fold	—

Source : Retail Marketing Division, GCC, Corporate Office, Visakhapatnam, Andhra Pradesh.

Sustaining the Growth and Tribal Dependence on NTFP over a period of time

With concerted efforts like : harnessing the NTFP potential, finding better market for the NTFP procured by tribals through various market strategies, value addition, and R&D, the procurement prices paid to tribals have witnessed tremendous growth. However, general deforestation, which is a global scenario is also seen in the country and in the State. The GCC has managed to sustain growth through quality practices and by imparting training to tribals on scientific tapping of NTFP, and through regeneration programmes. In the whole process, there is a sustained growth in dependence of tribals on NTFP. The GCC has managed to realise better value for NTFP and passed on better returns to tribals year after year.

Supply of Domestic Requirements through Public Distribution System (PDS)

(a) *The GCC has taken up the following initiatives to improve other D.R.s business in the interest of tribals*

(i) Introduction of *dals* (pulses) and other requirements in sachet form at affordable prices;
(ii) Conducting mobile sales in shandies;
(iii) Organising additional sale counters in tribal shandies;
(iv) Identifying needs of tribals by conducting household surveys in the interior tribal villages; and
(v) Distribution of LPG connections to members of women self-help groups.

(b) *D.R.s Performance from 2000–01 to 2004–05*

As per the data given below, there has been a significant improvement in the GCC—D.R.s performance of over the period from 2000-01 to 2004-05.

(Value Rs. in lakh)

Year	Supply of other DRs
2000-01	1627.85
2001-02	2107.72
2002-03	3034.00
2003-04	4250.20
2004-05	4973.53

**Source* : Domestic Requirements Division, GCC, Corporate Office, Visakhapatnam, Andhra Pradesh.

These efforts have not only enabled the GCC to make the D.R. depots strategic business units (SBUs) but also to make them the centre of all activities like :

(i) Purchase of NTFP from tribals on day-to-day basis and pay the value across the counter and enable tribals to possess cash for their day-to- day requirements.
(ii) D.R. depots function as nodal agencies for identification and disbursement of agricultural credit and recover the same from tribals even in kind (by accepting NTFP / Agricuiltural produce) and by cash.
(iii) The D.R. depots supply essential commodities under the P.D.S.; from dry fish to match boxes, dals, oils, cosmetics, utensils, etc., at very fair and reasonable prices.

(c) GCC now depends on D.R. Depots to fulfil the following objectives

(i) To supply domestic requirements to the tribals in the required size and convenience, and to see that D.R.s activities are a majcr profit making component, that strengthen the financial base of GCC to make the D.R. depots self-supporting in a phased manner. For the convenience of tribals, all the essential commodities are supplied in small sachets which are not only of a high quality but are also packed in hygienic conditions. This has enabled the tribals to purchase other day-to-day requirements along with essential commodities (ECs).

(ii) All the D.R. depots of GCC are manned by employees belonging to tribals who are exclusively selected for the purpose, in order to provide them employment.

(iii) The GCC is implementing various schemes of the Government through D.R. depots like Food for Work, S.G.R.Y., etc.

(iv) By ensuring that the D.R. depots function effectively in the tribal areas and by making them the centres of all activities of GCC, the corporation could also plan for making the Girijan Primary Cooperative Marketing Societies (GPCMS) self-supporting.

Training Programmes

The GCC has initiated training programmes to all gum pickers in the State on the methods of scientific collection of Gum Karaya and Gum Kondagogu through the Kovel Foundation, an NGO working exclusively on training gum pickers and is imparting training to them on :

- The use of Gum Karaya in various applications;
- Selection of Gum Karaya tree for blazing;
- Scientific tapping method of Gum Karaya;
- Application of training kits;
- Collection, drying and storage of gum;
- Grading and rates of gum;
- Use of Giri Cards (provided by GCC) and their importance;
- Shandy (*haat*) monitoring;
- Regeneration of Gum Karaya plants by sapling and stem cuttings;
- Addressing the problems of tribal gum pickers and other related issues; and
- Live demonstration at the Gum Karaya tree to the gum pickers.

Following are the details of training programmes those that have been completed and those in progress* :

(Value Rs. in lakh)

Sl. No.	Training period	ITDA area	No. of Trainees	Remarks.
1.	1999-02	Parvathipuram	572	Completed during 2002-03
2.	2000-02	Paderu	756	Completed during 2002-03
3.	2000-02	Eturunagaram	625	Last spell of training is in progress
4.	2001-02	Utnoor, Eturunagaram, Bhadrachalam	—	Completed 3508 Gum pickers and 9664 NTFP collectors identified
5.	2002-03	Seethampeta	381	Commenced during March 2002
6.	2002-03	Tirupathi, Srisailam	200	Completed during 2002-03 on N.M. Bark and Maredu-gaddalu
7.	2003-04	R. Chodavaram, Paderu Parvathi-puram Seethampeta, Bhadrachalam	3968	Training commenced during March 2003 and completed by May 2003.
8.	2004-05	R. Chodavaram, Paderu Parvathi-puram, Seethampeta, Bhadrachalam	4000	Training on Gum Karaya and Gum Kondagogu commenced during January 2005 and in progress.

* *Source* : Marketing Division, GCC, Corporate Office, Visakhapatnam, Andhra Pradesh.

The training programme for tribals on the scientific methods of collection of Gum Karaya has enabled the GCC to accomplish the following objectives :

(a) Promote gum tapping as a viable income generation programme (IGP) amongst tribal gum picking families;
(b) Impart skills, methods and scientific techniques of tapping, collection, and grading of Gum Karaya;
(c) Help tribals to realize better price and income;
(d) Help the GCC to improve its quantitative and qualitative procurement prospects, and value addition to Gum Karaya;
(e) Build awareness on preservation, maintenance, conservation, regeneration and judicious Gum Karaya tapping—maintenance of bio-diversity; and
(f) Increase life span of the gum trees and promote superior and export grade gum.

*Increase in Purchase Prices of Gum Karaya due to Training Programmes**

(Value in Rs.)

Sl. No.	*Name of the Commodity*	*1993-94 (Rs. per Kg.)*	*2004-2005 (Rs. per Kg.)*	*Increase (Rs. per Kg.) over 1993-94*	*% of Increase*
1.	Gum Karaya Grade I	80.00	140.00	60.00	75%
	Gum Karaya Grade II	48.00	100.00	52.00	108%
	Gum Karaya Grade III	26.00	90.00	64.00	246%
2.	Gum Kondagogu Gr. I	50.00	120.00	70.00	140%
	Gum Kondagogu Gr. II	35.00	80.00	45.00	128%
	Gum Kondagogu Gr. III	22.00	60.00	38.00	172%
3.	Honey	25.00	80.00	55.00	220%
4.	Maredugaddalu	10.00	20.00	10.00	100%
5.	Naramamidi Bark	12.00	23.00	11.00	92%

* *Source* : Marketing Division, GCC, Corporate Office, Visakhapatnam, Andhra Pradesh.

Regeneration of NTFP Species

In the economic interest of the tribals, the GCC has initiated regeneration of species of minor forest produce by entrusting to the forest department. The focus of GCC is to raise important NTFP species like: Gum Karaya, Amla, Myrobalans, Tamarind, Cleaning nuts, Chiranji, Pungam, Mohua, Ssheekakai, Soap-nuts, Naramamidi, etc., and hand over the maintenance work to the tribals.

Credit Activity

The GCC is acting as a lending institution in the tribal areas, as far as agricultural credit to the tribal members for their agricultural operations are concerned. This activity was grounded by the GCC during 1990–91 in 15 tribal districts of Andhra Pradesh through its 43 affiliated societies (GPCMs). The objective of GCC in this direction is to discourage private money lenders and provide loans at a low rate of interest and facilitate the tribals to repay the loans even in cash or in kind.

Statement showing the year-wise Disbursement and Recovery of Credit from 1999–2000 to 2004–05

(Rs. in lakh)

Sl. No.	Year	Total	
		Disbursement	Recovery
1.	1999-2000	493.93	198.58
2.	2000-2001	502.45	341.46
3.	2001-2002	356.18	371.95
4.	2002-2003	283.85	265.21
5.	2003-2004	251.65	317.44
6.	2004-2005	364.99	348.30

Source : Credit Division, GCC Corporate Office, Visakhapatnam, Andhra Pradesh.

Summing Up

On the recommendations of Malayappan Committee the Government of Andhra Pradesh set up the "Andhra Pradesh Scheduled Tribes Finance & Development Corporation" to protect the tribals from the exploitation by private traders and money lenders, and improve their level of living. In 1970, this institution was renamed as the Girijan Co-operative Corporation (GCC). The objectives of GCC are: (i) to ensure payment of remunerative prices for the NTFP collected by the tribals by eliminating middlemen and private traders; (ii) to ensure availability of essential commodities even in the interior agencies through a network of D.R. depots; and (iii) to provide support to the tribals in their agricultural activities through extending credit facilities. Over a period of roughly 50 years, the institution achieved remarkable growth in terms of the membership, share capital, and the various activities undertaken. As on 2005, it had a membership of 323,334 with a paid-up share capital of Rs. 3769139.17. By this time, the share capital received from the government accumulated to the tune of Rs. 2011.53 lakh.

One of the major activities of the GCC is the marketing of NTFP. Although the GCC has monopoly power on the procurement of NTFP due to non-viability, it has delisted certain items and is instead concentrating on the marketing of only the prominent products. For providing remunerative prices to the NTFP gatherers, the GCC has revised the method of fixing the prices, considering the labour costs involved in the collection. Although this method of fixing the prices is more or less the same as one for fixing the minimum support prices for farm products, the operation of this price scheme is totally different from MSP scheme. For improving incomes of the tribals in recent times, the GCC has initiated a number of innovative activities such as: grading and standardization and storing of products, establishing processing centres for creating employment to tribal women, securing value addition to the products, retail marketing, R&D initiatives, conducting training programmes, regeneration of NTFP stock, ensuring the regular supplies of essential commodities to the tribals, etc.

All these initiatives are on desirable lines. Yet the way in which they are being taken up has attracted some criticism. For instance, the GCC established the processing units in the urban areas and they are creating employment opportunities to the urban people but not to the tribals. The GCC also lacks professional marketing management to compete with the private sector in the open market. The GCC is also criticised for underweighment of the product and for not offering remunerative prices to the NTFP gatherers. All this calls for initiating steps to improve the efficiency in carrying out various newly introduced activities.

ANNEXURE 6.1

GIRIJAN COOPERATIVE CORPORATION LIMITED, VISAKHAPATNAM ORGANISATION CHART

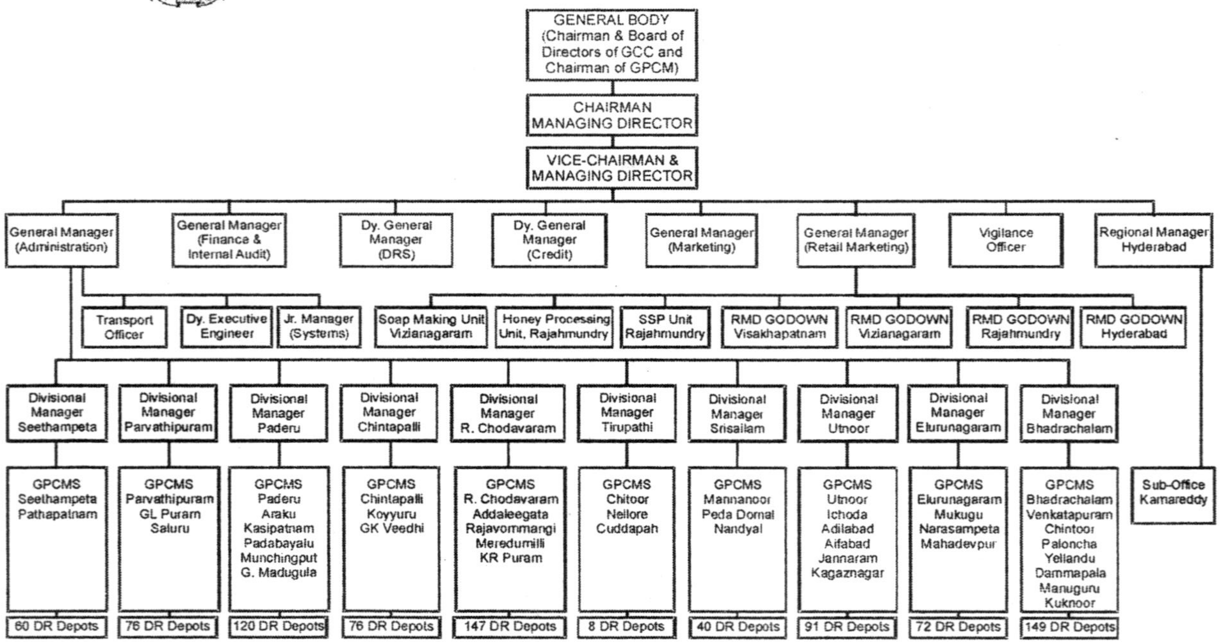

7

Policy Suggestions for Sustainable Management of NTFP and Improvement of Tribal Livelihoods

Introduction

The discussion in the earlier chapters suggests that there are certain limitations in the forest policies, NTFP policies, production of NTFP, value addition and marketing of NTFP, and pricing policy of NTFP. For sustaining the production of NTFP and improving the livelihoods of NTFP gatherers, there is a need to formulate the policies and design a model which transcends all these limitations. This chapter is aimed at making an attempt in this direction.

Forest Policies, Limitations and Recommendations

In Chapter 3, the national forest policies and their impact on the tribals access to NTFP, and the deprivation opportunities in the light of different State policies have been discussed in detail.

National Forest Policies

The national forest policies introduced in the years 1894, 1952, and 1988 have gradually abandoned the interest of tribals. The rights and privileges conferred on tribals in 1894 forest policy, with absolutely no restrictions being imposed on them, and regarded them as the lords of the forests have subsequently been whittled down to a bundle of mere concessions and permissions to use forest wealth.

Joint Forest Management (JFM)

The JFM policy of GoI was notified in 1990, which recommended State governments to involve local communities in the management of forests. Twenty Two State governments including the Government of Andhra Pradesh had resolved to constitute forest protection committees to manage the forest area.

Limitations of Joint Forest Management

In the light of origination of the concept of VSS, the NTFP trade in the State of Andhra Pradesh, is caught between the monopoly of GCC and informal trading by VSS members. The GCC's monopoly and other norms restrict non-tribal and VSS members from selling the produce through legal means, which eventually lead to rise in tribals and non-tribals conflicts, and in the process pitting one community against the other. The issue of sharing the benefits between the two categories has to be examined more carefully in view of the tribal laws and protective legislations conferred on them according to which usufruct rights lie with tribals.

Moreover, the forest department does not have perfect inventory of the NTFP items and quantities so as to assess the exact needs. The marketing of NTFP in non-scheduled areas is also not properly organized and the VSS is not equipped to market the NTFP either. In the Scheduled Areas, the GCC clientele includes the tribals while the VSS provides membership to all communities.

PESA and Limitations in its Implementation by the States

A plethora of problems have arisen in the States such as Orissa, which have diluted the provisions of PESA, though they had no legal jurisdiction to do so, as the PESA is a Central Act. Jharkhand has not conducted elections to panchayats and is the only State without panchayats.

In Andhra Pradesh too, there is a clear contradiction between PESA and the G.O.Ms. 173 of Environment, Forests, Science and Technology Department, on the usufruct rights of VSS prescribed therein which includes all NTFP except those for which the GCC holds monopoly rights. There is a contradiction between the ownership rights vested in Gram Panchayats/Sabhas clause and monopoly rights vested in the GCC.

Such indifference to PESA can be seen in many other States too. The irony is that while PESA remains unimplemented, the GoI has proposed amending Schedule-V of Constitution itself, to open up tribal areas for commercial exploitation by national and multinational corporate bodies.

PESA **Vs.** *Joint Forest Management*

The policies related to NTFP for the benefit of tribals come in conflict with the principle of joint forest management on one hand and with PESA (Panchayat Law applicable to the Fifth Scheduled Areas) on the other. The details are as follows :

(a) According to PESA, panchayats and government are owners of NTFP. But the forest department contends that villages do not have control over reserve forests, as they are outside village boundaries and, therefore, PESA is not applicable to reserve forests. The two ministries of the GoI, i.e., Rural Development and Environment and Forest have different views about applicability of PESA over reserve forests.

(b) There is a contradiction between JFM and PESA as JFM encourages community based on informal groups whereas PESA recognizes formal panchayats and Gram Sabhas. Even the revised JFM guidelines issued by the Ministry of Environment and Forest in 2002 do not mention PESA, showing how priority and significance given to its provisions and their potential bearing on the JFM framework in Schedule-V areas.

(c) PESA bestows ownership rights on the entire Gram Sabha/Panchayat with no condition that people need to protect forest before they enjoy the usufruct whereas joint forest management is based on the principle of care and share.

Need for an Active Role of State Level Agencies/TDCCs in implementing PESA

(a) In the absence of TDCCs and government regulated trade, and due to poor literacy levels and low bargaining power of the tribals, the market forces came into existence and exploited them.
(b) The private traders/merchants, contrary to TDCCs would purchase select commodities of select quality, and limited quantity or outrightly stop purchasing them when there is excessive supply of those NTFP items in the market or when there is any glut in the market. Thus the tribals would get into the threshold of the exploitative middlemen and exposed to volatile market fluctuations.
(c) Further, the industry or direct user is not assured of the requirement as the small VSS/village level Gram Sabhas may not be able to fulfil the needs of the end user/big buyer.
(d) In the absence of State level agencies, the rates of NTFP will not be uniform and would be susceptible to fluctuations due to the crop conditions and the influx of NTFP.

Thus, in the absence of a single controlling agency with authority to check and control smuggling of NTFP, middlemen and petty traders will always exploit the situation, depriving the tribal community of legitimate value for their items.

Proposed Policy to Link TDCCs and Panchayats

Gradual stabilization of prices in the market overcoming all vagaries of supply and demand conditions, is only possible with a single channelizing agency and creating markets, and this should be the aim of the governments so as to command reasonable and sustainable prices.

Working Arrangements with Gram Sabhas in the context of GCC

The policy recommendations for procurement of NTFP from the tribal areas would be that the GCC should enter into an MoU with the Gram Sabhas for procurement of NTFP and make efforts to realize better value for the NTFP and plough back the returns in terms of enhanced purchase prices to Gram Sabhas year after year.

Limitations and Policy Recommendations for Strengthening TDCCs

In Chapter 3, the institutional structure of the States controlling NTFP, the functional arrangements and NTFP trade practices by the TDCCs adjoining the tribal areas of Andhra Pradesh (i.e., Chattisgarh, Orissa, Maharashtra, and Madhya Pradesh) have been discussed in detail. The number of NTFP handled by the various State federations varies from 4 to 30. In some States, NTFP units are entrusted to State federations, local cooperatives, and private contractors simultaneously, which is contrary to, and far from the objective of serving the tribals.

The varying policies rights from nationalized/non-nationalized NTFP to the extension of PESA in some States have not given any comfort to tribals. Instead, they face challenges like different prices for their produce depending on the State they reside, differential treatment on the basis of boundaries, and illegal border transactions by them for price advantage. The present practices of the States and lack of information sharing from one another, are resulting in federations wasting precious resources as the traders exploit the opportunity through numerous loopholes in the policy at the expense of primary gatherers. However, it is inevitable to point out the limitations of TDCCs as on date.

Limitations of TDCCs

(a) The major constraint of TDCCs is shortage of funds. The allocations from the government—both State and central—are meagre and the TDCCs are hard pressed to run the business of procurement. The TDCC plans have a short term and are implemented on a day-to-day basis by rotating the working capital available with them and as a result, they are not able to look at the long term economic objectives of the tribals. The support from the governments is regrettably inadequate and the TDCCs are left to function on their own.

(b) And another major problem encountered by TDCCs is the loss of market for certain NTFP (viz., Myrobalans, Soapnuts, Sal seed, etc.), and the fluctuating market conditions (Kendu / Beedi leaf, Adda leaf, Tamarind etc.). Whenever the TDCCs try to rescue the tribals from market glut, they (the TDCCs) suffer huge losses. On the contrary, if the TDCCs act as business organizations, tribals are put to untold misery. The TDCCs should, therefore, balance between these two extremes.

(c) The Tribal Co-operative Marketing Development Federation (TRIFED) which was set up under the Ministry of Social Welfare in 1987, under the Multi-State Co-operative Societies Act to support the State co-operatives to find market for NTFP of the TDCCs and to train the tribals on scientific methods of collection of NTFP, is neither functioning on sound lines nor able to guide the TDCCs.

Need for Strengthening TDCCs

Creating markets and ensuring reasonable prices for NTFP should be the top priority of the government. Gradual stabilization of prices in the market to offset the vagaries of supply and demand conditions is only possible with single channelizing agencies like the TDCCs functioning in the States.

In the absence of these agencies with authority to check and control smuggling of NTFP, middlemen, and petty traders always exploit the situation depriving the tribal community of the legitimate value for their produce.

Therefore, the TDCCs should be given a substantial role in the collection of NTFP, instead of phasing out TDCCs from the role of collection and storage of NTFP and entrusting the same to panchayats which have to commence the work from a scratch. It would be more appropriate to strengthen the TDCCs for more active participation of tribal community in coordination with other institutions.

Recommendations for Strengthening TDCCs

The author recommends constituting an *NTFP Board* at the national level and *Confederation of Regional States* for strengthening TDCCs in order to protect interests of the tribals.

(a) Policy Prescriptions for a National Level NTFP Board

The TDCCs of the States shall register themselves with the Board and the NTFP Board comprising the representatives from each of the TDCCs (Chief Executives), TRIFED, the National Commission on Scheduled Areas and Scheduled Tribes, nominee of Ministry of Tribal Welfare, GoI, nominees from the forest departments of the respective States, and Commodity specialists, who shall oversee the objectives of the Board and evolve following strategies :

(i) The Board shall fix up minimum support prices and monitor procurement prices prevailing in the market and intervene whenever the market prices fall below the recommended minimum support price to ensure a steady level of income to NTFP collectors.

(ii) The Board shall recommend and pursue with the government for evolving a Uniform National Policy and bring NTFP into the fold of State tribal federations for equal justice, equal social and economic status to all tribals in the country.

(iii) For administrative convenience, the TRIFED shall be the nodal agency for the implementation of minimum support price for NTFP through State Tribal Development Federations and the Government of India shall provide funds to the NTFP Board to implement the MSP for NTFP and support the TDCCs through adequate funding.

(iv) The NTFP Board shall persuade the Ministry of Tribal Affairs for creation of a fund to the tune of Rs. 750 to Rs. 1000 crore for undertaking various activities by the Board like market intervention, price stabilization, minimum support price, value addition, R&D, trainings, regeneration, etc.

Recommendations for a Regional NTFP Policy

Looking at the social, economic, and political importance of NTFP in the whole region with a rich forest patch from eastern Maharashtra to western Orissa (covering the States of Maharashtra, Madhya Pradesh, Chhattisgarh, Andhra Pradesh and Orissa) which is home to about 60 million tribals of the country, it is advisable for the GCC to work in the direction of bringing out a common NTFP policy for seven States including Gujarat and Jharkhand.

The GCC should play a key role in coordinating with different stakeholders, State federations dealing with NTFP in the region, to arrive at common consensus among the States. The ultimate objective of GCC should be to form a *Confederation of Regional States* and the members of such a confederation will be the State agencies engaged in NTFP such as, the TDCCs and the departments of forest and rural development of the concerned respective States.

The confederation should work towards sharing knowledge and market intelligence to enable the State agencies to become more cooperative in nature rather than merely being competitive. The region as a whole can think of information network that will go a long way to end the clandestine nature of trade. Forest resources thus can then become a truly important means to the alleviation of poverty in the whole region.

Role of Funding Agencies in implementing Tribal Development Activities

(a) The European Union (EU) which is the biggest trade partner and the largest source of Foreign Direct Investment (FDI) in India, aims at improving the quality of life amongst the poor and most disadvantaged members of the society. A major part of the funds are used for bilateral projects implemented by various government departments. The government institutions, rural development agencies, and NGOs act as intermediary agencies responsible for channelling and monitoring the project funds for implementing tribal development project in the States. Similarly, the NABARD (National Bank for Agricultural and Rural Development) is taking care of the infrastructure development in the tribal areas under the Rural Infrastructure Development Fund-XI Programme.

(b) The Asian Development Bank (ADB), a multilateral development finance institution which is engaged in promoting economic and social progress of its developing member countries, is also implementing certain projects in the tribal areas.

(c) A World Bank project implemented by the Government of Andhra Pradesh under the name Indira Kranthi Patham (IKP) in the Scheduled Areas aims at livelihood development of the poor. The IKP with its recent expansion to certain tribal districts in Andhra Pradesh proposes to work around NTFP-based livelihood opportunities and one of their prioritized areas is finding market for certain types of NTFP.

(d) The United Nations is implementing a project called the United Nations Development Fund for Women (UNIFEM) in the tribal areas of Andhra Pradesh for empowering the women, by strengthening their economic capacities through the NTFP livelihood opportunities.

(e) To improve the self-reliance and socio-economic status of the tribals in north coastal districts, the European Commission (EC) is implementing a project called the Sustainable Tribal Empowerment Project (STEP) through CARE International and CARE India. The project aims to enhance the capacity of two lakh households to plan and manage their own development.

(f) The Ford Foundation is working to improve rural livelihoods in the tribal areas for sustainable management and development of natural resources, JFM, etc.

(g) The Government of Andhra Pradesh, through the Ministry of Rural Development is implementing a World Bank funded project, i.e., Andhra Pradesh Rural Livelihoods Project (APRLP) in the tribal areas.

(h) Similarly, the Ministry of Rural Development, Government of Andhra Pradesh is implementing the National Food for Work Programme, and other central, and State sponsored programmes in the tribal areas for providing additional employment to tribals and development of infrastructure.

(i) The Indian funding agencies like Sir Ratan Tata Trust, Infosys Foundation, etc., are also working in the tribal areas of Andhra Pradesh, to improve the quality of the NTFP procured by the tribals by providing for value addition through primary processing.

Limitations of NGOs

(a) The tribal development projects sponsored by the funding agencies have not been assigned uniformly among the institutions functioning for the purpose but were taken up unilaterally by the agencies leading to duplication of activities.

(b) One of the major limitations of the voluntary agencies is their working in isolation as they are scattered, un-organized and operating at micro level. They lack cooperation and coordination among themselves and with other institutions as well.

The author recommends the following policy options and role for the agencies working for the tribal development.

(i) The donors should encourage NGOs to work with the government agencies, since this would contribute to strengthening and improving the efficiency of both the institutions. The NGOs working in co-ordination with other institutions would provide better opportunities for replication and scaling up of achievements and innovative approaches. Mid-course correction would be quicker by all institutions when they work in a collaborative environment.

(ii) Poverty alleviation programmes to build the economy of the socially vulnerable sections are though very essential, the inflow of funds to various developmental activities should be planned rationally without any duplication of activity by agencies working for the same purpose.

Recommendations for Active Convergence between State Agencies

The author recommends active coordination and convergence between the State agencies for a meaningful service to tribals dependent on NTFP for their livelihood.

(a) The forest department being the custodian of forests can still concentrate on its activities of conservation, regeneration, and propagation. The VSS members may be involved and their main thrust should be on nursery raising, plantation, preservation, and procurement of NTFP, and other NTFP species of economic value like medicinal plants. The forest department through the VSSs has to take steps to protect and propagate the species listed under endangered category.

The existing institutions such as: the forest department, VSS, self help groups, IKP, or SERP have to stick to their roles which include: protection of forests, regeneration of forest species, conducting of training programmes for scientific collection of NTFP, sharing of market intelligence without duplicating their individual activities. The forest department has to take up the conservation activity with special focus on the marketable NTFP and IKP by giving suitable training to the tribal NTFP collectors, in order to improve the quality of the items, build awareness about prices, prepare the NTFP pickers for collective bargaining .

(b) However, as the VSS members are new to the organized trade of forest produce, they need consistent and long term training in collection, grading, holding stocks, identifying the appropriate market channels, and managing the affairs on their own. The GCC with its long-standing expertise and experience should support them by offering services to the VSS members, so that efforts in that direction by the forest department need not be duplicated again.

(c) The GCC has trading experience and NTFP clientele across the State and 43,133 sq metres of built-up storage accommodation in the tribal areas across the State and transport fleet for timely despatch and delivery of NTFP. The GCC should undertake the responsibility of NTFP marketing for tribals as well as for the VSS members, NGOs, and SHGs.

Recommendations for Effective Coordination among the Ministries under Government of India for Effective Implementation of Policies

Lack of co-ordination and focused approach among the ministries under GoI are resulting in inadequate services being provided to tribals depending on NTFP. Therefore, there is a dire need to redefine the role of ministries at the GoI level and integrate their activities in the best interest of tribals.

The following are some of the suggested roles proposed for a holistic approach to be adopted by the various members for securing tribal welfare :

Ministry of Environment & Forests (MoEF)

(a) The MoEF should modify the existing forest policy of 1988 or make a new policy exclusively catering to NTFP.

(b) The Ministry MoEF should initiate special schemes for *in situ* conservation of rich areas. This scheme should have components of resource inventory, conservation, good collection practices, capacity building of collectors of NTFP/JFM committees, processing, and value addition of NTFP.

(c) Standardization of sustainable harvesting and good collection practices of NTFP for securing maximum benefit for the tribals.

(d) Make transit rules for national transit permits for avoiding unnecessary delays in the transit of forest produce, due to change of transit permit at State borders and issue necessary guidelines.

(e) Appropriate and proactive guidelines should be issued under Forest Conservation Act to promote the cultivation of NTFP in the forest areas.

Ministry of Tribal Affairs (MoTA)

(a) The Tribal Ministry should provide funds regularly for procurement, storage, value addition, capacity building of TDCCs/Federations to ensure food security for the tribals.

(b) The funds should be earmarked every year on the basis of quantum of service provided by the TDCCs to tribals, progress of schemes under implementation, tribal population *vs* forest area, and potential of forest produce. The allotment of funds should be at the beginning of the financial year and utilization of funds by the TDCCs should be monitored during the procurement season.

National Scheduled Tribes Finance & Development Corporation (NSTFDC)

Currently, the focus of NSTFDC is on tribes residing in the plain areas through its various schemes. There is every need that the NSTFDC concentrate on tribes depending on NTFP for their sustenance.

(a) The NSTFDC should launch special loans/schemes to TDCCs for establishing godowns, cold storages, and processing units based on NTFP, and should provide soft loans with low interest on working capital.
(b) Consumption loans should be extended to all NTFP collectors in the lean seasons.

Ministry of Health

With increasing health consciousness in particular and side effects of allopathic drugs, people are switching over to indigenous drugs which are basically of herbal origin.

(a) The MHA should provide funds to State Medicinal Plants Board to develop traditional knowledge in herbal medicines, identification and recognition of *traditional herbal healers,* and documentation of their additional knowledge.
(b) The State Medicinal Plants Boards should be funded for the schemes of cultivation, processing, value addition, and marketing of medicinal plants.
(c) The Ministry should collect information on source and quantity of various raw materials, used by the pharmaceutical companies and pass it on to the TDCCs.

Ministry of Commerce

It should insist on NTFP-based industries to declare the source, the type of materials used by them, and develop data base at the national level for arriving at a strategy to promote domestic trade and export promotion.

Ministry of Rural Development (MoRD)

(a) The MoRD should issue guidelines to promote NTFP based procurement and value addition activities, through self help groups and earmark adequate funds under various programmes like: Food for Work, SGSY, SGRY, etc.

(b) It should step up assistance for NTFP based procurement and value addition efforts by SHGs at par with irrigation schemes.

Policy Recommendations for Qualitative Procurement, Sustainable Management and Regeneration Programmes for NTFP

In chapter 4, an attempt has been made to analyze: the trends in the growth and collection of NTFP; the methods of extraction of NTFP; whether the methods adopted for extraction cause any damage to the trees or quality of the produce; distance travelled; and time spent for the collection *vs.* quantity collected per person engaged in the collection, etc.

In chapter 5, an attempt has been made to examine the open market systems *vis-à-vis* marketing by the GCC; the inefficiencies, if any exist and to suggest a suitable strategy for marketing and pricing.

The analyses indicate that there was no significant growth in the total collection of NTFP, sometimes even showing downward trend in the case of some NTFP. There is a decline in the number of days engaged in collection by the tribals due to non-viability, increase in the time spent, and distance travelled, for the collection of NTFP.

In the prevailing situation, the author suggests that the TDCCs should aim to secure the following objectives :

(a) Improving the Quality of NTFP

The TDCCs should aim at improving the quality of NTFP by giving training to tribals in various forest-based operations such as scientific tapping of NTFP, intensive collection of medicinal herbs, and on other skills for gainful employment in the forestry operations all round the year.

As the NTFP are generally voluminous, their transportation in raw form reduces the net margins that are due to tribal collectors. Therefore, the TDCCs should train the tribals on segregation and grading (e.g., gums); bundling (e.g., brooms); simple processing (i.e., de-seeding of soapnuts/tamarind, etc.) to add value to NTFP. The TDCCs should take up value addition process for all NTFP and to opt for primary processing wherever possible.

(b) Standardizing NTFP through Quality Control Norms

The author recommends developing quality specifications and standardization of all the NTFP and packing techniques and drying methods to improve the shelf life of the NTFP.

(c) Tie-up with Research Institutions for assessing Resource Potential and Sustainable Harvesting Techniques

The author recommends the tie-up with research institutions like: the Indian Institute of Forest Management, Tropical Forest Research Institutes, R.R. Labs, Centre for Food Technological Research Institute, Central Bee Research & Training Institute etc., to achieve the following objectives :

(i) *Assess Resource Potential* : There are myriad forms and varieties of NTFP spread over vast areas. The Research institutions should assess resource potential and recommend new uses, and new end users, so that tribals get additional revenues from NTFP.

(ii) *Sustainable Harvesting* : Research institutions should carry out studies on the optimum period of harvesting, optimum quantities, which are sustainable without affecting the future regeneration.

(iii) Ex situ *Cultivation* : Certain NTFP, medicinal and aromatic plants are having great demand in trade and industries. This is resulting in excessive harvesting and resource depletion. There is a need to develop agro-techniques for these species after due experimentation. As the availability of plant material is a problem, there is a strong need to identify superior germ plasm and to produce quality plant material. For sorne species, plants have to be raised through tissue culture and vegetative propagation.

Research institutions have to take up the above work and recommend proper cultivation, prescribe packaging methods for various species including collection of seeds/propagation and techniques of raising seedlings in nurseries, planting, maintenance, and harvesting.

(iv) *Post-harvest Operations* : Research institutions should also prescribe procedures on post-harvest operations including: proper drying, processing, value addition, storage, and packaging, etc., for high value realization of NTFP.

(d) Regeneration of NTFP Species

The author recommends that the TDCCs should undertake protective measures to prevent deforestation of the tribal habitats and promote healthy forests. This is possible by involving tribals as shareholders and encouraging regeneration of NTFP species. The TDCCs should constantly persuade the forest departments for raising the NTFP species and to educate the tribals through awareness building activities at procurement points, shandies / village *haats*, D.R. depots, etc., in the tribal areas as the basis for a rational approach in tapping and harvesting the NTFP, raising saplings, etc.

Summing Up

The gradual loss of *foci* of the various national forest policies from the interests of tribals, the limitations in implementing JFM programme by the States, the problems in implementation of PESA in Orissa, and its dilution in other States. The different NTFP policy scenarios in the States are leading to deprived opportunities for the tribals living in each State. Therefore, the following policy suggestions are recommended by the author for the sustainable management of NTFP and improving the livelihood of tribals :

(a) Strengthen TDCCs to function as Single Channelizing Agencies in the State with proper co-ordination and integration with government agencies in the activity of tribal development.
(b) Constitute a national NTFP Board with TDCCs as its members to persuade with government on uniform national policy and to implement Minimum Support Price Policy for NTFP.
(c) Confederation of regional States including Gujarat covering Andhra Pradesh, Orissa, Chattisgarh, Madhya Pradesh, and Jharkhand to arrive at common consensus and to work in a collaborative environment.
(d) The Funding Agencies to implement the bilateral projects in the tribal areas through institutions already existing for the purpose without any duplication.
(e) Active convergence between the State agencies with prescribed roles to play: Forest Departments to take up conservation of forests through JFM/CFM, TDCCs to look after the NTFP markets, voluntary organizations to work with government institutions to improve the bargaining power of the tribals.
(f) For effective coordination among the various ministries under the GoI for scaling up their achievements in the best interest of tribals, the author recommends certain policy options for implementation by the departments working under the various ministries.

8

Summary and Conclusions

An Appraisal

Of Tribals and Governance

For the tribals, agriculture cannot provide full sustenance and they depend on the forest produce as a major source of income and food security. In fact, for some tribals in the interior areas, particularly the Primitive Tribal Groups (PTGs), collection of forest produce is their only major source of livelihood. The forest produce that tribals generally collect includes: bamboo, gums, seeds, nuts, barks, fruits, herbs, leaves, and other plant materials. These are called as Non-Timber Forest Produce (NTFP). There has been an increasing recognition that the NTFP plays crucial role in improving tribal livelihoods by ensuring nutrition, income, employment, and food security. However, due to unfavourable forest policies, poor literacy level of tribals and consequent bargaining power; the tribals are subjected to exploitation while selling their produce.

The area under forest cover has shown a declining tendency up to the early 1990s, adversely affecting the tribals dependent for ages on the forests for their sustenance. The forest policy has undergone many changes in the past and the forest policy of 1988 was more in favour of protection of the forests than tribals. Increasing the production of NTFP through silvicultural practices did not find a significant place in its agenda. The collection of NTFP has also been subjected to various regulations and they differ from State to State. Although these rules and regulations are framed for the better cause of protecting the forests and making the production of NTFP sustainable, they are very often acting against the interests of the tribals. The complexity in understanding these rules and the way in which they are being implemented, sometimes lead to the harassment of NTFP gatherers.

The various State governments have relaxed policies by opening the forests through long term agreements for the supply of NTFP at low prices to industrial houses, resulting in overharvest of the NTFP and affecting the bio-diversity in the process. Similarly, as for the monopoly factor in the trade of NTFP is concerned, the tribals have to sell their produce only to the State organizations and they have no right to make any direct sale to any outside party. Although the State monopoly of trade in NTFP was created in the interest of NTFP gatherers, there are, however, complaints against the functioning of these State organizations. All the factors discussed herein prompt us to believe that the tribals access to NTFP has been declining and posing a problem for the sustainable livelihoods of NTFP gatherers. Therefore, for improving and sustaining the livelihoods of NTFP gatherers, intervention on the lines of sustaining the production of NTFP, increasing the accessibility of tribals to NTFP, and removing the constraints in marketing assume importance. The sustainable production of NTFP requires: sustainable development of forests, improvement in silvicultural practices to increase the production of NTFP, and promotion of scientific methods of collection. Further, protecting the NTFP gatherers, i.e., tribals from exploitation requires market regulation and institutional support.

Of Physical, Human, and Economic Geography of Tribals

In this background, a detailed study examining the various aspects relating to production, collection, processing, value addition, and marketing of NTFP assume special importance. As all these factors are region-specific, regional studies have great significance. In Andhra Pradesh, the NCA region, comprising the districts of Visakhapatnam, Vizianagaram, and Srikakulam has a significant size of forest cover and tribal population. Huge quantities of NTFP are produced in the region and they are a major source of livelihood for a large number of NTFP gatherers, i.e., tribals. The marketing of NTFP in the region is done through the Andhra Pradesh Girijan Cooperative Corporation (GCC). This study analyses the aspects relating to production of NTFP, trends in growth, and cyclical variations in the collection of NTFP, changes in the collection related parameters such as, the number of tribals engaged in collection, quantities collected, time taken for collection, distance travelled, etc., pricing of NTFP, variations in the price of prominent NTFP, the price spread, the marketing techniques adopted by GCC and the other activities taken up by the GCC for improving the welfare of the tribals in NCA. Based on the analysis, an attempt has been made to suggest policy measures for sustainable production of NTFP and its marketing, to improve the livelihood opportunities open to NTFP gatherers.

Of Objectives, Methodology, and Sources

The specific objectives of the study are: to examine the forest and NTFP policies and assess their impact on NTFP gatherers, i.e., tribals access to NTFP; the production related aspects of NTFP such as: the type of the tree, the conditions under which it grows, the months in which the product is available, method of extraction, and primary processing method of the product; the trends in growth, instability, and cyclical variations of the collection of NTFP; whether the production/collection of NTFP is sustainable; the marketing channels and price determination of NTFP; the variations in the GCC's procurement and sale prices of NTFP; to document the origin, objectives, growth; and various activities taken up by GCC for the welfare of the tribals engaged in NTFP collection and identify the constraints if any; and suggest policy for the sustainable production / collection and marketing of NTFP to improve the economic condition of the NTFP gatherers by showing sustainable livelihood.

This study is based on both the secondary and primary data. The secondary data are drawn from the office of the GCC, Census Figures, and various Reports of Mandal Revenue Statistics. The data drawn from GCC form the basis for the analysis of trends in the growth, instability, and cyclical variations of the quantities of NTFP procured, and sold by GCC, and their prices. Trends in growth are analyzed in terms of trend in growth rates. Instability is measured in terms of instability indices. The cyclical variations are measured in terms of cyclical components estimated by using additive and multiplicative models. The information relating to the activities of GCC, other than procurement and sales is also obtained from the office of the GCC.

The description of the socio-economic profile of the tribal areas of NCA is based on the data drawn from the population census and the reports of Mandal Revenue Statistics. The primary data collected through a sample survey is used for estimating the parameters like: the tribal population engaged in the NTFP collection, the average quantities collected, average time taken for collection, etc. The change in these parameters over a period of past 5 years, formed the basis for assessing whether the collection of NTFP is sustainable or not.

Major Conclusions

(a) The NCA region comprising the districts of Visakhapatnam, Vizianagaram, and Srikakulam, has a relatively higher share of both forest area and tribal population in the State. The density of the tribal population is also relatively more in this region. Within this region, the concentration of both area and population is much higher in Visakhapatnam district. The forest area in the region is endowed with different types of forests, which are rich in both flora and fauna, and provide many varieties of NTFP.

Some major tribes living in this region are: Bhagatha, Konda Dora, Valmiki, Kondu, Konda Kapu, Kotia, Yerukala, Mooka Dora, Jathapu, Savara, and Manne Dora. The literacy levels of these tribes are very low and they vary considerably across the communities. The major occupation of these groups is agriculture. As the income derived from agriculture is not sufficient to meet their requirements, many tribals take up collection and sale of NTFP as their only economic activity. In fact, for a good number of tribals, collection of NTFP is a major source of livelihood. However, due to rapid destruction of forests, population pressure, incomes accruing from the sale of NTFP may be low in this region. The access to infrastructure facilities like: irrigation, power, transport, marketing, health care, and education which are essential for increasing the incomes and welfare of the tribals, is also very low.

(b) The National Forest Policy underwent significant changes over the last century. The first National Forest Policy came into existence in 1894 and was mostly concerned with the tribals and their rights over the forests. The subsequent policies of 1952 and 1984 had departed from the 1894 policy by restricting the rights of the tribals on the forests in the name of national interest. Under these policies, many restrictions were imposed on the use of forests and the privileges enjoyed by the tribals which were treated as laws and concessions. These policies affected the tribal people very deeply and were the root cause of the strained relations between them and the forest department, which continues even to the present time.

However, realizing the importance of the forests in maintaining ecological balance, the national forest policy was revised in 1988. This revised policy emphasizes the creation of massive people's movement through involvement of village communities living in and close to forests in the areas of protection, regeneration, and development of the forest, as well as in the creation of gainful employment to the people living in and around forests. This movement has been popularized through the Joint Forest Management Programme. Under this programme, 36,130 Forest Protection Committees are managing a total of 10.25 million hectares of forest area in the country and Andhra Pradesh contributes 1.63 million hectares with 6,575 JFM committees. The present policy is in favour of promoting sustainable production of NTFP, through the development of forests and improving the welfare of the tribals.

(c) The NTFP policies have been subjected to drastic changes in the country. The rights for the collection of NTFP enjoyed by the tribals since time immemorial and even under the colonial rule have been slowly hampered by various regulations introduced after independence. There has been a frequent change in these rules and regulations and many rules have been in operation contradicting each other. The complexity in understanding these rules and the way in which they are being implemented sometimes leads to corruption, harassment of NTFP gatherers, and ultimately deprivation of their sources of livelihood. The NTFP policies differ from State to State and each State has its own institutional structures to deal with NTFP. The approaches followed by various agencies/institutions are conflicting with one another in several aspects. The conflicting approaches of these State agencies in the field of: procurement and sales, benefit sharing, tax structure in NTFP trade, and the consequent cross-border transactions for price advantage, influx, erratic market situation with up-swing and down-swing trends are resulting in deprived and deferring opportunities for tribals living in each State.

(d) The most prominent NTFP available in NCA include Adda leaf (*Bauhania Valhi*), Cleaning nuts (*Strychnos potatorum*), Tamarind (*Tamarindus indica*), Gum Dikamali (*Gardenia gummifera*), Gum Karaya (*Sterculia urens*), Gum Kondagogu (*Cochlospermum religiasum*), Gum Tiruman (*Anegessua Catifolioc*), Gum Olibanum (*Boswellia serrata*), Hill brooms, Honey, Maredugaddalu (*Decalepis hamiltoni*), Marking nuts (*Semicarpus anacardium*), Mohua flower (*Madhuca longifolia*), Mohua seed (*Madhuca longifolia*), Myrobalans, Naramamidi bark (*Litsa glutinosa*), Nux vomica (*Strychnus Nux vomica*), Pungam seed (*Pungamia glabra*), Sheekakai (*Acacia concinna*), Soapnuts (*Spindus emerginatus*), and Wild brooms.

The sources of some of these products are big trees, while others are climbers, which have a life-span of about 50 to 60 years. Some of these products are extracted by shaking the branches of the trees, while the others are extracted by cutting or blazing the bark of trees without causing any damage to trees. Most of these produce serve as a basic raw material in many industries such as: pharmaceuticals, Ayurveda and Unani medicines, soap-making, paints, varnishes, tanning, confectionery, etc., and also in the form of ready-to-use consumer products. Some of these produces are also consumed directly with a little processing like honey, tamarind, etc.

(e) Among the NTFP produce available in this region, in terms of the value realized through sales in recent times, the most prominent one is Gum Karaya (*Sterculia urens*) followed by tamarind, naramamidi bark, gum kondagogu (*Cochlospermum religiasum*), Mohua seed and flower (*Madhucal longifolia*), honey, Nux vomica (*Strychnus Nux vomica*), hill brooms, adda leaf, maredugaddalu, sheekakai (*Acacia concinna*), myrobalans, marking nuts (*Semicarpus anacardium*), gum dikamali, cleaning nuts (*Strychnos potatorum*) and pungam seed.

The trends in the growth of collection of these products during the period from 1990–91 to 2002–03 exhibits a very gloomy picture. Only the collection of three products namely: Adda leaf, Gum Kondagogu and Marking nuts, which are not very prominent in terms of value increased significantly. The collection of Gum Karaya, the most prominent product in terms of the value and Cleaning nuts had declined significantly. The rates of growth of the collection of the other products are not statistically significant although some positive growth rates and some recorded negative growth rates. However, the values realized through the sale of these products recorded an upward trend in respect of many products. This may be due to increase in the prices of these products over time. A decline in the value realized from the sale of products is observed only in the case of Cleaning nuts, Gum Karaya, Gum Tiruman, and Wild brooms. However, the rates of growth are not statistically significant. The collection of all these products over time except for Gum Kondagogu are quite unstable and they have been subjected to cyclical fluctuations, with cycles of amplitude ranging from 2 to 5 years.

(f) For the tribals, collection of NTFP is not only a way of life, but also one of the major sources of livelihood next only to agriculture. About 40 per cent of them are engaged in this activity, and this proportion is relatively higher in the interior areas, and especially in the regions close to plains. This activity is a major source of livelihood for nearly one-fourth of the tribals living in NCA. But this proportion has been declining over time. It may be due to the increase in the efforts to be made for collection and decline in the quantities available. In respect of most of the NTFP, the average number of days engaged in collection per crop season is declining and the average time spent and the average distance travelled per unit of collection is increasing over time. The stock of NTFP in the region is also decreasing over time due to unscientific methods of extraction of the products. The rates of change in these parameters are relatively lower in the interior areas and higher in the areas close to plains. From these changes, it appears that the production/collection of NTFP in the NCA region is not sustainable, and the tribal livelihoods are at a risk, unless proper intervention is made.

(g) Although the GCC has a monopoly over the marketing insight of NTFP, in the NCA region, it does not cover certain products, for one or more reasons that, they are not available in adequate quantities or perishable in nature or the forest department wants to protect them. Even for the produce covered by GCC, private trade is still going on through the clandestine operations of the traders. The corporation is not in a position to curtail the operations of the private traders and protect the tribals from exploitation by the traders due to entry of various agencies like Vana Samrakshna Samithies, Village Organizations of the Society for Elimination of Rural Poverty, a World Bank funded project whose members include non-tribals also.

(h) The prices of NTFP received by the tribals are not determined by the forces of demand and supply in the market. They are either dictated by private traders or fixed by the GCC. The GCC fixes the procurement prices based on the prices in the open market or by taking the procurement prices in the past 3 to 4 years into consideration. Recently, it started a method of determining the prices taking into consideration the cost of collection. Therefore, fixing the procurement prices for NTFP on scientific lines is an issue that has yet to be settled.

(i) The GCC has been passing on more than 85 per cent of the sale price to the NTFP gatherers. But, very often the sale prices of GCC are less than the wholesale prices, in the open market, indicating the need for improving its marketing efficiency. The prices received by the tribals do not cover even the labour costs involved in the collection and processing of NTFP and thus they end up being exploited.

(j) The trend in growth rates of both the procurement and sale prices of most of the NTFP in the NCA region has been both positive and statistically significant. The procurement prices are increasing at a faster rate than sale prices, and it is a welcome feature in the interest of the tribals. But these rates of growth are associated with higher levels of instability. There are wider year-to-year fluctuations in both procurement and sale prices of some NTFP causing price uncertainty to both the tribals and GCC. The price uncertainty may cause damage to the stock of NTFP through over-exploitation and poses a threat to the sustainability of NTFP. The prices of some products are also exhibiting cyclical fluctuations with different amplitudes of the cycles. This type of movement in prices calls for a price policy, which can remove price uncertainties and provide remunerative prices to the tribals.

(k) Apart from procuring the NTFP, selling them, and passing on a part of the sale price to the tribals for improving their incomes, the GCC has initiated a number of activities such as: grading, standardization and storing the product, establishing the processing centres for creating employment for tribal women, value addition to the NTFP, retail marketing, R&D initiatives, conducting training programmes on methods of extraction and primary processing of the products, regeneration of the NTFP stock, and ensuring the regular supply of essential commodities to the tribals. For improving the livelihoods of NTFP gatherers, all these initiatives taken up by the GCC are highly desirable and its vision needs to be appreciated. However, the way in which various activities are being undertaken has been subjected to some criticism. For instance, the GCC established the processing units for value addition in the urban areas and they are also creating employment for urban people thus, depriving the opportunity to that extent to the tribals. The GCC lacks professional marketing management skills to compete with the private sector in the open market. The GCC has also been criticized for under-weighment of the product and for not offering remunerative prices to the tribals. All these facts call for initiating steps to improve efficiency in carrying out all these newly introduced initiatives.

Policy Suggestions

The analysis made in the study indicates that if the past trends in the collection and marketing of NTFP and present level of policy interventions by the governments were continued, NTFP production would not only become unsustainable but also pose a threat to livelihood opportunities to tribals, i.e., NTFP collectors. Seen against this background, there is a need for positive policy interventions to improve the living standards of tribals, who are depending on NTFP for their livelihood. The following policy options are being recommended.

TDCCs to act as Single Channelizing Agencies

The TDCCs should be given a substantial role in collection of NTFP, instead of phasing out TDCCs from the role of collection, storage, and marketing of NTFP. The TDCCs should be strengthened to function as *single channelizing agencies* of the States to stabilize NTFP markets and protect the tribals from all vagaries of supply and demand conditions. The Panchayats and TDCCs are to be properly integrated, by making TDCCs responsible for management of NTFP in a profitable way and plough back the returns in terms of enhanced purchase prices payable to tribals through the Panchayats/Gram Sabhas year after year.

Forming a National Level NTFP Board to Monitor and Guide the NTFP Activities of TDCCs

For effective functioning of TDCCs, an NTFP Board should be constituted with TDCCs of the States as members of the board. The TRIFED, National Commission on Scheduled Areas and Tribes, and a nominee each from the ministries of Tribal Welfare and forest departments of the respective States shall oversee the objectives of the board like: minimum support price (MSP), sustainable harvesting, value addition, export market, and R&D. The board shall persuade the government for a uniform NTFP policy, minimum support price, price stabilization fund, and timely and adequate financial support from the GoI to TDCCs for NTFP operations and other developmental activities netted around NTFP like: training programmes, value addition, research and development, regeneration of NTFP species, etc.

Confederation of Regional States

Looking at the socio-economic and political importance of NTFP in the region with the rich forest patch covering the States of Gujarat, Maharashtra, Madhya Pradesh, Chhattisgarh,

Andhra Pradesh, Orissa and Jharkhand, which are home to 60 million tribals of the country, i.e., 7 per cent of India's population: a confederation of regional States has to be formed with State agencies like the TDCCs, forest department, rural development departments of the respective States as members.

The Confederation shall work towards implementing a uniform NTFP policy and uniform pricing of NTFP in the interest of NTFP gatherers in these States. Further, it should work towards sharing of knowledge and market intelligence, common transit policies, tax policies, uniform purchase prices for NTFP at least for nationalized items, value-addition, common branding, common tenders for NTFP, sharing of knowledge and findings, etc., in order to enable the State agencies to work in a collaborative environment.

Active Convergence between State Agencies

The various government departments and NGOs should actively converge for a meaningful service to tribals depending on NTFP for their survival. The forest department should concentrate on conservation, regeneration, and propagation of NTFP species through Vana Samrakshana Samithies (VSS). The VSS members should be involved in nursery raising, plantation, preservation, and procurement of NTFP and other NTFP species of economic value like medicinal plants. The forest department through VSS has to take steps to protect and propagate the species listed under the endangered species category.

The TDCCs should take the responsibility of marketing of NTFP collected by the tribals, whether they are members of GPCMS, VSS, forest department, village organisations of the Society for Elimination of Rural Poverty (SERP), or NGOs. The funding agencies should implement the bilateral projects in the tribal areas through institutions already existing for the purpose without any duplication. The NGOs should work with the government agencies for better utilization of funds and expansion of activities through innovative approaches in implementing schemes aimed at tribal development.

Effective Coordination between the Ministries under Government of India for Effective Implementation of Policies

Various ministries of the GoI should effectively coordinate among themselves for scaling up their activities in the best interest of tribals.

(a) *Ministry of Tribal Affairs* should earmark funds to TDCCs based on the quantum of service provided by TDCCs to the tribals. The ministry should also provide funds regularly and in time for procurement, storage, value addition, and capacity building of the TDCCs.

(b) *Ministry of Environment & Forests (MoEF)* should modify existing forest policy or make a new policy exclusively for NTFP. The MoEF should standardize sustainable harvesting and good collection practices of NTFP, make Transit Rules, issue National Transit Permits, and issue guidelines to forest department for cultivation of NTFP.

(c) *Ministry of Health* should provide funds to the State Medicinal Plants Board to develop traditional knowledge of NTFP gatherers, i.e., tribals, so that tribal medicine can be popularized.

(d) *Ministry of Commerce* should insist upon NTFP based industries to declare the source and type of materials used by them and to develop database at the national level, for arriving at an unified strategy to promote domestic trade and export promotion.

(e) *Ministry of Rural Development* has tc issue guidelines to the DRDAs to promote NTFP based procurement and value addition activities through Self-Help Groups and earmark adequate funds under various programmes like: EGS, SGSY, SGRY, etc. Further, the MoRD should step up assistance for NTFP based procurement and value addition efforts made by SHGs at par with irrigation schemes.

APPENDICES

Appendix Table 4.1 : Procurement of NTFP from NCA

(Quantity in Quintals, Value Rs. in Lakh)

Sl. No.	Name of the Commodity	1992-93 Qty.	1992-93 Val.	1993-94 Qty.	1993-94 Val.	1994-95 Qty.	1994-95 Val.	1995-96 Qty.	1995-96 Val.	1996-97 Qty.	1996-97 Val.	1997-98 Qty.	1997-98 Val.	1998-99 Qty.	1998-99 Val.
1.	Gum Karaya	9212	242.05	8273	351.03	5688	300.00	5838	321.09	5104	344.25	5079	331.80	4475	289.24
2.	Gum Thiruman	624	15.00	1493	34.14	274	6.58	82	1.97	13	0.30	22	0.49	34	0.75
3.	Gum Olibanum	575	8.17	769	11.15	606	8.79	277	4.02	256	3.96	496	11.98	991	23.84
4.	Gum Kondagogu	—	—	—	—	—	—	230	11.50	232	14.77	329	20.31	432	29.77
5.	Gum Dikamali	505	1.99	44	1.76	350	17.50	206	12.36	386	1.93	102	0.46	323	2.59
6.	Myrobalans	5380	13.45	11762	24.09	6775	13.55	16742	50.23	7329	23.75	11812	46.81	13664	81.02
7.	Nux vomica	5327	15.98	5616	53.30	1930	9.49	3443	13.77	1157	4.12	4967	18.22	785	3.00
8.	Seeded Tamarind	54796	147.03	56042	199.74	47991	221.96	2991	11.91	56906	293.26	48743	256.26	46196	309.49
9.	Deseeded Tamarind	8356	36.37	5502	35.25	6529	45.23	5988	44.91	4925	50.84	11546	116.61	5085	60.25
10.	Tamarind Seed	13380	6.69	7358	5.52	8973	6.73	13927	13.93	7101	10.64	4829	9.64	7718	15.44
11.	Pungam Seed	1363	5.45	6516	24.98	3121	12.48	6507	23.54	1076	4.16	4561	16.30	995	3.95
12.	Cleaning nuts	6052	47.94	3407	28.32	353	1.41	1133	4.53	496	1.99	254	1.01	153	0.61
13.	Marking nuts	828	1.66	1107	1.35	1290	3.22	1779	5.34	8325	36.70	3650	9.17	4606	13.27
14.	Mohwa Seed	7685	53.79	6790	40.99	3899	27.29	9868	69.08	4071	30.46	11439	78.67	2539	25.18
15.	Mohwa Flower	9203	18.22	17710	42.76	7024	17.56	13295	39.92	1931	5.67	3474	10.16	365	1.37
16.	Honey	1428	41.93	729	18.07	621	24.79	1653	69.43	1610	64.87	2030	79.73	984	30.22
17.	Sheekakai	652	6.13	2026	29.06	789	12.34	673	5.38	1299	12.21	1149	7.95	1843	9.08
18.	Soapnuts	3863	25.92	2491	17.29	2783	20.87	1573	12.58	2327	17.26	610	4.68	1054	10.12
19.	Hill Brooms (Nos)	67862	2.72	39130	2.34	122722	5.98	252322	15.14	354839	27.81	114822	10.10	202840	12.36
20.	Hill Brooms (Qtls.)	—	—	—	—	—	—	—	—	—	—	—	—	—	—
21.	Wild Brooms (Qtls.)	—	—	—	—	—	—	—	—	1355	14.80	1486	15.54	1578	14.58
22.	Wild Brooms (Nos.)	—	—	—	—	—	—	—	—	—	—	—	—	—	—
23.	Adda leaf	21848	26.26	20948	32.56	18530	37.06	26293	52.59	14764	36.88	16597	10.24	10656	34.80
24.	Naramamidi Bark	—	—	224	1.79	1149	11.49	3158	32.33	7896	91.44	7971	93.44	6023	34.82
25.	Teripods	—	—	480	4.53	292	8.44	—	—	--	—	—	—	—	—
26.	Maredugeddalu	—	—	—	—	—	—	—	—	595	6.81	4013	57.94	396	4.06
	Others	—	69.90	—	52.75	—	0.35	—	145.81	—	33.15		56.27	—	68.45
	Total	—	**786.65**	—	**1012.77**	—	**813.11**	—	**961.36**	—	**1132.03**	—	**1263.78**	—	**1078.26**

Appendix Table 4.1 (contd.)

APPENDIX TABLE 4.1 (*contd.*)

(Quantity in Quintals, Value Rs. in Lakh)

Sl. No.	Name of the Commodity	1999-00 Qty.	1999-00 Val.	2000-01 Qty	2000-01 Val.	2001-02 Qty.	2001-02 Val.	2002-03 Qty.	2002-03 Val.	2003-04 Qty.	2003-04 Val.	2004-05 Qty.	2004-05 Val.
1.	Gum Karaya	5096	390.15	5986	448.06	6842	493.71	6935	516.01	5086	389.52	7689	678.82
2.	Gum Thiruman	78	1.68	84	1.95	56	1.54	187	4.85	186	7.60	101	5.33
3.	Gum Olibanum	896	21.76	1063	25.61	370	7.48	415	20.22	437	8.46	209	4.57
4.	Gum Kondagogu	863	62.87	1160	86.82	115885	85.40	1297	101.90	1244	100.81	1184	116.63
5.	Gum Dikamali	171	1.71	455	4.55	522	8.87	1127	16.90	676	7.43	363	4.28
6.	Myrobalans	18540	129.49	19507	100.86	10685	34.80	12058	19.45	7606	11.41	14246	30.66
7.	Nux vomica	1312	4.53	1938	9.34	1860	10.14	5399	53.35	2348	29.98	13118	236.64
8.	Seeded Tamarind	61577	384.75	110573	645.51	54295	329.56	58846	235.17	47842	319.42	70256	486.14
9.	Deseeded Tamarind	7317	100.74	12168	163.00	10656	94.19	3506	25.86	4007	28.16	5211	68.01
10.	Tamarind Seed	7586	22.83	14365	22.81	10128	18.23	2765	5.53	4611	11.50	7508	36.06
11.	Pungam Seed	3481	15.78	2607	11.72	6542	29.35	1946	10.17	4870	26.81	981	6.03
12.	Cleaning nuts	1384	5.57	762	3.02	338	1.37	1520	12.12	275	3.09	8942	319.33
13.	Marking nuts	8379	2.88	7751	19.09	5791	11.43	8108	20.05	4794	14.52	6906	25.19
14.	Mohua Seed	11934	111.40	9394	65.80	6671	40.75	6252	55.07	4950	49.25	11944	121.30
15.	Mohua Flower	12101	42.22	3795	17.88	11360	54.37	10003	40.02	4238	18.74	26545	154.64
16.	Honey	856	27.68	1995	79.78	1650	65.95	2078	87.74	1108	58.13	3802	302.05
17.	Sheekakai	1292	7.20	1734	14.70	2577	24.72	2600	30.58	2697	29.06	3869	38.78
18.	Soapnuts	2185	25.69	1660	20.06	2419	26.40	2564	14.62	2532	14.74	1912	10.60
19.	Hill Brooms (Nos)	159330	12.72	189835	16.10	243315	25.15	436637	57.82	409037	63.49	332961	55.66
20.	Hill Brooms (Qtls.)	—	—	—	—	—	—	—	—	368	6.96	115	2.08
21.	Wild Brooms (Qtls.)	852	9.24	350	3.53	1134	12.65	1079	11.73	878	10.26	292	3.67
22.	Wild Brooms (Nos.)	—	—	—	—	—	—	—	—	—	—	57860	3.16
23.	Adda leaf	3521	10.99	10506	46.30	3912	12.86	12625	42.50	9867	34.93	13645	51.54
24.	Naramamidi Bark	6233	99.81	3316	62.99	1079	21.58	8192	163.81	3261	70.67	2906	47.72
25.	Teripods	—	—	—	—	—	—	—	—	—	—	—	—
26.	Maredugeddalu	378	4.48	2065	28.91	1030	15.42	2651	44.34	1833	31.16	470	8.14
	Others	—	62.64	—	41.90	—	62.04	—	71.01	—	19.34	—	132.67
	Total	**—**	**1558.81**	**—**	**1940.29**	**—**	**1487.96**	**—**	**1660.82**	**—**	**1365.44**	**—**	**2949.70**

Appendix Table 4.2 : Estimated Values of the Parameters of Linear Trend Equations of the Collection of NTFP (Quantity) in NCA 1991-92 to 2002-03

Commodities	*a*	*b*	t_b	R^2	*F-Value*
Adda leaf	22150.8	–1072.6	2.69*	0.3968	7.236
Cleaning nuts	6917.65	–630.14	2.9741*	0.4457	8.845
Deseeded Tamarind	5907.19	156.643	0.6834	0.0407	0.467
Gum Dikamali	232.192	25.8956	1.1695	0.1106	1.368
Gum Karaya	17472.7	–1209.7	2.9826*	0.4471	8.896
Gum Kondagogu	–985.71	178.786	8.5967*	0.9249	73.904
Gum Olibanum	567.538	5.6264	0.2766	0.0069	0.077
Gum Thiruman	580.154	–45.066	–1.5901	0.1869	2.528
Hill Broom	129337	8654.02	0.9190	0.0713	0.845
Honey	1738.69	92.6154	0.2989	0.0081	0.089
Maredugeddalu	–3642.2	439.8	1.2302	0.4308	1.513
Marking nuts	1202.42	485.995	2.7572*	0.4087	7.602
Mohua flower	1235.3	-474.06	1.0401	0.0895	1.082
Mohua seed	7342.46	20.8901	0.0806	0.0006	0.006
Myrobalans	12861.6	33.0659	0.0746	0.0005	0.006
Naramamidi bark	3017.77	205.432	0.7421	0.0577	0.551
Nux vomica	3036.77	–24.11	–0.1697	0.0026	0.029
Pungam seed	3285.12	20.0055	0.1219	0.0014	0.015
Seeded Tamarind	36802.7	2309.3	1.1495	0.1548	2.015
Sheekakai	518.5	128.478	3.5812*	0.5383	12.825
Soapnuts	2995.54	–103.82	1.6638	0.2011	2.768
Tamarind	10561.5	–224.87	0.8606	0.0631	0.741
Wild Broom	2104.86	–98.571	–1.3093	0.2553	1.714

* Significance at 1 per cent level.

Appendix Table 4.3 : Estimated Values of the Parameters of Linear Trend Equations of the Collection of NTFP (Value) in NCA 1991-92 to 2002-03

Commodities	*a*	*b*	t_b	R^2	*F-Value*
Adda leaf	26.1281	1.4438	1.4014	0.1515	1.964
Cleaning nuts	–7.4153	3.6429	2.0874*	0.3035	4.357
Deseeded Tamarind	16.0411	6.0516	1.9430	0.2555	3.775
Gum Dikamali	–2.9089	0.9129	3.0758*	0.4624	9.460
Gum Karaya	489.5888	6.3684	0.5649	0.0282	0.319
Gum Kondagogu	–98.8477	17.4823	6.1157*	0.8617	37.402
Gum Olibanum	6.6365	0.8808	2.2291**	0.3112	4.969
Gum Thiruman	14.2558	–1.0125	1.2546	0.1252	1.574
Hill Broom	0.6077	1.6877	5.6279*	0.7422	31.673
Honey	2.4362	6.0687	1.4165	0.1543	2.006
Maredugeddalu	–8.306	2.359	0.3031	0.0439	0.092
Marking nuts	–0.7165	1.8227	3.9101*	0.5816	15.289
Mohua flower	13.9939	1.9075	1.2692	0.1277	1.611
Mohua seed	52.5308	0.7296	0.3322	0.0099	0.110
Myrobalans	23.5692	4.9645	1.6784	0.2039	2.817
Naramamidi bark	109.8857	1.3821	0.0917	0.0017	0.008
Nux vomica	11.4404	1.9759	1.1132	0.1013	1.239
Pungam seed	9.975	0.7795	0.9016	0.0688	0.813
Seeded Tamarind	94.8442	19.5810	2.2200**	0.3094	4.928
Sheekakai	3.015	1.4532	2.1032**	0.2868	4.424
Soapnuts	11.0642	0.2894	0.5811	0.0298	0.338
Tamarind	11.1331	0.992	1.9718**	0.2611	3.888
Wild Broom	18.897	–0.058	0.0497	0.0012	0.002

* Significance at 1 per cent level.
** Significance at 5 per cent level.

Appendix Tabl 4.4 : Estimated Values of the Parameters of Exponential Trend Equations of the Collection of NTFP (Quantity) in NCA 1991-92 to 2002-03

Commodities	*a*	*b*	t_b	R^2	*F-Value*
Adda leaf	10.1353	–0.0973	2.616*	0.3836	6.845
Cleaning nuts	8.5035	–0.2129	2.6335*	0.3867	6.935
Deseeded Tamarind	8.6874	0.0093	0.2407	0.0052	0.058
Gum Dikamali	5.2273	0.071	1.0827	0.0963	1.172
Gum Karaya	9.6048	–0.0971	3.0668*	0.4609	9.405
Gum Kondagogu	3.5672	0.2928	9.1761*	0.9335	84.200
Gum Olibanum	6.3158	–.0002	0.0063	0.00004	0.0000
Gum Thiruman	5.9428	–0.169	1.8694**	0.2411	3.495
Hill Broom	11.5923	0.0161	0.1490	0.0020	0.022
Honey	6.6930	0.0795	1.2651	0.1270	1.601
Maredugeddalu	1.7897	0.4573	1.4751	0.5211	2.176
Marking nuts	7.2106	0.1361	2.6893*	0.3967	7.233
Mohua flower	9.2037	–0.0652	0.7914	0.0539	0.626
Mohua seed	8.7735	0.0058	0.1501	0.0020	0.023
Myrobalans	9.2667	0.0177	0.5203	0.0240	0.271
Naramamidi bark	7.3001	0.0964	0.9201	0.0861	0.848
Nux vomica	7.8202	–0.0091	0.1735	0.0027	0.030
Pungam seed	7.8504	0.0118	0.2198	0.0044	0.0048
Seeded Tamarind	10.3611	0.0477	0.7478	0.0484	0.559
Sheekakai	6.5129	0.0909	3.5634*	.05358	12.698
Soapnuts	7.9466	–0.0451	1.2462	0.1237	1.553
Tamarind	9.3092	–0.0413	1.2542	0.1251	1.573
Wild Broom	7.9039	–0.0975	0.9976	0.1659	0.995

* Significance at 1 per cent level.
** Significance at 5 per cent level.

Appendix Table 4.5 : Estimated Values of the Parameters of Exponential Trend Equations of the Collection of NTFP (Value) in NCA 1991-92 to 2002-03

Commodities	*a*	*b*	t_b	R^2	*F-Value*
Adda leaf	3.1804	0.0470	1.5527	0.4239	2.411
Cleaning nuts	0.2551	0.2561	2.7044*	0.4224	7.314
Deseeded Tamarind	2.9269	0.1289	3.2494*	0.4898	10.558
Gum Dikamali	–1.5636	0.2358	1.8897	0.2451	3.571
Gum Karaya	6.1013	0.0207	1.0294	0.0879	1.060
Gum Kondagogu	1.1707	0.2951	8.3209*	0.9203	69.238
Gum Olibanum	1.8429	0.0832	2.4521**	0.3534	6.013
Gum Thiruman	2.3069	–0.1533	1.8668	0.2406	3.485
Hill Broom	1.3117	0.1469	7.0562*	0.8919	49.791
Honey	–1.8334	0.5327	3.4430*	0.5187	11.854
Maredugeddalu	–0.7588	0.2929	0.5658	0.1379	0.320
Marking nuts	0.4766	0.2247	4.0397*	0.7729	16.319
Mohua flower	2.3603	0.0480	0.3898	0.0136	0.152
Mohua seed	3.7378	0.0265	0.6241	0.0342	0.389
Myrobalans	3.1082	0.0993	1.7265	0.2132	2.981
Naramamidi bark	8.1234	–0.4197	0.8145	0.1171	0.663
Nux vomica	2.5692	0.0405	0.5929	0.0309	0.352
Pungam seed	0.9574	0.1675	1.3481	0.1418	1.817
Seeded Tamarind	4.2873	0.1271	2.0144**	0.2695	4.058
Sheekakai	0.2950	0.2276	1.8731	0.2418	3.509
Soapnuts	2.2951	0.0198	0.4496	0.179	0.200
Tamarind	2.4284	0.0555	1.9853**	0.2638	3.941
Wild Broom	2.9298	–0.0026	0.0401	0.0008	0.002

* Significance at 1 per cent level.
** Significance at 5 per cent level.

Appendix Table 4.6 : Estimates of Cyclical Component of the Collection of Gum Karaya in NCA

Year	Quantity (Qtls.)	Index	Five Years Moving Average	Cyclical Component from		Value (Rs.)	Index	Five Years Moving Average	Cyclical Component from	
				Additive Hypothesis	Multiplicative Hypothesis				Additive Hypothesis	Multiplicative Hypothesis
1.	27716	100.00	—	—	—	681.32	100.00	—	—	—
2.	20815	75.10	—	—	—	499.76	73.35	—	—	—
3.	9212	33.24	51.74	-18.50	64.24	242.05	35.53	61.10	-25.57	58.15
4.	8273	29.85	35.95	-6.11	83.02	351.03	51.52	51.18	0.35	100.68
5.	5688	20.52	24.62	-4.10	83.37	307.24	45.09	46.61	-1.52	96.75
6.	5838	21.06	21.64	-0.57	97.36	343.26	50.38	49.24	1.14	102.31
7.	5104	18.42	18.89	-0.48	97.46	344.25	50.53	47.43	3.10	106.53
8.	5079	18.33	18.47	-0.14	99.23	331.79	48.70	49.86	-1.17	97.66
9.	4475	16.15	18.57	-2.43	86.93	289.24	42.45	52.94	-10.49	80.19
10.	5096	18.39	19.83	-1.44	92 73	390.15	57.26	57.33	-0.06	99.89
11.	5986	21.60	21.17	0.43	102.03	448.06	65.76	62.74	3.03	104.83
12.	6842	24.69	—	—	—	493.7	72.46	—	—	—
13.	6935	25.02	—	—	—	516.01	75.74	—	—	—

Appendix Table 4.7 : Estimates of Cyclical Component of the Collection of Gum Thirumun in NCA

Year	Quantity (Qtls.)	Index	Five Years Moving Average	Cyclical Component from		Value (Rs.)	Index	Five Years Moving Average	Cyclical Component from	
				Additive Hypothesis	Multipli-cative Hypo-thesis				Additive Hypothesis	Multipli-cative Hypo-thesis
1.	169	100.00	—	—	—	2.92	100.00	—	—	—
2.	327	193.49	—	—	—	7.11	243.49	—	—	—
3.	·624	369.23	577.40	–208.17	63.95	15	513.70	448.42	65.27	114.56
4.	1493	883.43	560.00	323.43	157.76	34.14	1169.18	442.26	726.92	264.36
5.	274	162.13	497.20	–335.07	32.61	6.3	215.75	395.62	–179.86	54.54
6.	82	48.52	376.80	–328.28	12.88	2.02	69.18	296.23	–227.05	23.35
7.	13	7.69	85.00	–77.31	9.05	0.3	10.27	67.53	–57.26	15.21
8.	22	13.02	45.80	–32.78	28.42	0.49	16.78	35.96	–19.18	46.67
9.	34	20.12	46.20	–26.08	43.55	0.75	25.68	35.48	–9.79	72.39
10.	78	46.15	54.40	–8.25	84.84	1 69	57.88	43.90	13.97	131.83
11.	84	49.70	87.40	–37.70	56.87	1.95	66.78	73.70	–6.92	90.61
12.	54	31.95	—	—	—	1.53	52.40	—	—	—
13.	187	110.65	—	—	—	4.84	165.75	—	—	—

Appendix Table 4.8 : Estimates of Cyclical Component of the Collection of Gum Olibanum in NCA

Year	Quantity (Qtls.)	Index	Five Years Moving Average	Cyclical Component from		Value (Rs.)	Index	Five Years Moving Average	Cyclical Component from	
				Additive Hypothesis	Multiplicative Hypothesis				Additive Hypothesis	Multiplicative Hypothesis
1.	698	100.00	—	—	—	7.45	100.00	—	—	—
2.	490	70.20	—	—	—	7.35	98.66	—	—	—
3.	575	82.38	89.91	–7.54	91.62	8.17	109.66	115.01	–5.34	95.35
4.	769	110.17	77.85	32.32	141.52	11.15	149.66	105.83	43.84	141.43
5.	606	86.82	70.80	16.02	122.62	8.72	117.05	95.92	21.13	122.03
6.	277	39.68	68.54	–28.85	57.90	4.03	54.09	108.86	–54.77	49.69
7.	244	34.96	74.90	–39.94	46.67	3.66	49.13	142.93	–93.80	34.37
8.	496	71.06	83.21	–12.15	85.40	12.99	174.36	177.93	–3.57	97.99
9.	991	141.98	105.73	36.25	134.28	23.84	320.00	235.84	84.16	135.69
10.	896	128.37	109.34	19.03	117.40	21.76	292.08	246.09	45.99	118.69
11.	1063	152.29	107.02	45.27	142.30	25.60	343.62	232.81	110.82	147.60
12.	370	53.01	—	—	—	7.48	100.40	—	—	—
13.	415	59.46	—	—	—	8.04	107.92	—	—	—

Appendix Table 4.9 : Estimates of Cyclical Component of the Collection of Gum Kondagogu in NCA

Year	Quantity (Qtls.)	Index Average	Five Years Moving Average	Cyclical Component from Additive Hypothesis	Cyclical Component from Multiplicative Hypothesis	Value (Rs.)	Index Average	Five Years Moving Average	Cyclical Component from Additive Hypothesis	Cyclical Component from Multiplicative Hypothesis
1.	—	—	—	—	—	—	—	—	—	—
2.	—	—	—	—	—	—	—	—	—	—
3.	—	—	—	—	—	—	—	—	—	—
4.	—	—	—	—	—	—	—	—	—	—
5.	—	—	—	—	—	—	—	—	—	—
6.	230	100.00	—	—	—	13.45	100.00	—	—	—
7.	233	101.30	—	—	—	14.77	109.81	—	—	—
8.	329	143.04	181.48	–38.43	78.82	20.30	150.93	209.90	–58.97	71.90
9.	432	187.83	262.35	–74.52	71.59	29.78	221.41	319.00	–97.59	69.41
10.	863	375.22	342.78	32.43	109.46	62.86	467.36	424.04	43.32	110.21
11.	1160	504.35	426.96	77.39	118.13	86.82	645.50	545.37	100.13	118.36
12.	1158	503.48	—	—	—	85.41	635.02	—	—	—
13.	1297	563.91	—	—	—	101.89	757.55	—	—	—

Appendix Table 4.10 : Estimates of Cyclical Component of the Collection of Gum Dikamali in NCA

Year	Quantity (Qtls.)	Index	Five Years Moving Average	Cyclical Component from		Value (Rs.)	Index	Five Years Moving Average	Cyclical Component from	
				Additive Hypothesis	Multiplicative Hypothesis				Additive Hypothesis	Multiplicative Hypothesis
1.	169	100.00	—	—	—	0.54	100.00	—	—	—
2.	814	481.66	—	—	—	2.46	455.56	—	—	—
3.	505	298.82	222.72	76.09	134.17	1.99	368.52	242.22	126.30	152.14
4.	44	26.04	227.10	–201.07	11.46	0.17	31.48	252.96	–221.48	12.45
5.	350	207.10	176.45	30.65	117.37	1.38	255.56	233.70	21.85	109.35
6.	206	121.89	128.76	–6.86	94.67	0.83	153.70	177.04	–23.33	86.82
7.	386	228.40	185.56	42.84	123.09	1.94	359.26	325.93	33.33	110.23
8.	102	60.36	164.38	–104.02	36.72	0.46	85.19	338.15	–252.96	25.19
9.	524	310.06	193.85	116.21	159.95	4.19	775.93	475.93	300.00	163.04
10.	171	101.18	209.94	–108.76	48.20	1.71	316.67	732.59	–415.93	43.23
11.	455	269.23	331.24	–62.01	81.28	4.55	842.59	1341.48	–498.89	62.81
12.	522	308.88	—	—	—	8.87	1642.59	—	—	—
13.	1127	666.86	—	—	—	16.90	3129.63	—	—	--

Appendix Table 4.11 : Estimates of Cyclical Component of the Collection of Myrobalans in NCA

Year	Quantity (Qtls.)	Index	Five Years Moving Average	Cyclical Component from		Value (Rs.)	Index	Five Years Moving Average	Cyclical Component from	
				Additive Hypothesis	Multiplicative Hypothesis				Additive Hypothesis	Multiplicative Hypothesis
1.	25665	100.00	—	—	—	62.47	100.00	—	—	—
2.	10291	40.10	—	—	—	22.53	36.07	—	—	—
3.	5380	20.96	46.66	–25.69	44.93	8.75	14.01	42.11	–28.11	33.26
4.	11762	45.83	39.70	6.13	115.43	24.09	38.56	38.03	0.53	101.40
5.	6775	26.40	37.40	–11.00	70.59	13.70	21.93	38.42	–16.49	57.07
6.	16742	65.23	42.41	22.82	153.82	49.72	79.59	50.61	28.98	157.27
7.	7329	28.56	43.89	–15.33	65.05	23.76	38.03	68.84	–30.80	55.25
8.	11812	46.02	53.06	–7.03	86.74	46.80	74.92	105.91	–39.99	70.74
9.	13664	53.24	55.21	–1.97	96.43	81.03	129.71	122.28	7.43	106.08
10.	18540	72.24	57.83	14.41	124.92	129.49	207.28	125.81	81.47	164.75
11.	19507	76.01	58.02	17.99	131.00	100.86	161.45	117.06	44.40	137.93
12.	10685	41.63	—	—	—	34.80	55.71	—	—	—
13.	12058	46.93	—	—	—	19.45	31.13	—	—	—

Appendix Table 4.12 : Estimates of Cyclical Component of the Collection of Nux vomica in NCA

Year	Quantity (Qtls.)	Index	Five Years Moving Average	Cyclical Component from		Value (Rs.)	Index	Five Years Moving Average	Cyclical Component from	
				Additive Hypothesis	Multiplicative Hypothesis				Additive Hypothesis	Multiplicative Hypothesis
1.	1098	100.00	—	—	—	3.31	100.00	—	—	—
2.	2452	223.92	—	—	—	5.92	178.85	—	—	—
3.	5327	485.15	299.14	186.01	162.18	43.84	1324.47	700.79	623.69	189.00
4.	5616	511.48	341.86	169.62	149.62	53.30	1610.27	763.75	846.53	20.84
5.	1930	175.77	318.27	–142.50	55.23	9.61	290.33	752.87	–462.54	38.56
6.	3443	313.57	311.71	1.86	100.60	13.73	414.80	598.07	–183.26	69.36
7.	1157	105.37	223.72	–118.34	47.10	4.12	124.47	294.08	–169.61	42.33
8.	4967	452.37	212.46	239.91	212.92	18.22	550.45	263.38	287.07	208.99
9.	785	71.49	185.05	–113.55	38.64	2.99	90.33	236.80	–146.47	38.15
10.	1312	119.49	197.85	–78.36	60.39	4.53	136.86	273.17	–136.31	50.10
11.	1938	176.50	205.72	–29.22	85.80	9.33	281.87	485.44	–203.56	58.07
12.	1860	169.40	—	—	—	10.14	306.34	—	—	—
13.	5399	491.71	—	—	—	53.35	1611.78	—	—	—

Appendix Table 4.13 : Estimates of Cyclical Component of the Collection of Seeded Tamarind in NCA

Year	Quantity (Qtls.)	Index	Five Years Moving Average	Cyclical Component from		Value (Rs.)	Index	Five Years Moving Average	Cyclical Component from	
				Additive Hypothesis	Multiplicative Hypothesis				Additive Hypothesis	Multiplicative Hypothesis
1.	38009	100.00	—	—	—	102.31	100.00	—	—	—
2.	51616	135.50	—	—	—	124.35	121.54	—	—	—
3.	54796	144.17	130.73	13.43	110.27	147.03	143.71	149.57	–5.86	96.08
4.	56042	147.44	112.31	35.14	131.29	199.74	195.23	155.02	40.22	125.94
5.	47991	126.26	115.09	11.17	109.71	191.72	187.39	188.03	–0.64	99.66
6.	2991	7.87	111.91	–104.04	7.03	130.14	127.20	209.39	–82.19	60.75
7.	56906	149.72	106.73	42.99	140.28	293.26	286.64	230.84	55.80	124.17
8.	48743	128.24	113.87	14.37	112.62	256.26	250.47	268.58	–18.10	93.26
9.	46196	121.54	170.48	–48.94	71.29	309.49	302.50	363.32	–66.82	81.91
10.	61577	162.01	169.11	–7.10	95.80	384.75	376.06	376.42	–0.36	99.91
11.	110573	290.91	174.43	116.49	166.78	645.51	630.94	372.30	258.64	169.47
12.	54295	142.85	—	—	—	329.56	322.12	—	—	—
13.	58846	154.82	—	—	—	235.17	229.86	—	—	—

Appendix Table 4.14 : Estimates of Cyclical Component of the Collection of Deseeded Tamarind in NCA

Year	Quantity (Qtls.)	Index	Five Years Moving Average	Cyclical Component from		Value (Rs.)	Index	Five Years Moving Average	Cyclical Component from	
				Additive Hypothesis	Multiplicative Hypothesis				Additive Hypothesis	Multiplicative Hypothesis
1.	6820	100.00	—	—	—	41.66	100.00	—	—	—
2.	5650	82.84	—	—	—	29.63	71.12	—	—	—
3.	8356	122.52	96.35	26.17	127.16	36.37	87.30	90.70	–3.39	96.26
4.	5502	80.67	93.91	–13.24	85.90	35.35	84.61	93.63	–9.02	90.37
5.	6529	95.73	82.99	12.74	115.35	46.01	110.44	103.2	6.63	106.38
6.	5988	87.80	92.35	–4.55	95.08	47.78	114.69	142.34	–27.65	80.58
7.	1925	28.23	91.12	–62.90	30.98	50.84	122.04	154.34	–32.30	79.07
8.	11546	169.30	93.43	75.86	181.19	116.61	279.91	180.61	99.29	154.98
9.	5085	74.56	111.56	–37.00	66.84	60.25	144.62	235.92	–91.30	61.30
10.	7317	107.29	137.16	–29.87	78.22	100.74	241.81	256.74	–14.92	94.19
11.	12168	178.42	113.58	64.83	157.08	162.99	391.24	213.17	178.07	183.53
12.	10656	156.25	—	—	—	94.19	226.09	—	—	—
13.	3506	51.41	—	—	—	25.86	62.07	—	—	—

Appendix Table 4.15 : Estimates of Cyclical Component of the Collection of Tamarind Seed in NCA

Year	Quantity (Qtls.)	Index	Five Years Moving Average	Cyclical Component from		Value (Rs.)	Index	Five Years Moving Average	Cyclical Component from	
				Additive Hypothesis	Multiplicative Hypothesis				Additive Hypothesis	Multiplicative Hypothesis
1.	7633	100.00	—	—	—	6.12	100.00	—	—	—
2.	11074	145.08	—	—	—	8.85	144.61	—	—	—
3.	13380	175.29	126.86	48.43	138.17	11.18	182.68	137.94	44.74	132.43
4.	7358	96.40	143.36	–46.96	67.24	7.1	116.01	195.13	–79.12	59.45
5.	8973	117.56	132.95	–15.39	88.42	8.96	146.41	200.98	–54.58	72.85
6.	13927	182.46	110.54	71.92	165.06	23.62	385.95	195.85	190.10	197.06
7.	7101	93.03	111.48	–18.45	83.45	10.64	173.86	223.10	–49.25	77.93
8.	4829	63.26	107.85	–44.59	58.66	9.61	157.03	268.43	–111.41	58.50
9.	7718	101.11	109.00	–7.88	92.77	15.44	252.29	265.75	–13.46	94.93
10.	7586	99.38	116.93	–17.54	85.00	22.83	373.04	290•56	82.48	128.39
11.	14364	188.18	111.52	76.66	168.75	22.8	372.55	277.22	95.33	134.39
12.	10128	132.69	—	—	—	18.23	297.88	—	—	—
13.	2765	36.22	—	—	—	5.53	90.36	—	—	—

Appendix Table 4.16 : Estimates of Cyclical Component of the Collection of Pungam Seed in NCA

Year	Quantity (Qtls.)	Index	Five Years Moving Average	Cyclical Component from		Value (Rs.)	Index	Five Years Moving Average	Cyclical Component from	
				Additive Hypothesis	Multiplicative Hypothesis				Additive Hypothesis	Multiplicative Hypothesis
1.	1358	100.00	—	—	—	4.04	100.00	—	—	—
2.	4454	327.96	—	—	—	17.33	428.96	—	—	—
3.	1363	100.37	247.60	–147.23	40.54	5.45	134.90	311.04	–176.14	43.37
4.	6516	479.82	323.43	156.39	148.35	24.98	618.32	419.85	198.47	147.27
5.	3121	229.82	273.68	–43.86	83.97	11.03	273.02	354.65	–81.63	76.98
6.	6507	479.16	320.78	158.38	149.37	26.02	644.06	408.37	235.69	157.72
7.	1076	79.23	239.47	–160.24	33.09	4.16	102.97	304.28	–201.29	33.84
8.	4561	335.86	244.77	91.09	137.21	16.30	403.47	327.77	75.69	123.09
9.	995	73.27	187.33	–114.06	39.11	–3.95	97.77	256.98	–159.21	38.05
10.	3481	256.33	267.84	–11.50	95.71	15.78	390.59	381.68	8.91	102.33
11.	2607	191.97	229.32	–37.35	83.71	11.72	290.10	351.34	–61.24	82.57
12.	6542	481.74	—	—	—	29.37	726.49	—	—	—
13.	1946	143.30	—	—	—	10.17	251.73	—	—	—

Appendix Table 4.17 : Estimates of Cyclical Component of the Collection of Cleaning Nuts in NCA

Year	Quantity (Qtls.)	Index	Five Years Moving Average	Cyclical Component from		Value (Rs.)	Index	Five Years Moving Average	Cyclical Component from	
				Additive Hypothesis	Multiplicative Hypothesis				Additive Hypothesis	Multiplicative Hypothesis
1.	13312	100.00	—	—	—	59.55	100.00	—	—	—
2.	3423	25.71	—	—	—	19.61	32.93	—	—	—
3.	6052	45.46	39.88	5.58	113.99	47.94	80.50	52.99	27.51	151.92
4.	3407	25.59	21.59	4.01	118.56	28.32	47.56	34.51	13.04	137.80
5.	353	2.65	17.19	–14.54	15.43	2.36	3.96	28.59	–24.63	13.86
6.	1133	8.51	8.48	0.03	100.39	4.53	7.61	12.83	–5.23	59.28
7.	496	3.73	3.59	0.14	103.81	1.99	3.34	3.53	–0.18	94.76
8.	254	1.91	5.14	03.23	37.13	1.01	1.70	4.60	–2.91	36.83
9.	153	1.15	4.58	03.43	25.09	0.61	1.02	4.09	–3.07	25.02
10.	1384	10.40	434	6.05	239.36	5.57	9.35	3.89	5.47	240.71
11.	762	5.72	6.25	–0.52	91.65	3.01	5.05	7.62	–2.56	66.36
12.	338	2.54	—	—	—	1.37	2.30	—	—	—
13.	1520	11.42	—	—	—	12.12	20.35	—	—	—

Appendix Table 4.18 : Estimates of Cyclical Component of the Collection of Marking Nuts in NCA

Year	Quantity (Qtls.)	Index	Five Years Moving Average	Cyclical Component from		Value (Rs.)	Index	Five Years Moving Average	Cyclical Component from	
				Additive Hypothesis	Multiplicative Hypothesis				Additive Hypothesis	Multiplicative Hypothesis
1.	5948	100.00	—	—	—	5.67	100.00	—	—	—
2.	2295	38.58	—	—	—	1.83	32.28	—	—	—
3.	828	13.92	38.56	–24.64	36.10	0.63	11.11	39.75	–28.64	27.95
4.	1107	18.61	24.54	–5.93	75.83	1.35	23.81	37.67	–13.86	63.20
5.	1290	21.69	44.82	–23.13	48.39	1.79	31.57	160.67	–129.10	19.65
6.	1779	29.91	54.31	–24.40	55.07	5.08	89.59	190.79	–101.20	46.96
7.	8325	139.96	66.07	73.89	211.83	36.7	647.27	232.84	414.43	277.99
8.	3650	61.37	89.91	–28.54	68.25	9.17	161.73	404.51	–242.79	39.98
9.	4606	77.44	109.99	–32.55	70.40	13.27	234.04	453.90	–219.86	51.56
10.	8379	140.87	101.47	39.40	138.83	50.46	889.95	364.76	525.19	243.98
11.	7751	130.31	116.46	13.85	111.90	19.08	336.51	403.14	–66.63	83.47
12.	5791	97.36	—	—	—	11.43	201.59	—	—	—
13.	8108	136.31	—	—	—	20.05	353.62	—	—	—

Appendix Table 4.19 : Estimates of Cyclical Component of the Collection of Mohua Seed in NCA

Year	Quantity (Qtls.)	Index	Five Years Moving Average	Cyclical Component from		Value (Rs.)	Index	Five Years Moving Average	Cyclical Component from	
				Additive Hypothesis	Multiplicative Hypothesis				Additive Hypothesis	Multiplicative Hypothesis
1.	4129	100.00	—	—	—	24.77	100.00	—	—	—
2.	12682	307.14	—	—	—	88.78	358.42	—	—	—
3.	7685	186.12	170.43	15.69	109.21	53.79	217.16	191.63	25.53	113.32
4.	6790	164.45	198.23	–33.78	82.96	40.99	165.48	227.44	–61.95	72.76
5.	3899	94.43	156.62	–62.09	60.33	29	117.08	180.35	–63.27	64.92
6.	9868	238.99	174.70	64.29	136.80	69.12	279.05	200.44	78.61	139.22
7.	4071	98.60	154.11	–55.51	63.98	30.46	122.97	187.67	–64.70	65.53
8.	11439	277.04	193.03	84.01	143.52	78.67	317.60	254.21	63.39	124.94
9.	2539	61.49	190.73	–129.24	32.24	25.18	101.66	251.54	–149.88	40.41
10.	11934	289.03	203.33	85.70	152.15	111.41	449.78	259.85	189.93	173.09
11.	9394	227.51	178.20	49.31	127.67	65.81	265.68	240.78	24.91	110.35
12.	6671	161.56	—	—	—	40.75	164.51	—	—	—
13.	6652	151.42	—	—	—	55.05	222.24	—	—	—

Appendix Table 4.20 : Estimates of Cyclical Component of the Collection of Mohua Flower in NCA

Year	Quantity (Qtls.)	Index	Five Years Moving Average	Cyclical Component from		Value (Rs.)	Index	Five Years Moving Average	Cyclical Component from	
				Additive Hypothesis	Multiplicative Hypothesis				Additive Hypothesis	Multiplicative Hypothesis
1.	5864	100.00	—	—	—	11.11	100.00	—	—	—
2.	21263	362.60	—	—	—	41.68	375.16	—	—	—
3.	9203	156.94	208.27	–51.33	75.36	18.22	164.00	235.66	–71.67	69.59
4.	17710	302.01	233.61	68.40	129.28	42.76	384.88	283.69	101.19	135.87
5.	7024	119.78	167.68	–47.90	71.44	17.14	154.28	218.87	–64.59	70.49
6.	13295	226.72	148.14	78.58	153.05	37.79	340.14	204.36	135.79	166.45
7.	1931	32.93	88.98	–56.05	37.01	5.67	51.04	129.85	–78.81	39.30
8.	3474	59.24	106.30	–47.05	55.73	10.16	91.45	175.00	–83.55	52.26
9.	365	6.22	73.89	–67.67	8.42	1.37	12.33	139.15	–126.82	8.86
10.	12101	206.36	106.05	100.31	194.58	42.22	380.02	226.82	153.20	167.54
11.	3795	64.72	128.32	–63.61	50.43	17.88	160.94	280.58	–119.64	57.36
12.	11360	193.72	—	—	—	54.37	489.38	—	—	—
13.	10003	170.58	—	—	—	40.02	360.22	—	—	—

Appendix Table 4.21 : Estimates of Cyclical Component of the Collection of Honey in NCA

Year	Quantity (Qtls.)	Index	Five Years Moving Average	Cyclical Component from		Value (Rs.)	Index	Five Years Moving Average	Cyclical Component from	
				Additive Hypothesis	Multiplicative Hypothesis				Additive Hypothesis	Multiplicative Hypothesis
1.	488	100.00	—	—	—	9.8	100.00	—	—	—
2.	924	189.34	—	—	—	27.57	281.33	—	—	—
3.	1428	292.62	171.72	120.90	170.41	41.93	427.86	236.80	191.06	180.69
4.	729	149.39	219.47	–70.08	68.07	18.07	184.39	349.96	–165.57	52.69
5.	621	127.25	822.13	–694.88	15.48	18.66	190.41	426.12	–235.71	44.68
6.	1653	338.73	846.80	–508.07	40.00	65.25	665.82	503.27	162.55	132.30
7.	15629	3202.66	855.78	2346.89	374.24	64.89	662.14	528.10	134.04	125.38
8.	2030	415.96	865.49	–449.51	48.06	79.73	813.57	546.69	267.08	148.87
9.	948	194.26	879.51	–685.25	22.09	30.24	308.57	576.14	–267.57	53.56
10.	858	175.82	306.60	–130.7	57.35	27.67	282.35	578.31	–295.96	48.82
11.	1995	408.81	308.57	100.25	132.49	79.78	814.08	594.65	219.43	136.90
12.	1650	338.11	—	—	—	65.95	672.96	—	—	—
13.	2078	425.82	—	—	—	87.74	895.31	—	—	—

Appendix Table 4.22 : Estimates of Cyclical Component of the Collection of Sheekakai in NCA

Year	Quantity (Qtls.)	Index	Five Years Moving Average	Cyclical Component from		Value (Rs.)	Index	Five Years Moving Average	Cyclical Component from	
				Additive Hypothesis	Multiplicative Hypothesis				Additive Hypothesis	Multiplicative Hypothesis
1.	822	100.00	—	—	—	4.01	100.00	—	—	—
2.	976	118.73	—	—	—	5.54	138.15	—	—	—
3.	652	79.32	128.10	–48.78	61.92	6.13	152.87	277.46	–124.59	55.10
4.	2026	246.47	124.48	122.00	198.01	29.06	724.69	284.29	440.40	254.91
5.	789	95.99	132.34	–36.35	72.53	10.89	271.57	317.56	–45.99	85.52
6.	673	81.87	144.43	–62.55	56.69	5.38	134.16	326.63	–192.47	41.07
7.	1299	158.03	139.98	18.05	112.90	12.21	304.49	226.98	77.51	134.15
8.	1149	139.78	152.21	–12.43	91.83	7.95	198.25	208.58	–10.32	95.05
9.	1843	224.21	178.03	46.18	125.94	9.08	226.43	255.06	–28.63	88.78
10.	1292	157.18	209.12	–51.95	75.16	7.2	179.55	317.46	–137.91	56.56
11.	1734	210.95	244.43	–33.48	86.30	14.7	366.58	430.32	–63.74	85.19
12.	2577	313.50	—	—	—	24.72	616.46	—	—	—
13.	2600	316.30	—	—	—	30.58	762.59	—	—	—

Appendix Table 4.23 : Estimates of Cyclical Component of the Collection of Soapnuts in NCA

Year	Quantity (Qtls.)	Index	Five Years Moving Average	Cyclical Component from Additive Hypothesis	Cyclical Component from Multiplicative Hypothesis	Value (Rs.)	Index	Five Years Moving Average	Cyclical Component from Additive Hypothesis	Cyclical Component from Multiplicative Hypothesis
1.	2399	100.00	—	—	—	9.69	100.00	—	—	—
2.	3566	148.65	—	—	—	11.84	122.19	—	—	—
3.	3863	161.03	125.90	35.12	127.90	25.92	267.49	184.29	83.20	145.15
4.	2491	103.83	119.02	–15.18	87.24	17.29	178.43	185.84	–7.41	96.01
5.	2783	116.01	108.69	7.32	106.73	24.55	253.35	197.03	56.33	128.59
6.	1573	65.57	81.57	–16.00	80.39	10.44	107.74	153.19	–45.45	70.33
7.	2327	97.00	69.59	27.41	139.39	17.26	178.12	138.41	39.71	128.69
8.	610	25.43	64.60	–39.17	39.36	4.68	48.30	140.76	–92.47	34.31
9.	1054	43.93	65.33	–21.39	67.25	10.13	104.54	160.60	–56.06	65.09
10.	2185	91.08	66.09	24.99	17.80	25.69	265.12	179.46	85.66	147.73
11.	1660	69.20	82.38	–13.19	83.99	20.05	206.91	199.98	6.93	103.47
12.	2419	100.83	—	—	—	26.4	272.45	—	—	—
13.	2564	106.88	—	—	—	14.62	150.88	—	—	—

Appendix Table 4.24 : Estimates of Cyclical Component of the Collection of Hill Brooms in NCA

Year	Quantity (Qtls.)	Index	Five Years Moving Average	Cyclical Component from		Value (Rs.)	Index	Five Years Moving Average	Cyclical Component from	
				Additive Hypothesis	Multiplicative Hypothesis				Additive Hypothesis	Multiplicative Hypothesis
1.	300725	100.00	—	—	—	11.18	100.00	—	—	—
2.	185324	61.63	—	—	—	8.36	74.78	—	—	—
3.	67862	22.57	47.60	–25.04	47.41	2.72	24.33	56.87	–32.54	42.78
4.	39130	13.01	44.38	–31.37	29.32	2.34	20.93	71.50	–50.57	29.27
5.	122722	40.81	55.66	–14.85	73.32	7.19	64.31	106.31	–42.00	60.49
6.	252322	83.90	58.78	25.12	142.74	19.36	173.17	119.52	53.65	144.89
7.	354839	117.99	56.31	61.68	209.53	27.82	248.84	137.44	111.40	181.05
8.	114822	38.18	58.75	–20.57	64.99	10.1	90.34	147.33	–56.99	61.32
9.	2028	0.67	54.59	–53.92	1.24	12.36	110.55	141.48	–30.93	78.14
10.	159330	52.98	47.17	5.81	112.31	12.72	113.77	136.69	–22.92	83.24
11.	189835	63.13	68.58	–5.45	92.05	16.09	143.92	222.06	–78.14	64.81
12.	243315	80.91	—	—	—	25.14	224.87	—	—	—
13.	436637	145.19	—	—	—	57.82	517.17	—	—	—

Appendix Table 4.25 : Estimates of Cyclical Component of the Collection of Wild Brooms in NCA

Year	Quantity (Qtls.)	Index	Five Years Moving Average	Cyclical Component from		Value (Rs.)	Index	Five Years Moving Average	Cyclical Component from	
				Additive Hypothesis	Multiplicative Hypothesis				Additive Hypothesis	Multiplicative Hypothesis
1.	—	—	—	—	—	—	—	—	—	—
2.	—	—	—	—	—	—	—	—	—	—
3.	—	—	—	—	—	—	—	—	—	—
4.	—	—	—	—	—	—	—	—	—	—
5.	—	—	—	—	—	—	—	—	—	—
6.	—	—	—	—	—	—	—	—	—	—
7.	1355	100.00	—	—	—	14.8	100.00	—	—	—
8.	1486	109.67	—	—	—	15.54	105.00	—	—	—
9.	1578	116.46	82.97	33.49	140.37	14.58	98.51	77.97	20.54	126.34
10.	852	62.88	79.70	–16.83	78.89	9.25	62.50	75.07	–12.57	83.26
11.	350	25.83	73.70	–47.87	35.05	3.53	23.85	69.92	–46.07	34.11
12.	1134	83.69	—	—	—	12.65	85.47	—	—	—
13.	1079	79.63	—	—	—	11.73	79.26	—	—	—

Appendix Table 4.26 : Estimates of Cyclical Component of the Collection of Adda Leaf in NCA

Year	Quantity (Qtls.)	Index	Five Years Moving Average	Cyclical Component from		Value (Rs.)	Index	Five Years Moving Average	Cyclical Component from	
				Additive Hypothesis	Multiplicative Hypothesis				Additive Hypothesis	Multiplicative Hypothesis
1.	1666	100.00	—	—	—	25.6	100.00	—	—	—
2.	13487	80.93	—	—	—	16.07	62.77	—	—	—
3.	21848	131.09	109.78	21.31	119.42	26.26	102.58	106.01	–3.43	96.76
4.	20948	125.69	121.33	4.36	103.59	32.56	127.19	123.19	4.00	103.25
5.	18530	111.18	122.86	–11.68	90.49	35.2	137.50	139.45	–1.95	98.60
6.	26293	157.76	116.56	41.20	135.35	47.59	185.90	156.59	29.30	118.71
7.	14764	88.59	104.21	–15.62	85.01	36.88	144.06	159.79	–15.73	90.16
8.	16597	99.59	86.20	13.39	115.53	48.21	188.32	140.88	47.45	133.68
9.	10656	63.94	67.26	–3.32	95.07	36.65	143.16	139.87	3.30	102.36
10.	3521	21.13	54.23	–33.11	38.96	10.99	42.93	121.10	–78.18	35.45
11.	10506	63.04	49.47	13.57	127.44	46.3	180.86	116.64	64.22	155.06
12.	3912	23.47	—	—	—	12.86	50.23	—	—	—
13.	12625	75.75	—	—	—	42.5	166.02	—	—	—

Appendix Table 4.27 : Estimates of Cyclical Component of the Collection of Naramamidi Bark in NCA

Year	Quantity (Qtls.)	Index	Five Years Moving Average	Cyclical Component from		Value (Rs.)	Index	Five Years Moving Average	Cyclical Component from	
				Additive Hypothesis	Multiplicative Hypothesis				Additive Hypothesis	Multiplicative Hypothesis
1.	—	—	—	—	—	—	—	—	—	—
2.	5827	100.00	—	—	—	29.15	100.00	—	—	—
3.	—	—	—	—	—	—	—	—	—	—
4.	224	3.84	—	—	—	0.92	3.16	—	—	—
5.	1149	19.72	—	—	—	6.88	23.60	—	—	—
6.	3158	54.20	70.01	–15.82	77.41	21.1	72.38	146.68	–74.29	49.35
7.	7896	135.51	89.92	45.59	150.70	91.44	313.69	210.19	103.50	149.24
8.	7971	136.79	107.37	29.43	127.41	93.44	320.55	23.95	46.60	117.01
9.	6023	103.36	107.91	–4.54	95.79	93.49	320.72	302.69	18.03	105.96
10.	6233	106.97	84.51	22.46	126.57	99.81	342.40	255.88	86.52	133.81
11.	3316	56.91	85.27	–28.36	66.74	62.99	216.09	304.16	–88.08	71.04
12.	1079	18.52	—	—	—	23.22	79.66	—	—	—
13.	8192	140.59	—	—	—	163.81	561.96	—	—	—

Appendix Table 5.1 : Procurement and Sale Prices of NTFP

Sl. No.	Name of the Commodity	1992-93		1993-94		1994-95		1995-96		1996-97	
		Procurement Price paid to tribals	*Disposal Price (Sale Price)*	*Procurement Price paid to tribals*	*Disposal Price (Sale Price)*	*Procurement Price paid to tribals*	*Disposal Price (Sale Price)*	*Procurement Price paid to tribals*	*Disposal Price (Sale Price)*	*Procurement Price paid to tribals*	*Disposal Price (Sale Price)*
1.	Gum Karaya Gr.I	30.00-40.00	50.75	60.00-80.00	56.73	90.00	138.90	90.00	111.54	100.00	155.93
	Gum Karaya Gr.II	26.00-36.00	—	40.00-48.00	—	52.00	—	60.00	—	70.00	105.50
	Gum Karaya Gr.III	22.00	—	22.00-26.00	—	32.00	—	40.00	—	50.00	77.25
2.	Gum Thiruman Gr.I	25.00	26.28	30.00	34.12	30.00	39.97	30.00	37.17	30.00	66.36
	Gum Thiruman Gr.II	20.00	—	20.00	—	20.00	—	20.00	—	20.00	49.17
	Gum Thiruman Gr.III	—	—	—	—	—	—	—	—	—	—
3.	Gum Olibanum Gr.I	15.00	26.98	15.00	24.44	15.00	20.80	15.00	21.45	15.00	24.86
	Gum Olibanum Gr.II	12.00	—	12.00	—	12.00	—	12.00	—	12.00	17.98
4.	Gum Kondagogu Gr.I	—	—	50.00	—	64.00	—	72.00	79.72	90.00	151.53
	Gum Kondagogu Gr.II	—	—	35.00	—	44.00	—	48.00	—	56.00	96.10
	Gum Kondagogu Gr.III	—	—	22.00	—	26.00	—	32.00	—	40.00	54.46
5.	Gum Dikamali	—	—	4.00	21.00	5.00	7.78	6.00	6.67	6.00	7.20
6.	Myrobalans	2.50	2.55	1.50	2.08	2.00	2.60	3.00	3.32	3.00	4.36
7.	Nux vomica	3.00	3.67	8.00-10.00	12.81	4.00	15.61	4.00	5.04	4.00	4.98
8.	Seeded Tamarind	2.00-2.50	9.65	2.50-3.00	3.63	4.75	4.60	4.00	5.06	6.00	6.34
9.	Deseeded Tamarind	4.00-5.00	4.52	6.00	19.88	8.00	2.87	7.00	10.15	11.00	12.99
10.	Tamarind Seed	0.50	1.52	0.75	1.63	0.75	1.79	1.00	1.79	1.50	1.86
11.	Pungam Seed	4.00	7.14	3.85	3.80	4.00	4.41	4.00	5.22	4.00	5.86
12.	Cleaning nuts	6.00-8.00	7.47	8.00	—	4.00	7.80	4.00	9.52	4.00	9.41
13.	Marking nuts	2.00	2.04	2.00	0.46	2.50	1.67	3.00	3.26	4.40	4.70
14.	Mohua Seed	7.00	26.15	6.00	7.94	7.00	9.56	7.00	9.90	7.50	9.59
15.	Mohua Flower	2.00	2.95	2.50	3.43	2.50	4.11	2.00	1.31	3.00	4.36
16.	Rock Bee Honey	30.00	35.00	25.00	40.00	35.00	40.00	40.00	49.56	40.00	49.17
17.	Apiary Honey	35.00	35.00	35.00	40.00	41.00	40.00	45.00	—	45.00	49.17
18.	Bees wax	55.00	60.00	55.00	60.00	55.00	60.00	55.00	—	55.00	102.86
19.	Sheekakai	12.00	16.77	15.00	13.33	8.00	20.71	8.00	10.84	10.00	15.59
20.	Soapnuts (Forest)	6.50	10.09	7.00	9.36	8.00	7.42	6.00	7.23	6.00	8.11
	Soapnuts (Akkaram)	—	—	—	—	—	—	—	—	8.00	10.03
21.	Hill Brooms (Nos.) each	4.50	3.69	5.00	3.36	5.00	12.46	6.00	10.23	7.00	11.75
22.	Wild brooms	4.50	—	5.00	—	5.00	—	8.00	—	10.00	16.40
23.	Adda leaf	1.40-1.50	1.67	1.50	1.91	2.00	2.55	2.00	2.87	2.00	4.09
24.	R.S.Roots	20.00	—	30.00	29.00	30.00	3.00	40.00	—	40.00	40.00
25.	Naramamidi bark	8.00	10.00	10.00	11.00	10.00	—	10.00	—	12.00	19.59
26.	Amla pulp	—	—	—	—	—	—	4.00	—	4.00	—
27.	Maredugeddalu	—	—	—	—	—	—	—	—	13.00	18.84

APPENDIX TABLE 5.1 *(Contd.)*

Sl. No.	Name of the Commodity	1997-98 Procurement Price paid to tribals	1997-98 Disposal Price (Sale Price)	1998-99 Procurement Price paid to tribals	1998-99 Disposal Price (Sale Price)	1999-00 Procurement Price paid to tribals	1999-00 Disposal Price (Sale Price)	2000-01 Procurement Price paid to tribals	2000-01 Disposal Price (Sale Price)	2001-02 Procurement Price paid to tribals	2001-02 Disposal Price (Sale Price)
1.	Gum Karaya Gr.I	100.00	191.49	100.00	166.68	110.00	179.51	125.00	174.67	125.00	197.91
	Gum Karaya Gr.II	70.00	115.34	70.00	128.88	75.00	120.88	90.00	110.62	90.00	113.60
	Gum Karaya Gr.III	50.00	61.69	50.00	75.44	50.00	89.36	60.00	78.91	60.00	81.87
2.	Gum Thiruman Gr.I	30.00	62.50	30.00	70.00	30.00	34.08	30.00	70.00	50.00	35.43
	Gum Thiruman Gr.II	20.00	33.85	20.00	37.78	20.00	22.87	20.00	55.71	35.00	—
	Gum Thiruman Gr.III	—	—	—	—	—	—	—	—	17.00	—
3.	Gum Olibanum Gr.I	15.00	40.16	24.00	30.79	25.00	28.56	25.00	27.53	20.00	24.88
	Gum Olibanum Gr.II	12.00	28.44	20.00	26.64	20.00	22.80	20.00	—	15.00	—
4.	Gum Kondagogu Gr.I	90.00	157.40	100.00	161.62	100.00	136.03	100.00	114.38	100.00	130.35
	Gum Kondagogu Gr.II	60.00	89.03	60.00	104.92	60.00	110.99	60.00	89.95	60.00	92.60
	Gum Kondagogu Gr.III	42.00	50.29	42.00	50.49	42.00	76.96	42.00	70.86	42.00	73.60
5.	Gum Dikamali	8.00	14.00	10.00	11.55	10.00	86.67	10.00	14.01	17.00	22.30
6.	Myrobalans	3.25	5.86	4.00	8.14	7.00	8.93	7.00	7.41	3.00	5.01
7.	Nux vomica	3.50	4.60	3.75	14.80	3.00	4.35	5.00	5.53	5.50	7.26
8.	Seeded Tamarind	5.25	6.02	6.50	7.29	7.00	8.38	6.00	6.88	4.00	4.43
9.	Deseeded Tamarind	10.00	8.83	15.00	13.32	15.00	17.53	13.00	11.00	8.84	7.60
10.	Tamarind Seed	2.00	3.60	2.00	3.60	3.00	3.48	1.60	2.20	1.50	2.04
11.	Pungam Seed	4.25	4.26	3.75	5.03	5.00	6.85	5.00	4.73	4.50	5.51
12.	Cleaning nuts	4.00	7.98	4.00	6.72	4.00	5.46	4.00	4.75	4.00	11.02
13.	Marking nuts	2.75	4.06	3.00	4.62	3.00	5.79	3.00	5.29	2.00	2.43
14.	Mohua Seed	7.50	8.32	10.00	8.47	10.00	7.86	7.00	6.60	6.50	7.80
15.	Mohua Flower	3.75	2.95	4.00	3.71	3.50	5.49	3.50	5.99	4.80	4.57
16.	Rock Bee Honey	40.00	47.03	30.00	39.68	40.00	55.82	40.00	51.98	40.00	49.03
17.	Apiary Honey	45.00	52.59	35.00	—	40.00	55.82	40.00	—	40.00	49.03
18.	Bees wax	55.00	107.37	50.00	89.55	50.00	122.86	70.00	—	70.00	90.71
19.	Sheekakai	9.40	9.83	4.75	8.73	5.00	8.62	7.00	11.38	9.00	14.08
20.	Soapnuts (Forest)	7.40	7.81	11.00	11.11	12.00	12.17	10.00	14.00	8.00	8.21
	Soapnuts (Akkaram)	8.00	10.37	12.00	12.34	15.00	15.33	13.00	18.00	14.00	8.21
21.	Hill brooms (Nos.) each	8.00	4.43	9.00	5.48	9.00	8.95	9.00	11.41	8.00 to 16.00	13.57
22.	Wild brooms	11.00	13.62	11.00	12.05	11.00	16.52	11.00	15.43	10.00 to 12.00	19.97
23.	Adda leaf	2.50	5.01	2.50-5.00	4.92	2.50-3.50	4.95	4.40	7.48	3.50	4.18
24.	R.S.Roots	40.00	70.00	40.00	—	40.00	—	40.00	42.00	60.00	—
25.	Naramamidi bark	12.00	20.84	12.00	24.25	12.00	22.79	19.00	25.66	23.00	24.00
26.	Amla pulp	4.00	5.00	7.00	6.60	7.00	15.00	20.00	22.00	17.00	17.04
27.	Maredugeddalu	10.00	21.41	8.00	15.81	10.00	21.22	—	—	15.00	24.02

APPENDIX TABLE 5.1 *(Contd.)*

Sl. No.	*Name of the Commodity*	*2002-03*		*2003-04*		*2004-05*	
		Procurement Price paid to tribals	*Disposal Price (Sale Price)*	*Procurement Price paid to tribals*	*Disposal Price (Sale Price)*	*Procurement Price paid to tribals*	*Disposal Price (Sale Price)*
1.	Gum Karaya Gr. I	125.00	184.37	140.00	175.75	140.00	147.48
	Gum Karaya Gr. II	90.00	115.20	100.00	123.34	100.00	122.21
	Gum Karaya Gr. III	60.00	76.23	75.00	81.15	75.00	91.73
2.	Gum Thiruman Gr. I	40.00	60.00	80.00	75.00	80.00	92.50
	Gum Thiruman Gr. II	44.00	50.00	60.00	64.62	60.00	84.89
	Gum Thiruman Gr. III	30.00	31.43	50.00	48.52	50.00	65.74
3.	Gum Olibanum Gr. I	20.00	25.25	20.00	26.74	25.00	30.13
	Gum Olibanum Gr. II	15.00	16.56	15.00	17.55	20.00	18.01
4.	Gum Kondagogu Gr. I	100.00	125.87	120.00	129.67	120.00	131.73
	Gum Kondagogu Gr. II	60.00	78.94	80.00	86.40	80.00	92.90
	Gum Kondagogu Gr. III	42.00	65.49	60.00	74.45	60.00	78.42
5.	Gum Dikamali	11.00	18.16	12.00	14.11	12.00	13.31
6.	Myrobalans	1.50	8.33	1.50	1.97	2.25	1.48
7.	Nux vomica	13.00	16.35	17.00	148.24	19.00	25.62
8.	Seeded Tamarind	4.00	4.57	10.00	3.69	7.00	11.42
9.	Deseeded Tamarind	7.37	9.32	16.00	6.91	11.00	34.86
10.	Tamarind Seed	2.50	2.62	6.00	3.02	4.00	7.59
11.	Pungam Seed	5.50	6.29	6.00	7.38	6.50	7.62
12.	Cleaning nuts	10.00	9.35	30.00	13.86	35.00	35.03
13.	Marking nuts	2.50	3.07	3.00	3.95	4.00	4.61
14.	Mohua Seed	10.00	10.72	10.00	11.51	11.00	14.01
15.	Mohua Flower	5.00	5.40	5.00	6.10	6.00	8.96
16.	Rock Bee Honey	72.00	72.00	80.00	33.70	80.00	131.11
17.	Apiary Honey	60.00	72.00	80.00	—	80.00	—
18.	Bees wax	70.00	99.00	100.00	99.19	100.00	172.27
19.	Sheekakai	10.00	15.67	10.00	14.82	10.00	13.46
20.	Soapnuts (Forest)	12.00	6.54	12.00	5.78	5.54	6.28
	Soapnuts (Akkaram)	15.00	6.30	15.00	—	7.00	6.28
21.	Hill Brooms (Nos.) each	12.00	13.24	16..00	12.36	16..00	16.72
22.	Wild brooms	10.00 to 12.00	19.19	10.00 to 12.00	14.82	12.00	12.57
23.	Adda leaf	3.50	4.88	3.50	17.51	3.50	5.47
24.	R.S. Roots	60.00	—	60.00	—	60.00	—
25.	Naramamidi bark	23.00	29.48	23.00	31.22	23.00	37.36
26.	Amla pulp	25.00	32.00	25.00	19.00	20.00	18.67
27.	Maredugeddalu	17.00	27.46	17.00	21.10	20.00	21.67

Appendix Table 5.2 : Estimated Values of the Parameters of Linear Trend Equations of the Procurement Prices of the Prominent NTFP in NCA : 1991-92 to 2002-03

Commodities	*a*	*b*	t_b	R^2	*F-Value*
Adda leaf	87.1061	25.9196	7.08	0.8335	50.06
Cleaning nuts	575.0909	–2.5909	–0.16	0.0026	0.03
Deseeded Tamarind	536.7121	55.4546	2.66	0.4144	7.08
Gum Dikamali	15.2574	120.7167	6.96	0.8433	48.45
Gum Karaya	2940.9090	566.7832	8.51	0.8786	72.40
Gum Kondagogu	3610.1790	342.7143	2.54	0.5175	6.44
Gum Olibanum	1282.1210	90.6993	3.39	0.5343	11.47
Gum Thiruman	2206.0760	21.7448	1.61	0.2068	2.61
Hill Broom	3.3949	0.6695	7.26	0.8541	52.70
Honey	2461.0300	148.4441	3.50	0.5501	12.23
Maredugeddalu	58.0000	133.0000	6.40	0.9762	40.95
Marking nuts	123.4697	14.8252	1.90	0.2659	3.62
Mohua flower	155.1515	25.1434	8.24	0.8717	67.92
Mohua seed	675.5303	7.0979	1.25	0.1346	1.56
Myrobalans	181.0455	27.1853	1.76	0.2374	3.11
Naramamidi bark	37.2571	175.1075	11.26	0.9337	126.84
Nux vomica	236.4545	32.8147	2.55	0.3949	6.53
Pungam seed	347.8030	9.8636	3.49	0.5486	12.15
Seeded Tamarind	289.6212	27.5839	3.31	0.5222	10.93
Sheekakai	702.6515	20.1049	1.13	0.1131	1.28
Soapnuts	695.8030	18.6329	1.11	0.1099	1.23
Tamarind	73.0152	13.5105	3.66	0.5732	13.43
Wild Broom	983.2143	7.5000	0.56	0.0594	0.32

Appendix Table 5.3 : Estimated Values of the Parameters of Linear Trend Equations of the Sale Prices of the Prominent NTFP in NCA : 1991-92 to 2002-03

Commodities	*a*	*b*	t_b	R^2	*F-Value*
Adda leaf	113.1364	41.5175	4.80	0.6975	23.06
Cleaning nuts	727.9369	7.8093	0.45	0.0219	0.20
Deseeded Tamarind	589.5455	55.9546	2.01	0.2881	4.05
Gum Dikamali	123.7704	142.9786	5.50	0.7708	30.27
Gum Karaya	5059.1670	537.1923	3.62	0.5677	13.13
Gum Kondagogu	9450.7860	41.1429	0.18	0.0055	0.03
Gum Olibanum	1882.0910	99.0629	1.88	0.2616	3.54
Gum Thiruman	2480.8940	186.9650	1.99	0.2838	3.96
Hill Broom	256.3808	–20.6671	–1.41	0.1812	1.99
Honey	2516.3180	200.4091	1.53	0.2259	2.34
Maredugeddalu	–1272.8300	339.5000	6.57	0.9774	43.17
Marking nuts	149.3182	23.1049	2.25	0.3365	5.07
Mohua flower	252.3333	24.6539	4.05	0.6208	16.37
Mohua seed	954.9242	–10.8217	–1.07	0.1024	1.14
Myrobalans	240.3788	31.6084	1.61	0.2063	2.60
Naramamidi bark	-389.5960	296.1930	4.60	0.7791	21.16
Nux vomica	183.7424	61.3986	2.63	0.4079	6.89
Pungam seed	419.5303	14.3287	2.33	0.3522	5.44
Seeded Tamarind	350.0303	27.9056	2.33	0.3515	5.42
Sheekakai	852.6667	39.0385	1.74	0.2329	3.04
Soapnuts	824.7424	17.8986	0.77	0.0563	0.60
Tamarind	130.0000	14.7692	2.42	0.3701	5.88
Wild Broom	175.5811	151.7162	3.93	0.8374	15.45

Appendix Table 5.4 : Estimated Values of the Parameters of Exponential Trend Equations of the Procurement Prices of the Prominent NTFP in NCA : 1991-92 to 2002-03

Commodities	*a*	*b*	t_b	R^2	*F-Value*
Adda leaf	4.7251	0.1132	8.13*	0.8685	66.023
Cleaning nuts	6.3321	–0.0085	–0.30	0.0091	0.092
Deseeded Tamarind	6.2884	0.0695	2.96*	0.4674	8.774
Gum Dikamali	5.4831	0.1576	9.09*	0.9019	82.701
Gum Karaya	8.1076	0.0970	7.26*	0.8404	52.666
Gum Kondagogu	8.2446	0.0613	2.41**	0.4928	5.829
Gum Olibanum	7.1854	0.0497	3.65*	0.5711	13.317
Gum Thiruman	7.7018	0.0088	1.57	0.1969	2.452
Hill Broom	1.3949	0.0913	7.45*	0.8605	55.505
Honey	7.8054	0.0477	3.30*	0.5216	10.905
Maredugeddalu	6.3678	0.0869	7.54*	0.9827	56.818
Marking nuts	4.6238	0.0998	2.80*	0.4399	7.854
Mohua flower	5.1949	0.0809	10.17*	0.9118	103.429
Mohua seed	6.5176	0.0092	1.18	0.1222	1.393
Myrobalans	5.2892	0.0699	1.69	0.2215	2.846
Naramamidi bark	5.8718	0.1614	9.97*	0.9169	99.338
Nux vomica	5.6382	0.0631	2.81*	0.4405	7.874
Pungam seed	5.8671	0.0227	3.41*	0.5374	11.615
Seeded Tamarind	5.6689	0.0672	3.52*	0.5541	12.425
Sheekakai	6.5551	0.0211	0.90	0.0757	0.818
Soapnuts	6.5605	0.0184	0.95	0.0822	0.895
Tamarind	4.3861	0.0951	4.64*	0.6825	21.495
Wild Broom	6.8896	0.0073	0.55	0.0578	0.307

* Significance at 1 per cent level.
** Significance at 5 per cent level.

Appendix Table 5.5 : Estimated Values of the Parameters of Exponential Trend Equations of the Sale Prices of the Prominent NTFP in NCA : 1990-91 to 2002-03

Commodities	*a*	*b*	t_b	R^2	*F-Value*
Adda leaf	5.0132	0.1264	5.39*	0.7788	35.212
Cleaning nuts	6.6003	0.0047	0.19	0.0044	0.040
Deseeded Tamarind	6.3440	0.0683	2.44**	0.3796	6.119
Gum Dikamali	5.9201	0.1372	6.27*	0.8135	39.262
Gum Karaya	8.5121	0.0756	3.99*	0.6137	15.883
Gum Kondagogu	9.1515	0.0035	0.15	0.0036	0.022
Gum Olibanum	7.5269	0.0423	2.23**	0.3320	4.971
Gum Thiruman	7.8019	0.0549	2.14**	0.3138	4.573
Hill Broom	5.0764	−0.2299	−1.88	0.2821	3.536
Honey	7.8587	0.0443	0.81	0.0751	0.650
Maredugeddalu	6.2939	0.1371	8.73*	0.9870	76.168
Marking nuts	4.9264	0.1004	2.84*	0.4468	8.077
Mohua flower	5.5795	0.0626	4.03*	0.6186	16.222
Mohua seed	6.8639	−0.0135	−1.16	0.1188	1.348
Myrobalans	5.6086	0.0540	1.18	0.1229	1.402
Naramamidi bark	5.4629	0.2447	3.12*	0.6191	9.750
Nux vomica	5.7218	0.0841	3.34*	0.5279	11.182
Pungam seed	6.0485	0.0275	2.37**	0.3594	5.610
Seeded Tamarind	5.8373	0.0598	2.66*	0.4141	7.067
Sheekakai	6.7431	0.0361	1.81	0.2477	3.293
Soapnuts	6.7304	0.0128	0.56	0.0305	0.315
Tamarind	4.8636	0.0751	3.04*	.4803	9.240
Wild Broom	6.4475	0.0972	4.08*	.8474	16.662

* Significance at 1 per cent level.
** Significance at 5 per cent level.

Appendix Table 5.6 : Estimates of Cyclical Component of the Collection of Gum Karaya in NCA

Year	Procurement Price	Index	Five Years Moving Average	Cyclical Component from		Sale Price	Index	Five Years Moving Average	Cyclical Component from	
				Additive Hypothesis	Multiplicative Hypothesis				Additive Hypothesis	Multiplicative Hypothesis
1.	3000	100.00	—	—	—	4303	100.00	—	—	—
2.	4000	133.33	—	—	—	5277	122.64	—	—	—
3.	4000	133.33	153.33	–20.00	86.96	5277	122.64	148.27	–25.64	82.71
4.	4500	150.00	183.33	–33.33	81.82	5890	136.88	178.52	–41.64	76.67
5.	7500	250.00	200.67	49.33	124.58	11154	259.21	196.86	62.36	131.68
6.	7500	250.00	224.00	26.00	111.61	10811	251.24	220.40	30.85	114.00
7.	6600	220.00	246.67	–26.67	89.19	9222	214.32	244.15	–29.83	87.78
8.	7500	250.00	256.67	–6.67	97.40	10341	240.32	237.45	2.87	101.21
9.	7900	263.33	266.67	–3.33	98.75	11000	255.64	233.59	22.05	109.44
10.	9000	300.00	282.67	17.33	106.13	9714	225.75	235.54	–9.79	95.84
11.	9000	300.00	—	—	—	9980	231.93	—	—	—
12.	9000	300.00	—	—	—	9642	224.08	—	—	—

Appendix Table 5.7 : Estimates of Cyclical Component of the Collection of Gum Thirmun in NCA

Year	Procurement Price	Index	Five Years Moving Average	Cyclical Component from		Sale Price	Index	Five Years Moving Average	Cyclical Component from	
				Additive Hypothesis	Multiplicative Hypothesis				Additive Hypothesis	Multiplicative Hypothesis
1.	2174	100.00	—	—	—	2480	100.00	—	—	—
2.	2403	110.53	—	—	—	2227	89.80	—	—	—
3.	2286	105.15	106.95	46.38	98.31	3411	137.54	111.56	25.98	123.28
4.	2300	105.80	108.17	75.16	97.81	2000	80.65	137.85	–57.20	58.50
5.	2463	113.29	106.55	94.12	106.33	3716	149.84	152.61	–2.77	98.18
6.	2306	106.07	105.80	118.20	100.25	5739	231.41	158.57	72.84	145.93
7.	2227	102.44	104.57	142.09	97.96	4058	163.63	162.60	1.02	100.63
8.	2205	101.43	103.27	153.40	98.22	4150	167.34	178.87	–11.53	93.55
9.	2166	99.63	107.17	159.50	92.97	2500	100.81	170.17	–69.36	59.24
10.	2321	106.76	110.49	172.18	96.63	5733	231.17	167.12	64.05	138.32
11.	2730	125.57	—	—	—	4660	187.90	—	—	—
12.	2588	119.04	—	—	—	3680	148.39	—	—	—

Appendix Table 5.8 : Estimates of Cyclical Component of the Collection of Gum Olibanum in NCA

Year	Procurement Price	Index	Five Years Moving Average	Cyclical Component from		Sale Price	Index	Five Years Moving Average	Cyclical Component from	
				Additive Hypothesis	Multiplicative Hypothesis				Additive Hypothesis	Multiplicative Hypothesis
1.	1490	100.00	—	—	—	1698	100.00	—	—	—
2.	1470	98.66	—	—	—	1698	100.00	—	—	—
3.	1450	97.32	97.99	–0.67	99.32	2444	143.93	118.55	25.38	121.41
4.	1440	96.64	98.12	–1.48	98.50	2080	122.50	123.77	–1.27	98.97
5.	1450	97.32	110.60	–13.29	87.99	2145	126.33	148.86	–22.53	84.86
6.	1500	100.67	123.36	–22.68	81.61	2141	126.09	155.63	–29.54	81.02
7.	2400	161.07	136.64	24.43	117.88	3828	225.44	175.05	50.39	128.78
8.	2400	161.07	149.80	11.28	107.53	3019	177.80	182.21	–4.42	97.58
9.	2430	163.09	156.51	6.58	104.20	3729	219.61	186.28	33.33	117.89
10.	2430	163.09	151.14	11.95	107.90	2753	162.13	168.17	–6.04	96.41
11.	2000	134.23	—	—	—	2486	146.41	—	—	—
12.	2000	134.23	—	—	—	2291	134.92	—	—	—

Appendix Table 5.9 : Estimates of Cyclical Component of the Collection of Gum Kondagogu in NCA

Year	Procurement Price	Index	Five Years Moving Average	Cyclical Component from		Sale Price	Index	Five Years Moving Average	Cyclical Component from	
				Additive Hypothesis	Multiplicative Hypothesis				Additive Hypothesis	Multiplicative Hypothesis
1.	—	—	—	—	—	—	—	—	—	—
2.	—	—	—	—	—	—	—	—	—	—
3.	—	—	—	—	—	—	—	—	—	—
4.	—	—	—	—	—	—	—	—	—	—
5.	3887	100.00	—	—	—	7972	100.00	—	—	—
6.	6339	163.08	—	—	—	10046	126.02	—	—	—
7.	6170	158.73	157.30	1.43	100.91	9694	121.60	125.94	–4.34	96.55
8.	7283	187.37	175.84	11.53	106.56	10813	135.64	129.80	5.84	104.50
9.	6893	177.33	181.17	–3.83	97.88	11675	146.45	131.79	14.66	111.13
10.	7489	192.67	184.15	8.52	104.62	9511	119.31	127.18	–7.87	93.81
11.	7375	189.74	—	—	—	10837	135.94	—	—	—
12.	6750	173.66	—	—	—	7856	98.54	—	—	—

Appendix Table 5.10 : Estimates of Cyclical Component of the Collection of Gum Dikamali in NCA

Year	Procurement Price	Index	Five Years Moving Average	Cyclical Component from		Sale Price	Index	Five Years Moving Average	Cyclical Component from	
				Additive Hypothesis	Multiplicative Hypothesis				Additive Hypothesis	Multiplicative Hypothesis
1.	302	100.00	—	—	—	515	100.00	—	—	—
2.	394	130.46	—	—	—	554	107.57	—	—	—
3.	386	127.81	124.37	3.44	102.77	400	77.67	110.52	–32.85	70.27
4.	394	130.46	137.62	–7.15	94.80	777	150.87	118.49	32.39	127.34
5.	402	133.11	180.33	–47.22	73.82	600	116.50	151.34	–34.83	76.98
6.	502	166.23	154.77	11.46	107.40	720	139.81	167.42	–27.61	83.51
7.	1039	344.04	194.90	149.14	176.52	1400	271.84	171.55	100.29	158.46
8.	—	0.00	234.50	–234.50	0.00	814	158.06	210.44	–52.38	75.11
9.	1000	331.13	313.77	17.35	105.53	—	—	283.74	–283.74	0.00
10.	1000	331.13	344.30	–13.18	96.17	1401	272.04	303.93	–31.89	89.51
11.	1699	562.58	—	—	—	2230	433.01	—	—	—
12.	1500	496.69	—	—	—	1816	352.62	—	—	—

Appendix Table 5.11 : Estimates of Cyclical Component of the Collection of Myrobalans in NCA

Year	Procurement Price	Index	Five Years Moving Average	Cyclical Component from		Sale Price	Index	Five Years Moving Average	Cyclical Component from	
				Additive Hypothesis	Multiplicative Hypothesis				Additive Hypothesis	Multiplicative Hypothesis
1.	220	100.00	—	—	—	314	100.00	—	—	—
2.	165	75.00	—	—	—	269	85.67	—	—	—
3.	200	90.91	98.36	–7.45	92.42	208	66.24	88.09	–21.85	75.20
4.	200	90.91	107.91	–17.00	84.25	260	82.80	95.86	–13.06	86.38
5.	297	135.00	129.27	5.73	104.43	332	105.73	116.05	–10.32	91.11
6.	325	147.73	165.64	–17.91	89.19	436	138.85	133.25	5.61	104.21
7.	400	181.82	211.09	–29.27	86.13	586	186.62	173.57	13.06	107.52
8.	600	272.73	247.73	25.00	110.09	478	152.23	211.27	–59.04	72.05
9.	700	318.18	247.73	70.45	128.44	893	284.39	215.35	69.04	132.06
10.	700	318.18	226.00	92.18	140.79	924	294.27	187.58	106.69	156.88
11.	325	147.73	—	—	—	500	159.24	—	—	—
12.	161	73.18	—	—	—	150	47.77	—	—	—

Appendix Table 5.12 : Estimates of Cyclical Component of the Collection of Nux Vomica in NCA

Year	Procurement Price	Index	Five Years Moving Average	Cyclical Component from		Sale Price	Index	Five Years Moving Average	Cyclical Component from	
				Additive Hypothesis	Multiplicative Hypothesis				Additive Hypothesis	Multiplicative Hypothesis
1.	240	100.00	—	—	—	278	100.00	—	—	—
2.	352	146.67	—	—	—	432	155.40	—	—	—
3.	449	187.08	161.33	25.75	115.96	473	170.14	159.14	11.01	106.92
4.	497	207.08	171.00	36.08	121.10	525	188.85	174.89	13.96	107.98
5.	398	165.83	172.17	–6.33	96.32	504	181.29	176.83	4.46	102.52
6.	356	148.33	166.42	–18.08	89.13	497	178.78	177.19	1.58	100.89
7.	366	152.50	153.75	–1.25	99.19	459	165.11	170.72	–5.61	96.71
8.	380	158.33	160.67	–2.33	98.55	478	171.94	174.17	–2.23	98.72
9.	345	143.75	176.42	–32.67	81.48	435	156.47	190.65	–34.17	82.08
10.	481	200.42	228.25	–27.83	87.81	552	198.56	275.25	–76.69	72.14
11.	545	227.08	—	—	—	726	261.15	—	—	—
12.	988	411.67	—	—	—	1635	588.13	—	—	—

Appendix Table 5.13 : Estimates of Cyclical Component of the Collection of Seeded Tamarind in NCA

Year	Procurement Price	Index	Five Years Moving Average	Cyclical Component from		Sale Price	Index	Five Years Moving Average	Cyclical Component from	
				Additive Hypothesis	Multiplicative Hypothesis				Additive Hypothesis	Multiplicative Hypothesis
1.	240	100.00	—	—	—	266	100.00	—	—	—
2.	270	112.50	—	—	—	342	128.57	—	—	—
3.	375	156.25	143.50	12.75	108.89	380	142.86	146.92	–4.06	97.24
4.	400	166.67	166.42	0.25	100.15	460	172.93	174.59	–1.65	99.05
5.	437	182.08	187.67	–5.58	97.02	506	190.23	194.14	–3.91	97.99
6.	515	214.58	212.25	2.33	101.10	634	238.35	220.38	17.97	108.15
7.	525	218.75	231.00	–12.25	94.70	602	226.32	248.80	–22.48	90.96
8.	670	279.17	243.75	35.42	114.53	729	274.06	262.48	11.58	104.41
9.	625	260.42	249.17	11.25	104.52	838	315.04	250.53	64.51	125.75
10.	590	245.83	238.75	7.08	102.97	688	258.65	239.62	19.02	107.94
11.	580	241.67	—	—	—	475	178.57	—	—	—
12.	400	166.67	—	—	—	457	171.80	—	—	—

Appendix Table 5.14 : Estimates of Cyclical Component of the Collection of Deseeded Tamarind in NCA

Year	Procurement Price	Index	Five Years Moving Average	Cyclical Component from		Sale Price	Index	Five Years Moving Average	Cyclical Component from	
				Additive Hypothesis	Multiplicative Hypothesis				Additive Hypothesis	Multiplicative Hypothesis
1.	525	100.00	—	—	—	527	100.00	—	—	—
2.	435	82.86	—	—	—	452	85.77	—	—	—
3.	641	122.10	118.21	3.89	103.29	596	113.09	128.58	–15.48	87.96
4.	704	134.10	137.52	–3.43	97.51	798	151.42	157.87	–6.45	95.91
5	798	152.00	163.24	–11.24	93.12	1015	192.60	174.23	18.37	110.54
6.	1032	196.57	183.96	12.61	106.85	1299	246.49	202.20	44.29	121.90
7.	1110	211.43	209.56	1.87	100.89	883	167.55	238.44	–70.89	70.27
8.	1185	225.71	230.17	–4.46	98.06	1333	252.94	241.37	11.57	104.80
9.	1376	262.10	224.50	37.60	116.75	1753	332.64	220.87	111.76	150.60
10.	1339	255.05	210.32	44.72	121.26	1092	207.21	222.73	–15.52	93.03
11.	883	168.19	—	—	—	759	144.02	—	—	—
12.	738	140.57	—	—	—	932	176.85	—	—	—

Appendix Table 5.15 : Estimates of Cyclical Component of the Collection of Tamarind Seed in NCA

Year	Procurement Price	Index	Five Years Moving Average	Cyclical Component from		Sale Price	Index	Five Years Moving Average	Cyclical Component from	
				Additive Hypothesis	Multiplicative Hypothesis				Additive Hypothesis	Multiplicative Hypothesis
1.	80	100.00	—	—	—	100	100.00	—	—	—
2.	84	105.00	—	—	—	151	151.00	—	—	—
3.	97	121.25	132.75	–11.50	91.34	163	163.00	154.60	8.40	105.43
4.	100	125.00	150.25	–25.25	83.19	179	179.00	171.80	7.20	104.19
5.	170	212.50	179.25	33.25	118.55	180	180.00	213.60	–33.60	84.27
6.	150	187.50	205.00	–17.50	91.46	186	186.00	253.00	–67.00	73.52
7.	200	250.00	255.00	–5.00	98.04	360	360.00	286.80	73.20	125.52
8.	200	250.00	252.50	–2.50	99.01	360	360.00	293.80	66.20	122.53
9.	300	375.00	260.00	115.00	144.23	348	348.00	297.60	50.40	116.94
10.	160	200.00	262.25	–62.25	76.26	215	215.00	278.60	–63.60	77.17
11.	180	225.00	—	—	—	205	205.00	—	—	—
12.	209	261.25	—	—	—	265	265.00	—	—	—

Appendix Table 5.16 : Estimates of Cyclical Component of the Collection of Pungam Seed in NCA

Year	Procurement Price	Index	Five Years Moving Average	Cyclical Component from		Sale Price	Index	Five Years Moving Average	Cyclical Component from	
				Additive Hypothesis	Multiplicative Hypothesis				Additive Hypothesis	Multiplicative Hypothesis
1.	390	100.00	—	—	—	436	100.00	—	—	—
2.	400	102.56	—	—	—	500	114.68	—	—	—
3.	383	98.21	98.87	–0.67	99.33	400	91.74	105.46	–13.72	86.99
4.	355	91.03	98.72	–7.69	92.21	441	101.15	112.34	–11.19	90.04
5.	400	102.56	96.51	6.05	106.27	522	119.72	108.94	10.78	109.89
6.	387	99.23	97.28	1.95	102.00	586	134.40	113.67	20.73	118.24
7.	357	91.54	102.15	–10.62	89.61	426	97.71	124.86	–27.16	78.25
8.	398	102.05	104.72	–2.67	97.45	503	115.37	122.61	–7.25	94.09
9.	450	115.38	107.95	7.44	106.89	685	157.11	120.96	36.15	129.88
10.	450	115.38	116.46	–1.08	99.08	473	108.49	130.32	–21.83	83.25
11.	450	115.38	—	—	—	550	126.15	—	—	—
12.	523	134.10	—	—	—	630	144.50	—	—	—

Appendix Table 5.17 : Estimates of Cyclical Component of the Collection of Cleaning Nuts in NCA

Year	Procurement Price	Index	Five Years Moving Average	Cyclical Component from		Sale Price	Index	Five Years Moving Average	Cyclical Component from	
				Additive Hypothesis	Multiplicative Hypothesis				Additive Hypothesis	Multiplicative Hypothesis
1.	573	100.00	—	—	—	649	100.00	—	—	—
2.	750	130.89	—	—	—	747	115.10	—	—	—
3.	790	137.87	108.17	29.70	127.46	—	0.00	96.36	–96.36	0.00
4.	600	104.71	102.13	2.58	102.53	780	120.18	105.36	14.82	114.07
5.	386	67.36	89.91	–22.55	74.92	951	146.53	106.93	39.60	137.03
6.	400	69.81	76.30	–6.49	91.49	941	144.99	127.64	17.35	113.59
7.	400	69.81	69.32	0.49	100.70	798	122.96	120.40	2.56	102.12
8.	400	69.81	69.81	0.00	100.00	672	103.54	105.73	–2.19	97.93
9.	400	69.81	83.77	–13.96	83.33	545	83.98	110.63	–26.66	75.91
10.	400	69.81	97.73	–27.92	71.43	475	73.19	114.85	–41.66	63.72
11.	800	139.62	—	—	—	1100	169.49	—	—	—
12.	800	139.62	—	—	—	935	144.07	—	—	—

Appendix Table 5.18 : Estimates of Cyclical Component of the Collection of Marking Nuts in NCA

Year	Procurement Price	Index	Five Years Moving Average	Cyclical Component from		Sale Price	Index	Five Years Moving Average	Cyclical Component from	
				Additive Hypothesis	Multiplicative Hypothesis				Additive Hypothesis	Multiplicative Hypothesis
1.	80	100.00	—	—	—	121	100.00	—	—	—
2.	75	93.75	—	—	—	104	85.95	—	—	—
3.	125	156.25	176.25	–20.00	88.65	181	149.59	148.60	0.99	100.67
4.	140	175.00	266.25	–91.25	65.73	167	138.02	206.28	–68.26	66.91
5.	285	356.25	310.00	46.25	114.92	326	269.42	256.20	13.22	105.16
6.	440	550.00	351.25	198.75	156.58	470	388.43	303.14	85.29	128.14
7.	250	312.50	381.25	–68.75	81.97	406	335.54	321.65	13.88	104.32
8.	290	362.50	371.50	–9.00	97.58	465	384.30	355.21	29.09	108.19
9.	260	325.00	310.75	14.25	104.59	279	230.58	317.19	–86.61	72.69
10.	246	307.50	310.75	–3.25	98.95	529	437.19	300.66	136.53	145.41
11.	197	246.25	—	—	—	240	198.35	—	—	—
12.	250	312.50	—	—	—	306	252.89	—	—	—

Appendix Table 5.19 : Estimates of Cyclical Component of the Collection of Mohua Seed in NCA

Year	Procurement Price	Index	Five Years Moving Average	Cyclical Component from		Sale Price	Index	Five Years Moving Average	Cyclical Component from	
				Additive Hypothesis	Multiplicative Hypothesis				Additive Hypothesis	Multiplicative Hypothesis
1.	700	100.00	—	—	—	1038	100.00	—	—	—
2.	700	100.00	—	—	—	902	86.90	—	—	—
3.	605	86.43	100.00	–13.57	86.43	794	76.49	90.19	–13.70	84.81
4.	745	106.43	101.43	5.00	104.93	957	92.20	88.67	3.53	103.98
5.	750	107.14	101.14	6.00	105.93	990	95.38	87.32	8.05	109.22
6.	750	107.14	106.43	0.71	100.67	959	92.39	88.34	4.05	104.58
7.	690	98.57	105.14	–6.57	93.75	832	80.15	85.05	–4.89	94.25
8.	790	112.86	103.71	9.14	108.82	847	81.60	78.69	2.91	103.70
9.	700	100.00	100.86	–0.86	99.15	786	75.72	75.24	0.48	100.64
10.	700	100.00	106.29	–6.29	94.09	660	63.58	79.83	–16.24	79.65
11.	650	92.86	—	—	—	780	75.14	—	—	—
12.	880	125.71	—	—	—	1070	103.08	—	—	—

Appendix Table 5.20 : Estimates of Cyclical Component of the Collection of Mohua Flower in NCA

Year	*Procurement Price*	*Index*	*Five Years Moving Average*	*Cyclical Component from*		*Sale Price*	*Index*	*Five Years Moving Average*	*Cyclical Component from*	
				Additive Hypothesis	*Multiplicative Hypothesis*				*Additive Hypothesis*	*Multiplicative Hypothesis*
1.	196	100.00	—	—	—	230	100.00	—	—	—
2.	197	100.51	—	—	—	295	128.26	—	—	—
3.	241	122.96	118.57	4.39	103.70	342	148.70	148.17	0.52	100.35
4.	244	124.49	128.57	–4.08	96.83	411	178.70	166.09	12.61	107.59
5.	284	144.90	138.27	6.63	104.80	426	185.22	166.09	19.13	111.52
6.	294	150.00	152.04	–2.04	98.66	436	189.57	168.61	20.96	112.43
7.	292	148.98	162.76	–13.78	91.54	295	128.26	180.61	–52.35	71.02
8.	376	191.84	181.84	10.00	105.50	371	161.30	195.65	–34.35	82.44
9.	349	178.06	200.71	–22.65	88.71	549	238.70	197.48	41.22	120.87
10.	471	240.31	211.73	28.57	113.49	599	260.43	218.78	41.65	119.04
11.	479	244.39	—	—	—	457	198.70	—	—	—
12.	400	204.08	—	—	—	540	234.78	—	—	—

Appendix Table 5.21 : Estimates of Cyclical Component of the Collection of Honey in NCA

Year	Procurement Price	Index	Five Years Moving Average	Cyclical Component from		Sale Price	Index	Five Years Moving Average	Cyclical Component from	
				Additive Hypothesis	Multiplicative Hypothesis				Additive Hypothesis	Multiplicative Hypothesis
1.	2983	100.00	—	—	—	—	—	—	—	—
2.	1936	64.90	—	—	—	3000	100.00	—	—	—
3.	2478	83.07	96.49	–13.42	86.09	2500	83.33	—	—	—
4.	3048	102.18	103.20	–1.02	99.01	3100	103.33	119.85	–16.51	86.22
5.	3947	132.32	116.64	15.68	113.44	4436	147.87	131.53	16.34	112.42
6.	3983	133.52	120.63	12.89	110.69	4941	164.70	120.68	44.02	136.48
7.	3941	132.12	123.66	8.45	106.84	4752	158.40	100.01	58.39	158.38
8.	3073	103.02	124.02	–21.00	83.07	873	29.10	105.11	–76.01	27.69
9.	3500	117.33	124.13	–6.80	94.52	—	0.00	104.83	–104.83	0.00
10.	4000	134.09	126.01	8.08	106.41	5200	173.33	107.08	66.25	161.87
11.	4000	134.09	—	—	—	4900	163.33	—	—	—
12.	4222	141.54	—	—	—	5089	169.63	—	—	—

Appendix Table 5.22 : Estimates of Cyclical Component of the Collection of Sheekakai in NCA

Year	Procurement Price	Index	Five Years Moving Average	Cyclical Component from		Sale Price	Index	Five Years Moving Average	Cyclical Component from	
				Additive Hypothesis	Multiplicative Hypothesis				Additive Hypothesis	Multiplicative Hypothesis
1.	555	100.00	—	—	—	811	100.00	—	—	—
2.	840	151.35	—	—	—	713	87.92	—	—	—
3.	950	171.17	147.57	23.60	116.00	1333	164.36	120.91	43.45	135.94
4.	950	171.17	162.16	9.01	105.56	1050	129.47	139.36	–9.89	92.90
5.	800	144.14	157.12	–12.97	91.74	996	122.81	146.02	–23.21	84.11
6.	960	172.97	140.90	32.07	122.76	1559	192.23	134.67	57.56	142.74
7.	700	126.13	127.39	–1.26	99.01	983	121.21	130.04	–8.83	93.21
8.	500	90.09	130.63	–40.54	68.97	873	107.64	133.51	–25.87	80.62
9.	575	103.60	135.86	–32.25	76.26	862	106.29	129.59	–23.30	82.02
10.	890	160.36	152.97	7.39	104.83	1137	140.20	143.82	–3.63	97.48
11.	1105	199.10	—	—	—	1400	172.63	—	—	—
12.	1175	211.71	—	—	—	1560	192.36	—	—	—

Appendix Table 5.23 : Estimates of Cyclical Component of the Collection of Soap Nuts in NCA

Year	Procurement Price	Index	Five Years Moving Average	Cyclical Component from		Sale Price	Index	Five Years Moving Average	Cyclical Component from	
				Additive Hypothesis	Multiplicative Hypothesis				Additive Hypothesis	Multiplicative Hypothesis
1.	670	100.00	—	—	—	800	100.00	—	—	—
2.	850	126.87	—	—	—	1009	126.13	—	—	—
3.	700	104.48	106.99	–2.51	97.66	936	117.00	105.25	11.75	111.16
4.	700	104.48	109.07	–4.60	95.79	742	92.75	105.53	–12.78	87.89
5.	664	99.10	106.09	–6.99	93.42	723	90.38	99.80	–9.43	90.56
6.	740	110.45	114.30	–3.85	96.63	811	101.38	104.58	–3.20	96.94
7.	750	111.94	128.51	–16.57	87.11	780	97.50	120.00	–22.50	81.25
8.	975	145.52	144.75	0.78	100.54	1127	140.88	140.28	0.60	100.43
9.	1176	175.52	146.54	28.99	119.78	1359	169.88	140.55	29.33	120.86
10.	1208	180.30	141.16	39.13	127.72	1534	191.75	137.30	54.45	139.66
11.	800	119.40	—	—	—	822	102.75	—	—	—
12.	570	85.07	—	—	—	650	81.25	—	—	—

Appendix Table 5.24 : Estimates of Cyclical Component of the Collection of Hill Brooms in NCA

Year	Procurement Price	Index	Five Years Moving Average	Cyclical Component from		Sale Price	Index	Five Years Moving Average	Cyclical Component from	
				Additive Hypothesis	Multiplicative Hypothesis				Additive Hypothesis	Multiplicative Hypothesis
1.	4	100.00	—	—	—	70	100.00	—	—	—
2.	4	100.00	—	—	—	375	535.71	—	—	—
3.	6	150.00	137.60	12.40	109.01	400	571.43	247.78	323.65	230.62
4.	5.85	146.25	156.60	–10.35	93.39	12	17.14	231.13	–213.99	7.42
5.	7.67	191.75	180.60	11.15	106.17	10.22	14.60	250.56	–235.96	5.83
6.	7.8	195.00	150.60	44.40	129.48	11.75	16.79	136.28	–119.49	12.32
7.	8.8	220.00	161.25	58.75	136.43	443	632.86	136.35	496.51	464.15
8.	—	0.00	165.35	–165.35	0.00	—	0.00	136.69	–136.69	0.00
9.	7.98	199.50	178.00	21.50	112.08	12.25	17.50	137.21	–119.71	12.75
10.	8.49	212.25	200.45	11.80	105.89	11.4	16.29	14.72	1.57	110.64
11.	10.33	258.25	—	—	—	13.57	19.39	—	—	—
12.	13.29	332.25	—	—	—	14.3	20.43	—	—	—

Appendix Table 5.25 : Estimates of Cyclical Component of the Collection of Wild Brooms in NCA

Year	Procurement Price	Index	Five Years Moving Average	Cyclical Component from		Sale Price	Index	Five Years Moving Average	Cyclical Component from	
				Additive Hypothesis	Multiplicative Hypothesis				Additive Hypothesis	Multiplicative Hypothesis
1.	—	—	—	—	—	—	—	—	—	—
2.	—	—	—	—	—	—	—	—	—	—
3.	—	—	—	—	—	—	—	—	—	—
4.	—	—	—	—	—	—	—	—	—	—
5.	—	—	—	—	—	—	—	—	—	—
6.	1092	100.00	—	—	—	—	—	—	—	—
7.	1045	95.70	—	—	—	1200	100.00	—	—	—
8.	923	84.52	94.38	–9.85	89.56	—	0.00	—	—	—
9.	1085	99.36	94.80	4.56	104.81	1652	137.67	106.57	31.10	129.18
10.	1008	92.31	95.57	–3.26	96.59	1543	128.58	118.53	—	108.48
11.	1115	102.11	—	—	—	1999	166.58	—	—	—
12.	1087	99.54	—	—	—	1918	159.83	—	—	—

Appendix Table 5.26 : Estimates of Cyclical Component of the Collection of Adda Leaf in NCA

Year	Procurement Price	Index	Five Years Moving Average	Cyclical Component from		Sale Price	Index	Five Years Moving Average	Cyclical Component from	
				Additive Hypothesis	Multiplicative Hypothesis				Additive Hypothesis	Multiplicative Hypothesis
1.	119	100.00	—	—	—	160	100.00	—	—	—
2.	120	100.84	—	—	—	167	104.38	—	—	—
3.	155	130.25	128.57	1.68	101.31	170	106.25	129.88	–23.63	81.81
4.	190	159.66	150.59	9.08	106.03	255	159.38	160.50	–1.13	99.30
5.	181	152.10	179.16	–27.06	84.90	287	179.38	202.25	–22.88	88.69
6.	250	210.08	210.92	–0.84	99.60	405	253.13	243.50	9.63	103.95
7.	290	243.70	231.43	12.27	105.30	501	313.13	273.50	39.63	114.49
8.	344	289.08	274.96	14.12	105.13	500	312.50	331.00	–18.50	94.41
9.	312	262.18	288.24	–26.05	90.96	495	309.38	332.63	–23.25	93.01
10.	440	369.75	296.13	73.61	124.86	747	466.88	331.38	135.50	140.89
11.	329	276.47	—	—	—	418	261.25	—	—	—
12.	337	283.19	—	—	—	491	306.88	—	—	—

Appendix Table 5.27 : Estimates of Cyclical Component of the Collection of Naramamidi Bark in NCA

Year	*Procurement Price*	*Index*	*Five Years Moving Average*	*Cyclical Component from*		*Sale Price*	*Index*	*Five Years Moving Average*	*Cyclical Component from*	
				Additive Hypothesis	*Multiplicative Hypothesis*				*Additive Hypothesis*	*Multiplicative Hypothesis*
1.	500	100.00	—	—	—	—	—	—	—	—
2.	—	0.00	—	—	—	—	—	—	—	—
3.	440	88.00	—	—	—	—	—	—	—	—
4.	598	119.60	—	—	—	250	100.00	—	—	—
5.	668	133.60	88.24	45.36	151.41	785	314.00	—	—	—
6.	1158	231.60	114.56	117.04	202.16	1958	783.20	600.00	183.20	130.53
7.	1172	234.40	161.44	72.96	145.19	2083	833.20	762.24	70.96	109.31
8.	1552	310.40	205.92	104.48	150.74	2424	969.60	877.44	92.16	110.50
9.	1600	320.00	246.00	74.00	130.08	2278	911.20	720.80	190.40	126.42
10.	1899	379.80	295.24	84.56	128.64	2225	890.00	790.00	100.00	112.66
11.	2131	426.20	—	—	—	—	0.00	—	—	—
12.	2000	400.00	—	—	—	2948	1179.20	—	—	—

Bibliography

Benerjee, Debdas (1999), "State Regulation *versus* Market Forces", *Economic and Political Weekly*, Nos. 10 and 11, March 6-12/13/19.

Bose, Ashish (1991), *Demographic Diversity of India: A Report on State and District Level Data*, B.R. Publishing Corporation, Delhi.

Campbell, J.Y. (1988), *Putting People's Products First: Multiple Use and Management for Non-Wood Forest Products in India*, Mimeograph.

Campbell, J.Y. (1993), "Changing Objectives, New Products and Management Challenges Making the Shift Major *versus* Minor to Many Forest Products", Paper Presented at the Seminar on Forest Produce, Coimbatore.

Chopra, R.N. (1956), *Glossary of Indian Medicinal Plants*, ICSSR, New Delhi, p. 236.

Das, T.M. (1980), "The Value of a Tree", Proceedings of the Indian Science Congress.

De Beer and McDermott (1989), *Economic Value of Non-Timber Forest Products in South West Asia*, Council for the International Union of Conservation of Nature, Netherlands.

F.A.O. (1995), *Report of the International Expert Consultation on Non-Wood Forest Products*, FAO, Rome.

Fernandes, W. (1988), *Forests, Environment and Tribal Economy*, Indian Social Institute, New Delhi.

Forest Survey of India (1998), *State of India's Forests*, FSI, Dehradun, India.

Gaikwad, John S. (1988), *Role of Minor Forest Produce in Tribal Economy, Workshop on Integrated Tribal Development*, Administrative Staff College, Hyderabad.

Goel, C.L. (1990), *Improving Tribal Economy from Minor Forest Products through Government Efforts*, MFP Division, Forest Research Institute, Dehradun.

Government of Andhra Pradesh (1983) *Government Orders and Instructions on Tribal Development, Vol. II*, Office of the Tribal Welfare Department, Department of Tribal Welfare, Government of Andhra Pradesh.

Government of Andhra Pradesh (1997), *Andhra Pradesh : Four Decades of Development*, Government of Andhra Pradesh, Finance & Planning Department, Directorate of Economics and Statistics.

Government of Andhra Pradesh (2001), Andhra Pradesh District Gazetteers, Hyderabad.

Government of Andhra Pradesh (2004), *Basic Statistics of Tribal and Tribal Areas of Andhra Pradesh*, Tribal Cultural Research & Training Institute, Department of Tribal Welfare, Government of Andhra Pradesh.

Government of Andhra Pradesh (2004), *A.P. Community Forest Management Project*, Project Monitoring Unit, Department of Forest, Government of Andhra Pradesh.

Government of India (1984), *Report of the Committee for Review of Rights and Concessions in the Forest Areas of India.*

Government of India (1988), "Pattern of Consumer Expenditure of Scheduled Castes & Tribes Households", *NSSO, 38 Round, January–December 1993*, Directorate of Statistics, New Delhi.

Government of India (1993), *Housing and Amenities : A Brief Analysis of Housing and Demographic Tables of 2001 Census*, Office of the Registrar, Census of India, New Delhi.

Government of Orissa (1991), *Project Report for Development of Tribal Haats in Orissa"*, Ministry of Rural Development, Directorate of Marketing.

Haimendorf, Christiph Von Furer (1982), *Tribes of India : The Struggle for Survival*, Oxford University Press, Delhi.

Jain, P.C. (2001), *Globalization on Tribal Economy*, Rawath Publications, New Delhi.

Joshi, Vidyut (1998), "Tribal Situation in India : Issues in Development", *Sardar Patel Institute of Economic & Social Research*, Ahmedabad.

Kapur Mehta, Aasha (1998), *Sustainable Interventions for Poverty Alleviation: A Study by United Nations Development Fund for Women,* South Asia Region, Delhi.

Krisnamurthy, T. (1993), *Minor Forest Products of India,* New Delhi, Oxford & IBH Publishing Co. Pvt. Ltd, 1993, p. 331.

Lynch Owen J., (1992), *Securing Community Based Tenurial Rights in the Tropical Forests of Asia : Issues in Development,* World Resource Institute, Washington.

Malhotra *et al.* (1992), *Role of Non-Timber Forest Produce in the Village Economy,* IBRAD, Calcutta.

Mallik, R.M. (1994), *Study of Some Minor Forest Produce in Orissa : An Empirical Investigation,* NCDS, Bhubaneswar, Orissa.

Mallik, R.M. (1996), *Procurement and Marketing of Kendu Leaves in Orissa : A Study of Economic Deprivation and Benefits to Primary Collectors,* NCDS, Bhubaneswar, Orissa.

Mallik, R.M. (2000), Gupta T. and Guleria A. (1982), *Non-Wood Forest Products in India,* Oxford & IBH Publishing Co. Pvt. Ltd., New Delhi.

Mallik, R.M. (2000), Sustainable Management of Non-Timber Forest Products in Orissa—Some Issues and Options", *Indian Journal of Agricultural Economics,* Vol. 55, No. 3, July-Sept., pp. 384–397.

Mallik, R.M. and Panigrahi. N. (1998), *Study of Domestic and Commercial Use Including Marketing of NTFPs,* NCDS, Bhubaneswar, Orissa.

Muraleedharan, P.K. (1997), *Bio-diversity in Tropical Moist Forests : A Study of Sustainable Use of NTFPs in the Western Ghats,* Kenal Forest Research Institute, Trichur, Kerala.

Nadim, Husnine (2000), *Bharateeya Girijanulu,* Oriental Longman, Hyderabad.

Parthasarathy, G. and K. Uma Shankar Patnaik (2003), *Procurement and Marketing of Minor Forest Produce in Tribal Areas,* Atlantic Publishers, New Delhi.

Ramanujam, M.S. *et al.* (1998), *Pricing of Minor Forest Products Procured By GCC,* Government of Andhra Pradesh, IAMR Report No. 9/1997, IAMR, New Delhi, pp. 36–39.

Ratna Reddy, V. (2001), "Forest Degradation in India : Extent and Determinants"—*Indian Journal of Agricultural Economics.* Vol. 56, No. 4, Oct.-Dec., pp. 631-651.

Roy Burman, B.K. (1994), *Tribes in Perspective : Encyclopaedia on Scheduled Tribes, Scheduled Castes and Disadvantaged People (First Series)*, Mittal Publications, New Delhi.

Sankar, S.K. (1998), "Sustainability of JFM in South West Bengal : Case Study from Midnapur District", Paper presented in Rama Krishna Mission, Lokasikshya Parishad, West Bengal, March 24.

Saxena, N.C. (1995), "Forest Policy and the Rural Poor in Orissa", *Wasteland News (Oct.-Dec.)*, Society for Promotion of Wasteland Development, New Delhi.

Sharma, B.D. (1998), *Economic Development of Extremely Backward Tribal Regions*, Government of India, Ministry of Home Affairs, New Delhi.

Shukla, Hiralal (1988), *Tribal History : A New Interpretation*, B.R. Publishing Corporation, New Delhi.

Srinivasan & Agarwal (1968), *Bulletin of the Botanical Survey of India*, Calcutta, 1968, pp. 10, 381.

Sujit, Sikh Secunder (1990), *Economic Development of Tribal of India*, Ashish Publishing House, New Delhi.

Tewari, K.M. (1989), *A Plan for Creation of Employment Opportunities to Increase the Income of People Living Below the Grinding Poverty*. Forest Research Institute, Dehradun.

Tewari, D.D. (1993), *Economics and Management of Non Timber Forest Products: A Case Study of Gujarat*, Oxford & IBH Publishing Co. Pvt. Ltd.

Tewari, D.D. and Campbell J.Y. (1995), "Sustainable Management of NTFPs in India", *Journal of Sustainable Forestry*, pp. 53–79.

Troup, R.S. (1921), *The Silviculture of Indian Trees*, Oxford University Press, Oxford, p. 513.

World Resource Institute (1990), *World Bank in the Forest Sector : A Global Policy Paper*, World Resource Institute, Washington.

Index